LAND OF DISCONTENT

THE DYNAMICS OF CHANGE IN RURAL AND REGIONAL AUSTRALIA

edited by
Bill Pritchard & Phil McManus

UNSW
PRESS

A UNSW Press book

Published by
University of New South Wales Press Ltd
UNSW SYDNEY NSW 2052
AUSTRALIA
www.unswpress.com.au

National Library of Australia
Cataloguing-in-Publication entry:

  Land of discontent: the dynamics of change in rural and
  regional Australia.

  Includes index.
  ISBN 0 86840 578 7.

  1. Regional disparities — Australia. 2. Rural development —
  Australia — Economic aspects. 3. Rural development —
  Australia — Social aspects. 4. Australia — Rural
  conditions. 5. Australia — Economic policy — 1990–.
  6. Australia — Politics and government — 1990–.
  I. McManus, Phil, 1966–. II. Pritchard, Bill (William Noel).
  III. Title: Dynamics of change in rural and
  regional Australia.

  338.994

Printer Griffin Press
Cover illustration John Brack, born 1920. *The car.* 1955,
Melbourne. Oil on canvas, 41 x 101.8 cm. National Gallery of
Victoria, Melbourne. State Governmenmt funds 1956

CONTENTS

FOREWORD
CHRIS SIDOTI *Human Rights Commissioner*

Rural and remote communities across Australia are by no means homogenous — indeed there are great differences by state and territory, size of town, wealth and environment. What they have in common is a small population spread across a vast area. The challenges this poses for the rural economy and society and for the provision of infrastructure and services are immense. A study of women's labour market participation in regional Australia commissioned by the Sex Discrimination Commissioner in 1999, for example, noted the impact on job opportunities for rural women who, on the whole, are less able than men to commute long distances for work. During the Human Rights Commission's Bush Talks consultations in 1998 these challenges, and the contemporary failure to address them adequately, were made plain in every town and community we visited:

> This country 40–50 years ago was building physical and social infrastructure with far less rural population and far less GDP and government funding. Yet now we're being told the nation can't afford it.
>
> It's not possible to provide equal services everywhere. But Geraldton is close to Perth and a big city. Yet the services here are inadequate. If that's acceptable, then three-quarters of the State is written off in terms of improving anything.

Many communities in rural Australia are thriving; developing new industries with renewed optimism. Many others feel under siege. They have declining populations, declining incomes, declining services and a declining quality of life. The infrastructure and community life of many rural and remote towns has been slowly pared away.

There is a general sense of alienation and frustration in rural and remote Australia. During the 1990s this was reflected in the development of various political movements symptomatic of this sense of being forgotten by governments. On the whole these movements exploited the prevailing alienation without proposing real solutions. Globalisation is widely blamed with many people feeling unable to influence the direction of their lives and livelihoods.

Yet globalisation offers a range of potential solutions to the problems of distance and demography faced in Australia. The new information technologies, coupled with genuine inclusion of rural and remote communities as real players in policy, planning and implementation, can assist in the delivery of information essential to business, research tools, education and training, health, justice and other services. These are opportunities never before enjoyed in 'the bush' and they are still to be fully exploited.

The Human Rights and Equal Opportunity Commission's 1999–2000 national inquiry into rural and remote education examined education as one 'essential service' under threat in rural areas and still absent from many remote communities. We were particularly keen to explore solutions which contribute to the survival and growth of rural areas.

This book is an important contribution to the essential task of reframing the national relationship to regional Australia. There is enormous discontent. There is also tremendous energy, creativity, vibrancy and commitment to a future for rural Australia. As Bush Talks was reminded:

> This is one country as a whole, with the middle part included. The rest of the country has to remain connected so that we feel whole as a nation.

PREFACE

PHIL McMANUS & BILL PRITCHARD

L̲and of Discontent has been written at a time of great change in rural
and regional Australia. Our ambition in putting it together has
been to explore the significance and underlying causes of these changes.
Unfortunately much of the debate to date has over-simplified the complexities of rural and regional Australia. One aim of this book is to rem-
edy this situation.

This book takes the term 'rural and regional Australia' to mean the
areas outside the capital cities. This is consistent with current usage by
Australian governments and the media. In current policy and popular
discourse, 'regional issues' in Australia have come to mean issues outside the capital cities. Traditionally the term 'region' was interpreted
more broadly.

The contributors to this book are social scientists from a range of
disciplines including geography, sociology, political science and environmental studies. The range of perspectives brought from these disciplines enriches the analysis of the issues discussed here.

The choice of cover design was important to us. We believe that
John Brack's 1955 image *The Car* is an important statement about
Australian culture and values. In this image the car is not so much in the
landscape as the landscape is in the car (Burn, 1991). People and technology are part of rural scenes. The artificial divisions of human and

nature are blurred. Perhaps this seems clearer to people now, but Ian Burn (1991, 2) asked why Brack painted such an image in the 1950s:

> Did he see it as an historical companion to Frederick McCubbin's 1904 triptych *The Pioneer*? Was it an attempt to refute Russell Drysdale's 1940s outbackery, the image of 'real Australia'? Was the car meant as the modern-day symbol substituting for the pioneering spirit and daily hardships which supposedly forged our society of 'mates'? Was it a symbol of freedom and mobility, the ability to overcome the vastness of the country while keeping the family unit intact?

The image resonates with the issues raised in the chapters that follow. Concerns about people, mobility, security, gender roles, family structures, jobs and the environment permeate both the painting and this book. *Land of Discontent* is intended to be a contribution to developing a more nuanced and contemporary understanding of these issues.

A book like this one is not possible without the efforts of many different people. We are indebted to John Elliot from UNSW Press for his support throughout the project. We would also like to recognise the efforts of people who refereed each chapter but who, for professional reasons, have to remain anonymous. Their input, and the helpful suggestions by David Hedgcock on the entire manuscript, has brought to fruition the potential in this project. Finally, thanks to our partners Kerry Hart and Jenny Barrett for their support, and for Jenny in particular for her assistance with the choice of cover design.

REFERENCE

Burn I (1991, originally 1985) 'Is art history any use to artists?' in Burn I, *Dialogue: Writings in Art History*, Allen and Unwin, Sydney, pp 1–14.

CONTRIBUTORS

GLENN ALBRECHT is an environmental philosopher who teaches environmental studies at the University of Newcastle in the Hunter Region of New South Wales. Born in Perth, he moved to Newcastle in 1982 in order to complete his PhD on the theme of organicism. Glenn was a foundation member of the Hunter Wetlands Trust and played a major role in the creation of the Wetlands Centre at Shortland. He has a long involvement with conservation projects, especially those involving habitat for birds. He has published on the tradition in eco-anarchism known as 'Social Ecology', transdisciplinary approaches to human and environmental health and the ethical issues associated with the use of native Australian animals. He is committed to the idea of sustainability because the alternatives are unthinkable and unlivable.

NEIL ARGENT is a lecturer in human geography in the Department of Geography and Planning at the University of New England, Armidale, New South Wales. Prior to moving to Armidale in 1996, Neil lived on a small farm and vineyard in the ranges above the Barossa Valley, South Australia, for most of his life, working as a farm hand and shearer for several years. He moved to Bridgewater in the Adelaide Hills in 1990 to complete his university studies while still running a small farm in the Barossa. Neil presently lives in the centre of Armidale but plans to return to the land ... one day.

ANDREW BEER is a Senior Lecturer in the School of Geography, Population and Environmental Management, Flinders University, Adelaide. He was born in Adelaide and lived for nine years in Canberra before returning to the town of his birth in 1993. He has also lived in Plymouth in the United Kingdom. His notable publications include *Beyond the Capitals: Urban Growth in Regional Australia* (with Alaric Maude and Andrew Bolam, 1994) and *Home Truths: Property Ownership and Housing Wealth in Australia* (with Blair Badcock, 2000).

MAURICE DALY was Professor of Economic Geography at Sydney University for 19 years, and concurrently held positions as Director of the Planning Research Centre and the Research Institute for Asia and the Pacific. Since leaving the university some five years ago he has been active in applied research in Australia and in Asia. Maurice has been a Local Government Grants Commissioner in New South Wales for 10 years.

ROLF GERRITSEN is Principal of the Gerritsen Institute, a private think tank. He is also Professorial Associate at the Public Policy Program of the Australian National University, Canberra, where he convenes the local government program. He has taught or consulted in all Australian states and territories, including consultancy to Commonwealth, state, Aboriginal, regional and local government agencies. His principal research and consultancy interests are in the area of public policy, regional development and local government.

IAN GRAY is Associate Professor in Sociology at Charles Sturt University. His writing spans topics relating to rural communities and the culture of farming, covering issues related to rural society and social change. He has published in Australian and international journals, including *The Australian Journal of Social Issues, Sociologia Ruralis* and the *Journal of the Community Development Society*. Ian has authored *Politics in Place: Social Power Relations in an Australian Country Town* (1991), and co-authored *Immigrant Settlement in Country Areas* (1991), *Coping with Change: Australian Farmers in the 1990s* (1993) and *Australian Farm Families' Experience of Drought* (1999). His research interests include sociology of community, rural society, local government, urban society, occupations, and the environment. He is a former resident of Cowra, New South Wales, and now lives in Wagga Wagga. Having earlier shunned the urban atmosphere of both Sydney and Canberra, he is now a confirmed regional dweller.

FIONA HASLAM MCKENZIE is a lecturer and researcher in the Faculty of Business and Public Management at Edith Cowan University, Perth.

She grew up in Popanyinning in rural Western Australia before moving to Perth to study. She has also studied at a university in Salt Lake City, USA, and holds several undergraduate degrees and a Masters of Philosophy degree. Fiona is currently working towards a doctorate, researching the effects of demographic and economic change on rural communities in Western Australia. She has been widely published.

GEOFFREY LAWRENCE is Executive Director of the Institute for Sustainable Regional Development at Central Queensland University, Rockhampton. He spent his first 20 years in Sydney, attending James Ruse Agricultural High School and graduating in agricultural science at the University of Sydney in 1972. He worked for a short while as a research assistant in agricultural economics at the University of Queensland before completing a sociology degree at the University of Wisconsin (Madison). Geoffrey lectured in sociology at the (now) Charles Sturt University in Wagga Wagga, and in 1993 was appointed Foundation Chair in Sociology at Central Queensland University, Rockhampton.

STEWART LOCKIE is a Senior Lecturer in Rural and Environmental Sociology at Central Queensland University, Rockhampton, where he is also Associate Director of the Centre for Social Science Research. His current research focuses on the greening of food and agriculture, social impact assessment and coastal zone management. Stewart grew up in Sydney, and has since lived, studied and worked at or near Richmond (at the former Hawkesbury Agricultural College), Armidale, Wagga Wagga and Rockhampton. He currently enjoys the rural idyll on a few acres at Mt Chalmers, 30 kilometres from Rockhampton.

PHIL McMANUS is a lecturer in the School of Geosciences at the University of Sydney. He was born and raised in the Western Australian wheatbelt town of Northam, and has also lived in Perth and in Newcastle, New South Wales, where he co-edited *Journeys: The Making of the Hunter Region*. Phil's research interests include human-nature relationships, ecological cities and regions, forestry and sustainability. His inspiration for his current work is partly derived from memories of working for two hot, dry, long summers on a wheatbin downwind of a pig farm in Western Australia.

BILL PRITCHARD is a lecturer in Economic Geography at the University of Sydney, where his main research interests concern the strategies of large food companies, restructuring of the Australian wine industry, and regional economic issues in Australia's north. He spent his formative years in the Lismore area of the New South Wales north coast, before moving to Canberra to attend university. Over the past decade he has held a number of positions in the public and community sectors, spent considerable time in the Northern Territory, and completed a PhD at the University of Sydney on corporate restructuring in the Australian food industry.

FRAN ROLLEY is a lecturer in Human Geography at the University of New England where her recent research has focused on the health status and health-care behaviour of rural Australians, and the effects of service restructuring on rural residents and communities. She spent much of her childhood in the Riverina district of New South Wales. After undergraduate studies in economic geography at the University of New South Wales she worked as a research officer with the Australian Bureau of Statistics and managed a beef cattle property with her partner outside Canberra. Whilst raising three children she taught at the Universities of Wollongong and Sydney, before 'going bush' again to Armidale, where she completed her PhD in 1995 at the University of New England.

MATTHEW TONTS is a Reseach Fellow in the Centre for Social Research at Edith Cowan University, Perth. His current research focuses on issues relating to the social and economic wellbeing of rural people. He also has interests in regional development policy in Australia and Europe, rural service provision and rural planning. Matthew was born and raised in Narrogin, a town in Western Australia, and moved to Perth to attend university. He has since lived and worked in York (in Western Australia's Avon Valley), Canberra and in Plymouth, in the United Kingdom.

1
INTRODUCTION
PHIL McMANUS & BILL PRITCHARD

Events during the last few years of the 1990s raised the prospect of dramatic changes to Australia's political, social, economic and cultural landscapes. For most of the prior half century, 'the bush' had been quiescent in the face of dramatic changes to Australia's economic and social fabric. Rural anger about specific policies or events erupted episodically, but rarely did it dominate the national stage, or capture (sub)urban Australia's imagination. At the 1996 federal election, conventional wisdom amongst spin-doctors and social commentators was that the political character of rural and regional Australia was like the folklore personality of its individuals — laconic, long-suffering and, in party political terms, loyal.

These assumptions were thrown askew in the years immediately leading up to the turn of the century. The rise and subsequent decline of Pauline Hanson's One Nation, along with the electoral success of independent parliamentary candidates in many rural and regional seats, focused national attention on social and economic change outside the capital cities. The 'bush', it seemed, was no longer quiescent. In a short period of time, the national media and mainstream political organisations 'discovered' a so-called 'forgotten citizenry' (Badcock, 1998), and showered it with concern. This has meant that, at the turn of the new century, 'the bush' has come to town — the concerns of rural and regional Australians are now planted in the national consciousness.

The intention of this book is to explore the background to these processes and, by so doing, intervene in ongoing debates about the challenges facing people and communities in these parts of the nation. Each of the book's ten thematic chapters highlights and critiques a particular debate associated with recent discourse on the futures of rural and regional Australia. Although there is considerable diversity among the chapters, they are linked by two general arguments. First, the examination of contemporary changes in rural and regional Australia needs to be positioned within a broader analysis of socio-spatial inequality and division in contemporary Australia. In the past two decades there have been profound shifts within the geographical manifestations of wealth and income in Australia. Many parts of rural and regional Australia have been most adversely affected by these processes (Walmsley & Weinand, 1997). Study after study has shown that, in general, rural and regional Australia is disadvantaged when compared with the capital cities. In 1996, of the 15 federal electorates with the highest proportion of households earning less than $500 a week, 12 were located in rural and regional Australia (Kopras, 1998). Some 52 per cent of rural workers are paid basic award wages, whereas 73 per cent of capital city workers receive above-award pay rates (Long, 1999). In New South Wales, the five highest incomes postcodes for 1996–97 were in Sydney, while the 12 lowest were in country areas (Australian Taxation Office, 1999). An analysis of the 1996 census indicated that the 'top 10 regions in terms of household income are urban; the bottom 10 are in outer urban and rural areas' (Barker, 1999: 16). Research for Jesuit Social Services on social disadvantage found that, in 1996, the vast majority of rural and regional New South Wales and over half rural and regional Victoria possessed above-average levels of social disadvantage (Vinson, 1999). Rural and regional Australia also tends to be disadvantaged relative to the capital cities in the provision of medical services, the rate of youth suicide, the provision of commercial and financial facilities, and the lack of many educational and employment opportunities.

These developments are undeniably linked with contemporary processes of global restructuring. The sharper edge of global competition, combined with the rationalisation of both public and private sector services, has impacted harshly on many people in rural and regional Australia. Of course, these same forces have similarly affected many people in metropolitan Australia, and are highly uneven in their impacts in 'the bush'. Yet the rapidity of economic, social and cultural changes in the past two decades has generated particular difficulties for many communities outside the capital cities. Moreover, declining social and economic infrastructure in many parts of the nation has exacerbated these problems, making many institutions and individuals in rural and regional Australia poorly equipped to deal with change. In the eyes of many, rural and regional Australia has not only been extremely exposed to social and economic change, it has been without adequate resources to respond effectively to new challenges.

Notwithstanding these points, we do not wish to contribute to the burgeoning popular literature portraying Australia's contemporary geography of wealth and inequality in terms of urban 'winners' and rural 'losers'. Inequality within cities has grown significantly over recent decades (Gregory & Hunter, 1996), and there is considerable diversity in the distribution of income within rural and regional Australia (Productivity Commission, 1999). Claims in the popular media of a 'great divide' between urban and rural–regional Australia in terms of incomes, service provision, lifestyles and outlooks reflect a convenient simplification of complex processes. The point is that this book fully acknowledges the depth of problems facing rural and regional Australia, but does not clothe this in a stylised dichotomy. Indeed, we suggest that the tone of much popular debate on these issues is not only simplistic, but plays into the hands of rural populists who have little else to offer in the way of effective policy solutions to genuine problems.

This brings us to the book's second general argument, which is the need to critically evaluate the debates that were intensified by Pauline Hanson's high profile, but have continued beyond her political demise. Whilst in the political spotlight, Hanson became associated with a clutch of issues that appealed to her rural populist support base. These issues included government funding for Indigenous Australians, multiculturalism, the level and composition of immigration, social security support for single parents, the need for a 'flat' tax system, and gun ownership. These issues were raised in ways that were confused and at times contradictory, but this was largely immaterial to Hanson because the common theme in her rhetoric was the desire to instil a brand of rural populism in the Australian political scene. Hanson's claim was that other politicians, too cowered by political correctness, were unwilling to raise these issues.

The attempt to put blame on Aborigines, Asian immigrants, or various classes of welfare recipients, as an explanation for social disadvantage is akin to Cervante's 16th century tale of Don Quixote tilting at windmills. Yet, despite the untenable assumptions that underlay many of Hanson's claims, her agenda resonated with many Australians, particularly those living in rural and poorer outer-suburban areas. These supporters and quasi-supporters have survived beyond the political life of One Nation, and there is little doubt that their polling strength could decide key seats in future elections. Thus there is a need to continue to question certain arguments and assumptions that are still being used uncritically in contemporary debates about rural and regional Australia.

THE LEGACY OF PAULINE HANSON

If nothing else, Pauline Hanson assisted in focusing attention on rural and regional Australia. To understand how this legacy has formed, it is important to be aware of how she emerged and, for now, faded from the political scene. Other politicians and lobby groups have certainly learned the lesson of leaving a gap in the political spectrum for Hanson-like figures to emerge. The spectre of Pauline Hanson could be seen in John Howard's 'bush tour' in January 2000, in the Australian Labor Party running 'Country Labor' candidates in the 1999 NSW election, and in the reminders in almost every policy initiative that rural and regional Australia is not being forgotten.

The dramatic emergence on the national stage of Pauline Hanson — a renegade Liberal who successfully contested the ALP-held federal seat of Oxley in March 1996 — provided a figurehead to stimulate national debate on rural and regional Australia. Hanson had unsuccessfully contested the 1993 election in Oxley for the Liberal Party, and in 1996 she ran as an independent candidate after being disendorsed mid-campaign by the Liberals. The reason for disendorsement related to anti-Aboriginal comments she made, which Liberal spin-doctors feared could harm the party nationally. Without time to preselect an alternative candidate, Hanson effectively captured the anti-Keating protest vote in Oxley (Deutchman & Ellison, 1999).

Media coverage of Pauline Hanson in the national press (*Australian Financial Review* and *The Australian*) and in the Sydney, Melbourne, Adelaide and Hobart newspapers was minimal until her maiden speech in the House of Representatives on 10 September 1996 (Deutchman & Ellison, 1999: 43). From her foothold in the House of Representatives, however, Pauline Hanson — with significant help from her advisers, David Oldfield and David Etteridge, the sensationalist tabloid media, and the unctuous performances of commercial radio announcers such as Sydney's Alan Jones — effectively tapped into the disaffections of thousands of Australians.

The rise of right-wing political parties in Australia is not a new phenomenon. They are, in part, generated to fill the political vacuum left as the major parties fight for the hearts and minds of middle class Australians. Furthermore, a rich vein of radicalism — both from the left and right of the political spectrum — flavoured Australian rural politics up until the Menzies era (Blainey, 1999). The rise of fringe parties is geographical in that they appeal to some voters who are marginalised by distance from the political and economic 'centre', whether that centre be Canberra, Sydney, Brisbane and other Australian capitals, or New York, Washington and Brussels. Marginalisation through distance, however, is insufficient to explain the popularity of these parties. There are many more complex, interacting causes that feed the support for right-wing fringe parties and political instability in general.

Pauline Hanson emphasised and exaggerated perceptions of what were often measurable differences in material wealth, opportunities and service provision within Australia. She and her nascent party — Pauline Hanson's One Nation — challenged the political assumptions of many commentators and politicians. One Nation was popular in some parts of rural and regional Australia, and not others. It was particularly successful on the suburban fringe of the poorer sides of Australia's capital cities. While relying heavily on television, radio and newspaper coverage in the cities, Pauline Hanson's One Nation addressed itself to, and threatened to extensively change, the political landscape of rural and regional Australia.

At the time of writing it is unclear what all this means for Australian politics. Perhaps the most telling development to date has been the intense navel-gazing of the federal National Party, especially under the leader it elected in 1999, John Anderson. Anderson's 'two nations' speech of February 1999 (discussed below) certainly represented a pivotal moment in contemporary Australian rural politics. Since that speech, the National Party has adopted more forthright rhetoric on the need to more fully incorporate social issues within policy making. The evidence on the extent to which this rhetoric has been mirrored in fundamental shifts within the party's policies is equivocal.

For Pauline Hanson's One Nation, the future is even more difficult to forecast but, at the time of writing, it does not look rosy. The party pitched itself to the right of the National Party, which it accused of being slavish to the demands of economic rationalism from the Liberals in the federal Coalition. Pauline Hanson's One Nation reached into the concerns of many Australians, and gave them both voice and, in Pauline Hanson, body. Yet the entity was deeply troubled from within. From the outset, Pauline Hanson's One Nation was mired in controversy due to an alleged lack of democratic procedures and accountability. The implosion of the party since its dizzy success at the June 1998 Queensland election — where it captured 22.7 per cent of the primary vote and won 11 of 89 seats — has been due partly to the realisation by its elected members and office holders that the process of government is much more complicated than simply blaming Aborigines, Asians, single parents and 'dole-bludgers'.

This book is not about these soap operas. Nor is it about the characteristics of right-wing rural politics in general. Pauline Hanson is important to this book only in so far as her interventions have helped propel national debate on the future of rural and regional Australia. The arguments raised by her and her party provide a context in which to investigate the changing character of rural and regional Australia, and to critically explore key debates in media and academic establishments concerning the reasons for, and implications of, these changes.

CONTEMPORARY ACCOUNTS OF RURAL AND REGIONAL AUSTRALIA IN THE MASS MEDIA

To some extent our motivation in developing this book has been to engage with popular accounts of 'why Hanson emerged?' There is no simple answer to this question: the disaffection mobilised by Hanson and others responded to trying economic and social conditions in rural and regional Australia, but also moved beyond them. Furthermore, it responded to a particular moment in Australia's political life — an interregnum between the demise of the Hawke–Keating era and the Coalition taking control of government. This interregnum was undoubtedly lengthened by John Howard's invocation to abandon the alleged rhetorical straight-jacket of political correctness, an action that let racist sentiment bloom in the community.

The political uncertainty featured by the rise of Pauline Hanson unsettled the rhythm of Australia's two-party system, and sent shock waves through Australia's liberal media. Legitimate confusion appeared amongst many journalists and editors concerning how these developments should be read. Media debate on Pauline Hanson's One Nation swung between journalistic analysis and hectoring rancour: should she be regarded as a serious political force, or should she be reviled for the racist sentiments with which she was associated? The media gazed on Pauline Hanson's supporters alternatively as 'excluded citizens' living in 'forgotten places' (Badcock, 1998) — in other words, victims of economic rationalism and restructuring — or as an embittered minority vengefully and myopically using racial prejudice to account for their ills. What they were not was probably easier to typify than what they were. Evidently, they were 'the other' to the supposed 'Chardonnay set' which supported Prime Minister Keating's agenda on globalisation, engagement with Asia, Indigenous reconciliation and the Republic. Although they voted in droves to expel the Keating Labor government in 1996, they transgressed normal party lines, and this fact caused considerable unease within Australia's political establishment.

One of the more common discourses accompanying the rise of Hanson was the notion of a 'great divide' in Australian society, which we noted above. Feature stories on Australia's supposedly deepening rural–urban divide promised a rich harvest for newspapers such as *The Australian*, the *Sydney Morning Herald* and the *Age*; for television current affairs programs including the ABC's *7.30 Report*, *Lateline*, and the Nine's *Sunday* program; and for various programs on the ABC's Radio National. A series of features in the *Sydney Morning Herald* over

1999 captured the sensationalised reporting that formed much of this discourse. In February 1999, Craig McGregor wrote: 'The great divide that splits Sydney is bad enough, but the great divide between Sydney and the rest of the State is sometimes worse ... Right across the west, a new Rustbelt is developing' (1999: 6). Similarly, a few months later Debra Jopson intoned: 'Communities across NSW are battling for their existence as rural Australia continues to reel from an economic restructuring which has gutted jobs, stripped away services and forced families and young people from the bush' (1999: 4). Aside from their sensationalist tones, a problem in these accounts is that they easily become mantras. Rather than opening debates on rural and regional Australia, the mantras of globalisation and rural stereotype close potentially vital debates: their implicit message is that 'the bush is in decline, this is inevitable, and this explains the rise of Hanson'.

These accounts reached their apogee following the 1998 Queensland election. On 13 June 1998, Pauline Hanson's One Nation achieved 23 per cent of the primary vote and won 11 out of 89 seats in the Queensland parliament. An analysis of these electoral results by Davis and Stimson (1998) involved associating 1647 polling booths across Queensland with 1996 census data disaggregated to 6448 collector districts. From this methodology, the researchers observed that support for Pauline Hanson's One Nation was correlated spatially with the geographies of urban fringes and their hinterlands. Support was weak in town and city centres and quite variable in rural areas, but consistently strong in the rural–urban interface of Brisbane and in Queensland's major regional cities. Socio-economically, the researchers concluded:

> Where these areas contain unskilled workers in blue collar industries, few indigenous Australians or people born overseas, and have a high number of people either achieving or attempting to achieve the Australian dream of home ownership, then [One Nation] is likely to do well. [Davis & Stimson, 1998: 81]

It is apparent that many of the concerns that Pauline Hanson's One Nation raised on the political agenda, and which have since been taken up by the revamped leadership of the National Party, have existed in Australia for many years. Issues such as changing farm and settlement demographics, the withdrawal of financial services, and the rise of environmental and indigenous concerns are now high on the political agenda of all parties. Many of these issues were directly addressed by the leader of the National Party, John Anderson, in his speech to the National Press Club in Canberra on 17 February 1999 when he introduced the term 'two nations'. The crux of Anderson's speech was an attempt to explain the decline of rural and regional Australia by technological change (Anderson, 1999). Of course, technological change is important. It has helped farmers to make larger profits, it has improved the quality of education for children in remote parts of Australia, and it has provided many households with the information and entertainment available in the cities. Technological change has also improved personal mobility, reducing the reliance of residents on their local towns and communities, and thus facilitating economic dislocation. By wrapping his analysis within the overarching blankets of 'technology' and 'progress', however, the Anderson approach is technologically deterministic. As demonstrated in the following chapters, the causes, nature and extent of rural and regional change in Australia has complex roots. Although technological change is very real, its social and economic implications are determined via the interplay of processes and institutions operating at multiple scales within and outside rural communities.

THE RE-POSITIONING OF RURAL AND REGIONAL AUSTRALIA

Notwithstanding the limitations of Anderson's 'two nations' rhetoric, this and other contributions have encouraged Australians to think critically about rural and regional Australia: about how these spaces are being re-positioned within national political, social, economic and cultural arenas. This attention to rural and regional Australia has emerged in contrast to recent historical trends. For the past 50 years or so, the great issues affecting Australia have been played out in the nation's state capitals. Cities have been the places where the vast bulk of Australia's immigrants have settled and have been the heartlands of economic change — from the great Fordist manufacturing complexes of the immediate post-1945 period, to the 'new' economy of the information superhighway. Cities have also been the key sites for social problems such as unemployment, crime and drug addiction. Even national environmental debates — the Gordon-below-Franklin Dam; the Ranger, Coronation Hill and Jabiluka mines in Kakadu; and the conservation of forests — have been won and lost in the mediascapes of (sub)urban Australia. Political control in Australia has depended on managing these issues in ways that capture the votes of (sub)urban electorates.

In political terms, generally rural and regional Australia has been an arena of safe seats: Country–National Party members have been elected in the 'bush' and Labor members elected in resource and manufacturing regions (such as the Hunter Valley). Socially, rural and regional Australia has tended to attract fewer immigrants (especially non-English speaking immigrants) than the cities, and this has influenced its social character as a whole. Economically, sustained declines in farmers' terms of trade and the general impact of technological change have encouraged a steady pace of agricultural restructuring. Between the 1950s and the 1990s, the ratio of the costs of production relative to agricultural prices received fell four-fold (Productivity Commission, 1999: 66), and the number of Australian farms fell by about one per cent per annum (see Chapter 3). Consequently, rural and regional Australia has become increasingly diverse and less attached to traditional industries.

As these developments wrought change on the rural landscape, rural and regional Australia was repositioned in the national psyche. These changes are probably best exemplified through the ways that film makers have portrayed the regions. The yeoman 'everyman' travails of *Dad and Dave* in mid-century were supplanted towards the end of the century by the masculine mythologies of *Crocodile Dundee* and the sense of rural Australia as a strange and hostile place, as seen in films like *Wake in Fright* and *Priscilla: Queen of the Desert*. In different ways, the imagined geographies of these films problematise how we should view 'the bush'. The (basically urban) film makers engaged in these projects highlight a set of conflicting images about the place of rural and regional Australia within national landscapes.

Consistent with the increased complexity of economic and social processes in rural and regional Australia, political allegiances are also in flux. During the same period of Hanson's rise, rural and regional Australia elected a raft of independent parliamentarians, with different ideologies and priorities. In the 1996 Federal election, the rural seat of Calare (NSW) ousted its Labor candidate in favour of Peter Andren, a local independent. Unlike Hanson, Andren retained his seat in the 1998 federal election. The 1999 NSW election saw three rural independents elected to the Legislative Assembly, while the ALP ran candidates in rural areas under the banner of Country Labor. The election of the Bracks Labor government in Victoria in September 1999 was achieved by winning key seats in regional centres such as Ballarat and Bendigo, and obtaining the support of newly elected independent MPs in Gippsland East, Gippsland South and Mildura. The election of Craig Ingram as the member for Gippsland East is notable in that his main policy was related to the environmental management of the lower Snowy River system: a far cry from the racial and economic policies that underpinned Hanson's support. Evidently, rural and regional Australia is increasingly politically volatile.

STRUCTURE OF THIS BOOK

This book comprises twelve chapters, including this introduction. As noted, each chapter engages with contemporary debates relating to the futures for rural and regional Australia. The next chapter, by Stewart Lockie, questions the discursive construction of rural Australia and its inhabitants. Lockie challenges readers to consider what we know (or think we know) about 'the bush' and the people who live there. The organisation of knowledge influences how we talk, write and think about rural and regional Australia. Lockie analyses one form of organised knowledge; that is, representations of Pauline Hanson's One Nation in Queensland's major metropolitan newspaper — the *Courier-Mail*. Because content analysis of media sources provides a limited perspective on what underlies the discourses of rurality and regionality, Lockie draws on a diverse array of sociological research into the cultures of non-metropolitan Australia and the discourses that circulate to demonstrate that One Nation's understanding of rural and regional Australia was marked by significant absences. While One Nation's political campaign received extensive media attention, Lockie argues that programs like Landcare and issues such as Native Title are likely to have more lasting impact in rural and regional Australia.

In Chapter Three, Geoff Lawrence and Ian Gray provide an important overview of trends and changes in agriculture within Australia. This chapter uses qualitative and quantitative data to explore the characteristics of recent social, cultural and economic restructuring at the farm level. Lawrence and Gray assess restructuring processes within the national farm population, the impacts of these processes at regional scales, and constituent changes to the characteristics of Australian farming. The authors challenge stereotypical constructions of 'the average farm' and 'the average farmer'. They demonstrate that the homogenous image of the 'man on the land' is 'as flawed now as it has been in past generations'. The chapter highlights the diversity of lifestyles, sources of income and situations of participants in the Australian farming sector.

These arguments provide a context for Matthew Tonts to discuss the towns in rural and regional Australia in Chapter Four. Tonts highlights how some towns throughout rural and regional Australia have grown in population, while others have declined. Although population growth is not a guarantee of increasing or even maintaining the level of services, population decline makes towns particularly vulnerable. This is part of a vicious cycle, where the removal of services not only contributes to population decline, but often results in the more entrepreneurial and higher spending members of a community moving elsewhere in search of opportunities.

In the following chapter, Fiona Haslam McKenzie draws upon research she recently conducted in the central wheatbelt of Western Australia to ask: 'Where do people fit in the rural equation?' Haslam McKenzie highlights the social and cultural issues experienced by many people in rural and regional Australia. In this chapter, statistics of farm sizes and agricultural production provide the context, rather than the endpoint, for the stories of long distances travelled for education and medical needs, of the alienation experienced by women new to the area, and of farm succession. The extensive use of quotes highlights the personal feelings of a type that Pauline Hanson's One Nation tapped into, but which traditional political parties dismissed in their doctrines of international competitiveness and trade liberalisation.

In Chapter Six, Bill Pritchard explores the political economy of trade affecting rural and regional Australia. He highlights how Australia has been repositioned within a global marketplace, and the assumptions made by advocates of 'trade liberalisation' in order to convince other people of the necessity of this approach. The chapter explains the changes within trade policy for various sectors. The issue of trade and protectionism, particularly around the pig industry, was an important component on the Pauline Hanson's One Nation policy platform. Pritchard argues against both the Pauline Hanson's One Nation protectionist barriers and the deregulated utopia of trade liberalisation advocates. While seeing a change in recent government policy with regard to rural policy, he questions whether this is a significant change in direction or a knee-jerk reaction to electoral shifts.

Chapter Seven continues the theme of frustration and disempowerment by exploring the rise of environmental and indigenous concerns. This chapter is important given the centrality of indigenous issues to Pauline Hanson's rise to notoriety, but the almost total silence of Pauline Hanson's One Nation on environmental issues. In this chapter, Phil McManus and Glenn Albrecht highlight shifts in attitudes among environmentalists, Aborigines, mining companies and rural producers to these issues. The authors note that previous assumptions about allies and opponents no longer hold, and that increasingly there are conflicts within and between shifting alliances. Through the use of case studies, McManus and Albrecht demonstrate that, far from being disempowered by these issues, some corporations have actively engaged in setting an agenda of working together on potentially controversial issues. The benefits of this approach for the environment and indigenous people are questioned.

In Chapter Eight, Rolf Gerritsen considers the importance of governance in defining, contributing to, and solving the various and often related problems experienced in rural and regional Australia. His focus on the management of government links the macro-economic picture outlined in Chapter Six with the decline of many regional centres, as documented in Chapter Four and Chapter Nine. Gerritsen highlights how there is currently an imbalance between competition and equity in government policy, and how the effects are being felt most acutely in rural and regional Australia.

The withdrawal of financial services has been a major concern in many parts of rural and regional Australia. In Chapter Nine, Neil Argent and Fran Rolley highlight the timing and extent of bank closures in New South Wales and Western Australia. They focus on the growing number of towns that have recently been left without any bank. While this phenomenon is not unique to rural and regional Australia, it often highlights to people in the affected towns how little control they have over an important aspect of their lives. The continuing relevance of these issues is emphasised by the announcement of a proposed merger between the Commonwealth and Colonial State Banks in March 2000.

In earlier chapters, rural and regional Australia is exposed as heterogenous and constructed from multiple, competing discourses. The latter chapters explore possibilities for moving forward on the basis of these understandings. The restructuring of rural and regional Australia is a process involving a connectivity of changes at multiple scales. In Chapter Ten, Andrew Beer explores the history of regional policy in Australia. He concentrates on recent policy initiatives at the Commonwealth level and highlights the differences in approaches to regional development organisations by the States. This chapter demonstrates that inappropriate implementation of underfunded policy initiatives are often responsible for the ineffectiveness of government policy in addressing many of the issues raised in the earlier chapters. The chapter links Commonwealth and State government and provides an entry point for the following chapter on local government and communities.

In Chapter Eleven, Maurice Daly highlights the importance, potential and limitations of local government in improving the future of rural and regional Australia. Daly's chapter is derived from his personal experiences as Local Government Grants Commissioner for New South Wales over an extended period. Daly delves beneath the rhetoric of romantic localism to demonstrate that, far from being a panacea, local government as it is currently structured and operated is often part of the problem. He suggests, however, that this need not always be the case. In this chapter, local government is seen as a means to an end, not an end in itself. The chapter introduces current initiatives that may inspire other communities, individual local governments and municipal associations. The restructuring and redefining of local government is seen by Daly as an important step in improving the quality of life for people in rural and regional Australia. Following this chapter, McManus and Pritchard offer some brief concluding thoughts on the futures for rural and regional Australia.

Together, these chapters represent an important journey through many of the key issues and prospects for rural and regional Australia at the beginning of a new century. While it is impossible to cover every aspect in a single publication, the book explores many of the important matters that have affected rural and regional Australia in recent years, and that will continue to do so into the foreseeable future. It is these issues, rather than the ephemeral personalities in the shape of Pauline Hanson and others, that will influence the futures of communities and individuals living in rural and regional Australia.

REFERENCES

Anderson J (1999) 'One nation or two? Securing a future for rural and regional Australia', Address to the National Press Club, Canberra, 17 February. www. dot.gov.au/media/anders/speeches/as1_99.htm.

Australian Taxation Office (1999) *Taxation Statistics*, ATO, Canberra.

Badcock B (1998) 'Forgotten places, excluded citizens & the rise of One Nation', *Urban Policy and Research*, 16(3), pp 241–46.

Barker G (1999) 'One land, two nations', *Australian Financial Review*, 15 November, p 16.

Blainey G (1999) 'A radical harvest to be reaped', *Sydney Morning Herald*, 31 December (supplement), p 8.

Davis R & Stimson R (1998) 'Disillusionment and disenchantment at the fringe: explaining the geography of the One Nation Party vote at the Queensland election', *People and Place*, 6(3), pp 69–82.

Deutchman I & Ellison A (1999) 'A Star is Born: The roller coaster ride of Pauline Hanson in the news', *Media, Culture & Society*, 21(1), pp 33–50.

Gregory R & Hunter B (1996) 'Increasing regional inequality and the decline in manufacturing', in Sheehan P, Grewal B & Kumnick M (eds) *Dialogues on Australia's Future: In Honour of the Late Professor Ronald Henderson*, Center for Strategic Studies, Victoria University, Melbourne, pp 307–24.

Jopson D (1999) 'Heart ripped out of country towns', *Sydney Morning Herald*, 7 June, p 4.

Kopras A (1998) 'Electorate rankings: Census 1996', *Background Paper*, 14, Information and Research Services, Department of the Parliamentary Library, Canberra.

Long S (1999) '... but lean fare for battlers in the bush', *Australian Financial Review*, 15 December, p 19.

McGregor C (1999) 'The great divide', *Sydney Morning Herald*, 27 February (Spectrum), pp 1–6.

Productivity Commission (1999) *Impact of Competition Policy Reforms on Rural and Regional Australia*, Inquiry Report 8, AusInfo, Canberra.

Trinca H (1999) 'Third way to a rural revival', *Sydney Morning Herald*, 8 June, p 15.

Vinson T (1999) *Unequal in Life: The Distribution of Social Disadvantage in Victoria and New South Wales*, Ignatius Centre for Social Policy and Research, Richmond.

Walmsley D & Weinand H (1997) 'Is Australia becoming more unequal?', *Australian Geographer*, 28(1), pp 69–88.

2

CRISIS AND CONFLICT: SHIFTING DISCOURSES OF RURAL AND REGIONAL AUSTRALIA

STEWART LOCKIE

... it is time we told it like it is: that the bush, as we knew it, is no more. That it has been gutted beyond all recognition by political theorists and economic rationalists with their felt pens and whiteboards and fancy titles in the south ... The people have finally spoken ... and what they had to say at the ballot boxes sent the nation reeling. At last, it seems, the plight of the bush has become a part of the national political agenda: the rest of the nation is now shocked and dismayed at what was done to a part of the nation that they once took for granted. The discontent from the bush is now blazing across the nation. [*Courier-Mail*, 8 August 1998: 18]

This book is based on the proposition that one of the most significant social and political impacts of the rise of Pauline Hanson's One Nation Party has been a reassessment of many of the taken-for-granted assumptions that people make about rural and regional Australia. The election of 11 One Nation members to the Queensland parliament in June 1998 no doubt confirmed the 'redneck' status of rural and regional Australians in many people's minds. After all, nine out of the 11 One Nation MPs harked from non-metropolitan electorates. But it has also raised questions in the minds of others as to why so many people have become disaffected with the major political parties and the perceived failure of those parties to address a host of apparently endemic social and economic crises. It is easy enough to criticise One Nation for identifying simplistic solutions to complex problems — particularly when those solutions belie thinly veiled racial prejudice — but such criticism doesn't do much by itself to solve those problems. One Nation's electoral success has given new impetus to debates about the social and economic issues confronting those living outside metropolitan centres. It has forced reassessments of economic and social policy and the place of rural and regional Australians at all levels of politics. It has raised questions about what it means to be an Australian and about whose interests really count. Just as importantly, it has placed these issues on the front pages of both metropolitan and rural newspapers.

This chapter is not about One Nation or the issues or crises confronting 'the bush' — not directly anyway. Rather, it is about the changing ways in which we understand rural and regional Australia. It is about what we know (or think we know) about 'the bush' and the people who live there. It is about the ways we organise our knowledge and, consequently, the ways we talk, write and think about rural and regional Australia. My route into this will be through an analysis of the ways in which rural and regional Australia has been represented through media coverage of the One Nation phenomenon. In particular, I will analyse those representations through Queensland's major metropolitan newspaper — the *Courier-Mail*. [1] While this will be my route in, however, it won't be the only route we'll travel through the chapter. Alternatives are necessary, firstly, because while One Nation has promoted particular representations of non-metropolitan Australia, it is but one group among many involved in such activity; and, secondly, because content analysis of media sources will only give us a limited perspective on what underlies the discourses of rurality and regionality that we are interested in. Using representations of One Nation as our starting point will raise many of the key debates, but to flesh this picture out we need to draw on a diverse array of sociological research into the cultures and discourses of non-metropolitan Australia. Before doing so, however, we need to clarify just what concepts like discourse and rurality mean.

KEY CONCEPTS: DISCOURSE AND RURALITY

The term discourse has become extremely popular in the social sciences. In everyday use discourse means conversation. Thus, when linguists engage in discourse analysis it is the ways in which words and other symbols go together to create meaningful conversations that they are interested in. When sociologists use the terms discourse and discourse analysis, however, they are usually referring to something a little different (although not entirely unrelated, thankfully). In particular, sociologists and other social scientists are interested in the ways in which words, symbols and meanings are linked to power and knowledge. From this perspective discourses are understood as more than conversation. They are the ways of 'talking about something, organising knowledge and thereby classifying and regulating people' that come to be established as accepted knowledge (Haralambos et al., 1996: 159). The focus on discourse in contemporary social science reflects the proposition that the most powerful forms of coercion are often the most subtle. Although brute physical or economic force remain a salient feature of many social relationships (violence against women, for example), so too do a variety of strategies 'to change the minds of others in one's own interests' (van Dijk, 1993: 254). Power, in this sense, is dependent on the ability of actors 'to win the struggles that take place over the attribution of specific social meanings to particular events, actions and ideas' (Long, 1992: 24) or, in other words, to define the content of a discourse.

The relationship between discourse and power makes it seem obvious enough that discourses will not be fixed or universal, but will be contested, debated and resisted. The question is how? The mass media stands out as a social arena through which meanings are very clearly associated with particular events, actions and ideas and, therefore, through which discourses are circulated and contested. Access to the mass media is thus obviously a key resource of power in contemporary Australia. Importantly though, it is not the only resource. The media does not have the ability by itself to establish what counts and what doesn't as valid knowledge. In attempting to come to grips with discourses of rural and regional Australia, we need to cast our net more widely to consider the roles played by those with professional expertise in science, economics, policy formulation and accounting, through to those who resist or accommodate that expertise in their daily lives as farmers, tradespeople, activists, politicians, workers, citizens etc. in rural and regional Australia.

But where exactly is rural and regional Australia? To most the answer is obvious — it's where metropolitan Australia isn't. But that's only a statement of what isn't rural or regional. It says nothing about what is, or about the difference between rural and regional. Is rural and regional something to do with population size, land use, culture ...?

The reason for discussing this issue in the same section as discourse is to point out that even our understanding of something as seemingly straightforward as the question of what areas are rural or regional is a discursive construct, not an innate or fixed category. Depending on the definition used, between 10 per cent and 30 per cent of Australians live in rural or remote areas (Bourke & Lockie, forthcoming). The Australian Bureau of Statistics (ABS) classifies 'major urban' settlements as those with a population of over 100 000; 'other urban' as settlements in the range 1 000–99 999; 'localities' in the range 200–999; and less than 200 as the rural balance. Others prefer to use four categories: urban, regional, rural and remote (Cameron-Jackson, 1995). It is also common to discuss rurality, in particular, in terms of 'rural cultures' and 'identities', or in terms of dependence on agriculture. To paraphrase Dunn (1989), rurality thus appears to have something to do with getting cow dung on your boots, tractor diesel on your hands or a hot scone at a Country Women's Association function. I don't intend entering these definitional debates here (see Bourke & Lockie, forthcoming; Share, 1995). There is widespread agreement among sociologists that rurality is a multi-dimensional concept that means different things in different contexts. The key issue and the topic of this chapter is the different and competing meanings that are ascribed to the concept in public discourses of rurality and regionality in contemporary Australia.

'COUNTRYMINDEDNESS': RURAL AND REGIONAL IDENTITY IN HISTORICAL CONTEXT

Throughout this country's brief European context the archetypal Australian has often been represented as a rural Australian male — a hardworking and honest larrikin, true to his mates but fiercely independent and self-reliant, more at home under the sun and the stars than in the feminised confines of an office or home. Written in such extravagant language, this description may seem more cliched than archetypal, but it is clear nevertheless that rural imagery figures prominently in constructions of Australian national identity. From the 'bush poetry' tradition of Banjo Paterson's 'The Man from Snowy River' to the contemporary popularity of period furniture and the Driza Bone-filled shops that crowd our tourist districts, we, and our visitors, are surrounded by the association of Australianness with rurality. This is not the only image — beaches and diggers (returned soldiers) are also writ large — but it is an undeniably important one.

Despite this, rural people have often felt forgotten and have organised themselves politically around resistance to what they have seen as urban governments, which have not understood both the unique needs of rural Australia and its centrality to national economic and social well-being. According to Aitken (1985), an ideology that came to be known as 'countrymindedness' emerged during the period 1890–1920; a period during when increasing international competition in markets for food and fibre, the establishment of a system of arbitration to protect the incomes and employment conditions of workers, and the federation of the States contributed to a self-perception among rural Australians that they were both different and vulnerable. From the early 1920s, countrymindedness was manifested politically through the formation and electoral success of the Country (now National) Party. During what Aitken (1985: 35) describes as the 'high period' of the Country Party between 1925 and 1960, elements of countrymindedness included the beliefs that:

- Australia depends on its primary producers for its high standard of living, for only those who produce a physical good add to a country's wealth.

- Therefore all Australians, from city and country alike, should in their own interest support policies aimed at improving the position of the primary industries.

- Farming and grazing, and rural pursuits generally, are virtuous, ennobling and cooperative; they bring out the best in people.

- In contrast, city life is competitive and nasty, as well as parasitical.

- The characteristic Australian is a countryman, and the core elements of the national character come from the struggles of country people to tame their environment and make it productive. City people are much the same the world over.

- For all these reasons, and others like defence, people should be encouraged to settle in the country, and not in the city.

- But power resides in the city, where politics is trapped in a sterile debate about classes. There has to be a separate political party for country people to articulate the true voice of the nation.

The policies of the Country Party were both populist (Aitken, 1985) and 'agrarian socialist' (Lawrence, 1987). They were focused on: the protection of farmers' incomes through import restrictions and statutory marketing authorities; the redistribution of land from earlier land grants and squatters to family farmers through closer settlement schemes; and the promotion of higher productivity through public subsidisation of research and advisory services and infrastructure development such as irrigation projects and railways. Importantly, the discourses of rurality associated with countrymindedness had a degree of resonance in the city and thus the policies of the Country Party enjoyed support beyond the small electoral base of 'the bush' (Aitken, 1985). Yet despite their appeals to egalitarianism there were glaring absences from these discourses. The male family farmer was represented as the embodiment of countrymindedness and his interests were represented as the interests of all rural people — indeed, as the interests of all Australians. Absent was any sense that women, indigenous people, members of other non-British ethnic groups, wage workers or gays and lesbians may have constituted legitimate and unique interest groups in their own right (Share, 1995). Consequently, virtually every political arena from the federal (Aitken, 1985; Sher and Rowe-Sher, 1994) to the local (Dempsey, 1992; Gray, 1991; Poiner, 1990; Wild, 1974) equated rural policy with agricultural policy, while challenges to male hegemony on the farm were suppressed by denying many women access to property through inheritance (Voyce,

1994) and limiting their involvement in decision making (Alston, 1995).

The discourses of rurality underlying countrymindedness have become increasingly problematic. Challenges to male hegemony are discussed below, but it is important to note here the declining influence of the idea that all Australians ultimately depend on agriculture for prosperity (Aitken, 1985). Postwar immigration fuelled population growth in the cities and by the 1970s the relative importance of agriculture to the national economy was in decline. At the same time, the industrialisation of agriculture meant that fewer and fewer people were directly involved in agricultural production as farms amalgamated and workers were replaced by capital inputs. As the constituency for a political party founded on the ideology of countrymindedness shrank, the Country Party re-positioned itself as the National Party (Aitken, 1985) and abandoned its formerly agrarian socialist policies in favour of those guided by discourses of economic rationalism and managerialism. This is now reflected in policies that emphasise economic efficiency and competitive advantage (see Chapters 6, 9 & 10). In the case of agriculture, we have thus seen the dismantling of institutions such as statutory marketing boards that formerly acted to collectivise the risks associated with trading in volatile international commodity markets. Instead, contemporary policies argue that individual farmers must learn to manage these risks — through, for example, the use of property planning, forward selling and futures markets — and to increase their productivity. Those who don't should be 'adjusted' out of the industry, as the provision of assistance to them would only distort market signals and reduce the international competitiveness of Australian agriculture (Higgins, 1999). Rural communities, similarly, are expected to develop new economic opportunities for themselves if they are to retain population and services (Herbert-Cheshire, 2000). The particular 'ways of knowing' that undergird these discourses and policies are discussed below. More immediately, however, it is important to note that discontent with these discourses and policies has very clearly fed One Nation's electoral success.

CONTEMPORARY DEBATES: MEDIA REPRESENTATION OF ONE NATION AND RURAL AND REGIONAL AUSTRALIA

Courier-Mail coverage of One Nation is framed within notions of naivety, irresponsibility and threat. I do not wish to analyse these in great depth — nor to comment on the extent to which these negative framings are justified — but they do bear mention due to the dramatic extent to which One Nation is also framed as a rural phenomenon, despite Pauline Hanson's own political emergence from the metropolitan electorate of Oxley. One Nation's policies on guns are represented as a threat to public order and safety; its policies on economic reform and immigration as potentially (if not immediately!) responsible for the loss of markets, business opportunities, tourists and international students; its policies on social security as ill-informed; and its policies on Aboriginal affairs, Native Title and immigration as racist. Despite the publication of accusations by farming organisations that these policies, if implemented, would damage agricultural trade, One Nation's success in the 1998 State election has been consistently represented as a counterpunch from an angry and ailing rural and regional Queensland. In other words, the election gave rural and regional Queensland the opportunity to 'hit back' at politicians and a wider community which had refused to listen and acknowledge cries for help. Thus we are confronted with representations of rural and regional Queensland opposed to the granting of Native Title to indigenous people; to gun laws that outlaw the possession of semi-automatic and military-style rifles; and to the removal of the last vestiges of protectionism for agricultural commodities. A binary divide is constructed between the metropolitan — where One Nation polled comparatively poorly — and the rural; Brisbane thus being seen as having shaken off its 'country town image' and established itself as a 'cosmopolitan centre' (*Courier-Mail*, 15 June 1998: 5). By implication, of course, the rural and regional is associated with racism, violence and economic fatuity:

> The people of regional Australia increasingly appear to believe it is acceptable to be racist as Pauline Hanson's One Nation grows in popularity ... Human Rights and Equal Opportunity commissioner Chris Sidoti said that after months of listening to rural people, he had observed less restraint in making racist comments. [*Courier-Mail*, 27 July 1998: 2]

No wonder it is reported that Asian business people and tourists are afraid to leave the safety of metropolitan Brisbane and the Gold Coast for the 'hillbilly backwater' of 'redneck' rural Queensland (*Courier-Mail*, 17 August 1998: 9). And what of the economic consequences? The newspaper was unequivocal:

> Withdrawing ourselves in fear and loathing of a globalised, deregulated economy is a sure-fire way of mangling vital trade relationships and torpedoing foreign investment — in other words, of killing off job opportunities and future economic growth. [*Courier-Mail*, 26 May 1998]

But rural and regional Queensland is not tarred with quite the same brush as the One Nation Party. Increasing levels of rural and regional poverty; rapidly declining numbers of farms (down 40 000 nationally over 20 years and 2000 during the 12 months leading up to 1998 — *Courier-Mail*, 19 September 1998: 12); and cuts to key services such as banking and education are presented as issues that have hurt rural and regional Australians. The pressure placed on politicians to address these issues by the Queensland election resulted in a multitude of commitments in the lead-up to the 1998 federal election. In the words of Tim Fischer, former deputy leader of the federal Liberal–National Coalition: 'We must establish a human dimension, [and] a jobs dimension ... your government shares some of your concerns that competition policy has not had enough regard to "public interest" in country Australia' (*Courier-Mail*, 19 September 1998: 15).

In the apparently oppositional discourse to economic rationalism that thus appears to have developed, there are two key dimensions that must be addressed. The first of these is the manner in which a more 'human dimension' has been incorporated into dominant discourses of economic rationalism and managerialism with minimal alteration to their key elements. The second is the manner in which discourses of rural and regional Australia are still most notable for their absences. How else could the former federal Minister for Primary Industries, John Anderson, state that 'country people are concerned with the Wik Native Title problem' (*Courier-Mail*, 27 June 1998: 10) without acknowledging that the indigenous people at the heart of this so-called 'problem' live predominantly in rural and regional communities themselves? Why do they not figure in discourses of rurality? How can it be assumed that 'country people', indigenous and non-indigenous, have a universal interest in and concern for the 'problem' of Native Title when substantial numbers voted for neither the National nor One Nation parties?

And so again we are presented with an image of the rural Australian as a white farmer whose economic wellbeing is fundamental to the survival of 'the bush'. Little distinction is made between the interests of primary industries and the fortunes of the all too many unemployed in regional centres such as Wide Bay — despite the remote likelihood of their widespread employment in capital intensive agriculture. As Lawrence and Williams (1990) point out, capital intensification in agriculture, even when prices are buoyant, has negative consequences for economically dependent communities nearby, due to the downward pressure that constant productivity gains place on labour and service requirements. Despite the protests of particularly vulnerable producers as the last vestiges of protectionism have disappeared, key farm lobby and industry groups have enthusiastically embraced the project of trade liberalisation in the belief that internationally competitive Australian producers are disadvantaged by subsidies and barriers elsewhere. According to Brendan Stewart, the President of Queensland Graingrowers: 'Farmers must control their own destiny and overcome a handout mentality ... There is no use looking for government handouts to sustain the unsustainable. We have to seize the day and make our own opportunities (*Courier-Mail*, 28 July 1998: 2).

The human face of economic rationalism thus begins to emerge, not as an agrarian socialist challenge to the fetishisation of efficiency and competitiveness, but as a range of strategies designed to help rural and regional people help themselves within the 'deregulated' market environment. These range from the provision of basic services, such as community banking and telecommunications services that may enhance opportunities to develop alternative economic activities, to the provision of training and planning programs that allow people to calculate and manage for themselves the riskiness of alternate marketing and production options. The rationality, or way of thinking, underlying these strategies has been described by Foucault (1991) and others (Burchell, 1993; Miller & Rose, 1990; Rose, 1993) as neo-liberalism. This differs from the *laissez-faire*, or 'hands off', approach to government of classical liberalism by deliberately, although indirectly, attempting to shape the types of decisions individuals are likely to make by influencing: firstly, the environment within which those decisions are made; and, secondly, the ways people are likely to interpret and respond to that environment. Recent examples of the former strategy include trade deregulation, the abolition of drought relief programs, and the introduction of tradeable water rights; while examples of the second include property management planning programs, promotion of community Landcare groups, and rural adjustment programs. Discourses of rural crisis are thus incorporated within the neo-liberal rationality of governance just as easily as discourses of economic rationalism; the primary responsibility of governments being to remove impediments to the movement of capital and ensure that people are equipped to participate in this movement. The questions are whether this incorporation will achieve widespread acceptance and whether the strategies associated with it will actually address the social and economic 'problems' that have fed the discourse of crisis?

KNOWING RURAL AND REGIONAL AUSTRALIA

One of the striking features of contemporary discourses of crisis in rural and regional Australia is the extent to which what we actually think we know about rural and regional Australia is taken for granted. Just as we 'know' that the income gap between rural and city dwellers has grown, rates of male suicide have increased and the numbers of farmers have dropped; we also 'know' that a weak Australian currency during 1998 added 20 per cent to the cost of major farm inputs, while a number of commodity markets crashed due to the Asian economic crisis, and others were threatened by the prospect of a 'trade war' between Australia and Canada. The media reports on which much of this knowledge is based are themselves based on the research of agencies such as the ABS and the Australian Bureau of Agricultural and Resource Economics (ABARE). It is not my intention here to question this knowledge — I have no doubt it is based on sound and rigorous research — but to examine the ways in which knowledge generating activities such as the collection of statistics shape discourses of rural and regional Australia.

The collection of statistics renders otherwise highly complex and fluid social domains visible and thereby open to policy makers and other 'experts' seeking to manage those domains (Miller & Rose, 1990; Murdoch & Ward, 1997). As Murdoch and Ward (1997) show, the collection of agricultural statistics was fundamental to postwar British attempts to boost food production and restructure agriculture as a modern, specialised economic sector. Without statistics, policy makers and politicians would have had very little 'rational' basis on which to base policy decisions. Equally, farmers and farm lobby groups would have had very little basis on which to shape their responses to a changing policy and market environment. But as Murdoch and Ward (1997) also argue, these statistics did not simply provide a window onto an already existing reality, they shaped that reality in important ways. In the first instance, the collection of statistics was focused on what were defined as predominantly full-time commercial farming businesses, thereby excluding innumerable smallholdings and mixed enterprises. In the second instance, the collection of statistics required farmers to keep particular financial and production records, thereby also encouraging them to see themselves as modern business people. Together, these 'encouraged a view of agriculture as an economic sector in need of rationalisation and modernisation' (Murdoch & Ward, 1997: 320), and consequently as a sector dependent on those with expertise in accounting and agri-science to generate and use appropriate knowledge. Comparatively ignored were questions of farm family welfare or rural community development.

There are a number of parallels here with Australia, both historically and contemporarily. Beyond the five-yearly census of the Australian population, the collection of statistics about rural and regional Australia is overwhelmingly dominated by the collection of agricultural production and financial statistics — the ABS Farm Census (focused predominantly on farm production) and the ABARE Farm Survey (focused predominantly on detailed financial analysis). While many smaller independent studies have tried to assess broader social questions in relation to rural and regional communities or farm families, it is virtually impossible to find data that addresses such questions at a national level (see for example Coakes et al., 1999). Although the ABARE Farm Survey regularly asks supplementary questions — such as participation in Landcare groups and the adoption of recommended land management practices — virtually unquestioned is the assumption that agriculture is first and foremost an economic activity, and that ensuring its success as an economic activity is the primary task in ensuring the welfare of the farm families and rural communities, about which we know comparatively little. Statistical data concealing these assumptions subsequently becomes embedded in discourses of agriculture and the rural as economic sectors that reach far beyond the offices of policy makers. Headlines such as 'canegrowers warn on souring trade' (*Courier-Mail*, 5 June 1998: 2), 'rural gloom as markets wipe out dollar gains' (*Courier-Mail*, 24 June 1998: 4) and 'crisis slashes exports by two billion dollars' (*Courier-Mail*, 16 December 1998: 14) feature in the mainstream press far more consistently than the other 'crisis'-related issues that featured so prominently in 1998 following the Queensland election. Indeed, it is possible to suggest that it is the ubiquity of agricultural production and financial statistics that have facilitated the incorporation of discourses of rural crisis so easily within the neo-liberal project of 'deregulation' and 'rural adjustment' in Australia.

Before closing this section it is important to point out the almost complete absence of criticism of agri-science in recent debates over rural crisis. While the 'economic rationalists' who seek to manage 'rationally' on the basis of statistics have been targeted for their supposed lack of practical knowledge and expertise, agricultural science has been mentioned only in the context of being yet another service that is being lost from rural areas, and without which local farmers will progressively lose their competitiveness. And yet, according to rural sociologists, agri-science is highly implicated in the long-term decline of rural communities and environments (see Lawrence, 1987; Vernicle & Lawrence, 1995). Simply put, the intensification of agriculture is associated with declining labour inputs and increased pressure on natural resources. More important in terms of our discussion here, though, is the way in which agri-science constructs agriculture as a largely industrialised activity based on the efficient transformation of inputs into outputs. When this construct is combined with economic primacy and declining terms of trade, it is very difficult for farmers to address the environmental costs that may be associated with excessive or inappropriate use of inputs so long as production is maintained, at least in the short-term. Despite widespread awareness of problems of agricultural land and water degradation, and concerns about the long-term impacts of chemical use, most farmers believe they have little choice but to follow the dominant trajectory of agri-science (Lockie et al., 1995). To do otherwise is considered too risky as it essentially involves losing access to the knowledge and expertise of government advisory officers, researchers, input suppliers and neighbours (Lockie, 1997a, 1998a, 1999; Lockie et al., 1995). Whether or not agri-science, as we currently know it, is capable of constructing an ecologically sustainable agriculture is not an issue that can be addressed in this chapter (I would suggest that it cannot). The point is that agri-science provides a very powerful way of 'knowing' agricultural production systems and environments that has largely gone unchallenged in recent discourses of rural and regional Australia. The industrialised model of agriculture on which this way of knowing is based is *one* alternative for agriculture in Australia and *one* alternative for agriculture-dependent communities in Australia. But as the dominant alternative, it is one that is highly supportive of economic and agricultural primacy within discourses of rurality.

CONTESTING ECONOMIC AND AGRICULTURAL PRIMACY

In this final section we will explore some challenges to economic and agricultural primacy in discourses of rural and regional Australia that have either been 'glossed over' in the media 'feeding frenzy' surrounding the One Nation phenomenon, or have been constructed in negative terms — as part of the 'crisis' for rural and regional people — by One Nation. These include 'women in agriculture', Landcare and alternative uses and constructions of rural space, including Native Title.

'WOMEN IN AGRICULTURE': CHALLENGING MASCULINE AND PRODUCTIVIST AGRICULTURE

The Australian 'women in agriculture' movement — also known as the 'rural women's movement' — emerged in the mid-1980s when the Victorian government appointed women's advisers in the Department of Agriculture who established the Victorian Rural Women's Network and promoted annual 'Women on the Land' gatherings (Alston, 1996). This model has been adopted in most other States and has led to the development of a loose collective of women throughout rural Australia who identify in some way with the 'women in agriculture' movement, even though most are not members of formal movement organisations. While participants vary widely in age, the majority are Anglo–Australian women from owner-operator farm units (Liepins, 1998). Activism has thus focused more on farm-based issues than wider rural community issues. This activism has focused on two primary issues: firstly, a reversal of the historically invisible contribution women make to farming and to rural communities; and, secondly, a broadening of the rural policy agenda beyond commodity issues to include social and environmental considerations related to agriculture (Alston, 1996; Liepins, 1995). Important outcomes include both recognition and support from the federal government for the representation of rural women's interests in policy making (Alston, 1996);

and the transformation of women's self-identities from farmers' wives to farmers in their own right and legitimate political activists (Liepins, 1998). Thus, the contribution of 'women in agriculture' to the broadening of the agri-political agenda beyond production and profitability not only pre-dates One Nation, but is accorded substantially more legitimacy within mainstream political parties and arenas. It is important not to succumb to the temptation to conclude that increased involvement in decision making and politics among women will necessarily transform Australian agriculture — women farmers are, after all, subject to the same economic pressures and dependent on the same agri-scientific knowledges as any other farmer. Nevertheless, the archetypal rural Australian may still be a farmer, but the challenge has been issued to the conception that 'he' is strictly male.

LANDCARE: RECONSTRUCTING IMAGES OF THE RURAL LANDSCAPE

The National Landcare Program (NLP) was launched in 1989 with a principal focus on the promotion and support of a nationwide network of community Landcare groups based on localised watersheds or neighbourhoods. The emphasis in these groups was on addressing local environmental degradation in a co-operative and integrated manner, with government support available to assist with group co-ordination, trial and demonstration projects and, more recently, problems of particular regional significance. Groups have thus tended to focus on educational activities, farm and catchment planning projects, tree planting, and demonstrations and trials of new practices (Campbell, 1994; Curtis & De Lacy, 1997). The consistency of Landcare with the otherwise often competing discourses of ecological sustainability, community empowerment and economic rationalism has seen it achieve almost universal political support and widespread community involvement (Lockie, 1997b). Women's rates of involvement, for example, are considerably higher than in other farm-based organisations (Lockie, 1997c), as is involvement among smallholders and townspeople (Campbell, 1994).

The other remarkable feature of Landcare is the extent to which it has facilitated a transformation in the way land degradation is understood — from a problem that many farmers did not recognise, and that many more denied publicly, to one that is discussed openly and addressed co-operatively (Lockie, 1998b). What this represents is not simply a shift in farmer attitudes but a reconceptualisation of the ways in which agricultural landscapes are understood (Beilin, 1997). Agricultural landscapes through much of Australia are no longer seen by their managers solely as sites of production to be improved through the application of agri-science, capital and labour, but as fragile and complex agro-ecosystems incorporating a number of 'non-productive' elements, such as native flora and fauna, vegetated riparian (streambank) zones etc. In many districts 'good' farm management has become synonymous with acknowledging the presence of land degradation and attempting to do something about it. This does not mean that Landcare has led to a dismantling of industrialised agriculture. Farmers still face substantial economic pressure and a knowledge base that supports further intensification. Landcare has itself supported intensification in many ways by encouraging attempts to modify agricultural landscapes so that industrialised agriculture may be more comfortably accommodated (for example, through strategic tree planting to reduce wind, run-off etc.), rather than encouraging a fundamental reassessment of the goals and form of agriculture. For our discussion here though, the critical thing to remember is that Landcare has begun to change the way we think about rural environments and to transform the self-identities of farmers from isolated and self-reliant individuals (as encouraged by the notion of the farm as a business) to interdependent members of catchment communities (Lockie, 1998b; see also Ewing, 1997).

NATIVE TITLE AND THE RURAL AS NON-AGRICULTURAL SPACE

One of the more significant aspects of the High Court's decision in Wik (see Chapter 7) in the context of this chapter, was the legal finding that in the case of pastoral leases farmers are not the only ones who have a legitimate interest in rural landscapes. While the Wik decision found that some aspects of Native Title — such as access to land for ceremonial purposes — could co-exist with the rights of pastoral leaseholders, it has always been the case that, to varying degrees, more than one set of rights have existed across all land tenures (Reeve, forthcoming). Nevertheless, the recognition of the rights of indigenous Australians — as a group that has been so comprehensively marginalised by discourses of rurality — would seem bound to generate conflict and misunderstanding. How else, to repeat a question asked above, could the federal Minister for Primary Industries claim that Native Title is a concern for rural Australians as if indigenous people did not count among them? And so it does not seem surprising that the Wik decision has been used to generate fear among farming communities that their own rights — even rights over freehold land not affected by the Wik decision — were under threat. The resulting smokescreen has hidden the fact that farmers have not lost any rights over existing pastoral leases, while the federal Coalition's 10 Point Plan removed the rights of Aborigines to negotiate over mining developments on pastoral leases subject to native title (Watson, forthcoming).

As much as anything else, debate over Native Title in the wake of Mabo and Wik has demonstrated the depth of belief within much of rural and regional Australia that rural space is most rightfully agricultural space. But it is not only Native Title that is challenging this conception. Urban encroachment, sub-division of commercial farms into smallholdings ('hobby farms' or 'lifestyle blocks'), rural tourism and the diversification of town economies beyond dependence on agriculture have all led to conflict over the meaning of rural space. These are conflicts not only over what sorts of activities are most appropriate for rural areas, but over who counts as rural and the extent to which their interests should be considered by others. In conflict over chemical spray-drift from cotton farms near the New South Wales town of Gunnedah, for example, the suggestion was made by both farmers and local government representatives that Gunnedah was a farming community. People critical of that industry, they claimed, should either support the cotton industry or leave (McHugh, 1996). Such conflict is only likely to increase as rural and regional communities continue to pursue non-agricultural economic opportunities.

CONCLUSION

The 'bush' has once again become part of the national political agenda. Discourses of rurality have extended beyond notions of the rugged, independent, male farmer as the archetypal Australian and the idyllic images of intimate rustic communities selling 'country style' to urban consumers. Instead, crisis in rural and regional Australia and conflict over 'economic rationalism' are very much at the forefront of public debate. The aspects of crisis highlighted by the success of One Nation in the 1998 Queensland election provide only a partial perspective on change in contemporary discourses of rurality and regionality. 'Women in agriculture', Landcare and Native Title are each associated with cultural change that may be argued to be far more profound than those associated with One Nation. Where One Nation reinforces the absences that have dominated discourses of rurality and regionality (that is, the absence of non-farmers, non-whites and non-males), each of these other arenas of change go some way towards challenging those absences. It is important to note, however, that the extent of opposition to Native Title in recent discourses of rurality and regionality demonstrates that indigenous people continue to be constructed as the 'other' and a source of threat to a degree not experienced by members of 'women in agriculture' or Landcare.

To what extent can we expect to see transformation in the primacy accorded to the economic and agricultural in government and agri-industry policy and programs? The strength of this way of thinking lies in the enormous amount of 'knowledge' — in the form of both agri-science and production and financial statistics — that informs and reinforces it. Challenges to economic rationalist discourse must not only construct an alternative discourse that highlights human costs, they must construct an alternative knowledge base with which to inform alternative rationalities and strategies. More simply expressed, they must change what we know about rural and regional Australia. Again, we have to conclude that the challenge to dominant discourses laid down by 'women in agriculture', Landcare and Native Title are likely to be far more substantial in the long-term than that laid down by One Nation. Where One Nation's claims and policies are easily dismissed as irrational, counter-factual and prejudiced, 'women in agriculture', Landcare and Native Title have far more fundamentally changed what we know. We know that women's contribution to agriculture and rural communities has been marginalised because, as largely unpaid labour, it has not been accounted for; we know that land and water degradation costs something in the vicinity of $2 billion per annum (Madden et al., 2000) and has led to the establishment of a National Land and Water Resources Audit to account for this more thoroughly; and we know that indigenous people have legal rights to land that have been denied them. Still, for the moment at least, it seems that neo-liberal rationality — constructed discursively as 'economic rationalism' — is capable of accommodating discourses of social and environmental crisis. While these alternative discourses argue the need to consider the human dimension of economic change, neo-liberalism constructs this human dimension as the responsibility of those affected. Similarly, neo-liberalism constructs the environmental dimension of economic change as an example of market failure best dealt with by better information. For both dimensions the role of government remains one of maintaining suitable conditions for economic efficiency and production, and ensuring that people affected negatively by these conditions are provided with opportunities to help; that is, to participate in the neo-liberal project and to pursue efficiency and productivity themselves. Only time will tell whether the current focus on asking those in 'the bush' most affected by restructuring to help themselves will continue to provide adequate support for the neo-liberal project, or whether this will itself come to be seen as a nonsense.

NOTE

1 All editions of the *Courier-Mail* were reviewed from May 1998 through December 1998. All articles concerned with the One Nation Party or issues constructed as 'rural' or 'regional' were copied and content analysis was undertaken that focused on the ways in which these issues were 'framed'; that is, the ways in which they were represented, the meanings that were associated with them and the context in which they were placed (see Hannigan, 1995). A metropolitan newspaper was chosen as the basis for this analysis as it was believed that this would most clearly demonstrate the types of discursive representation of rurality and regionality that were deployed irrespective of whether they originated in rural or regional spaces.

ACKNOWLEDGMENTS

I would like to thank Kerry Buchholtz for his many hours at the microfiche reader.

REFERENCES

Aitken D (1985) '"Countrymindedness" — the spread of an idea', *Australian Cultural History*, 4, pp 34–40.

Alston M (1995) *Women on the Land: the Hidden Heart of Rural Australia*, UNSW Press, Sydney.

Alston M (1996) 'Backs to the wall: rural women make formidable activists', in Lawrence G, Lyons K & Momtaz S (eds) *Social Change in Rural Australia*, Rural Social and Economic Research Centre, Central Queensland University, Rockhampton, pp 77–84.

Beeline R (1997) 'The construction of women in Landcare: does it make a difference?', in Lockie S & Vanclay F (eds) *Critical Landcare*, Centre for Rural Social Research Key Papers No. 5, Charles Sturt University, Wagga Wagga, pp 57–70.

Bourke L & Lockie S (forthcoming) 'Rural Australia: an introduction', in Lockie S & Bourke L (eds) *The Social and Environmental Transformation of Rural Australia*, Pluto Press, Sydney.

Burchell G (1993) 'Liberal government and techniques of the self', *Economy and Society*, 22(3), pp 267–82.

Cameroon-Jackson BF (1995) 'Semantic complexities in defining rurality: towards a definition based on human considerations', *Education in Rural Australia*, 5(1), pp 1–7.

Campbell A (1994) *Landcare: Communities Shaping the Land and the Future: With Case Studies by Greg Siepen*, Allen & Unwin, Sydney.

Coakes S, Fenton M & Lockie S (1999) *Development of a Draft Framework for the Fitzroy Basin Theme 6 Implementation Project: Capacity of and Opportunity for Farmers and Other Land Managers to Implement Change at the Property, Community and Regional Level*, Rural Social and Economic Research Centre, Central Queensland University, Rockhampton.

Curtis A & De Lacy T (1997) 'Examining the assumptions underlying Landcare', in Lockie S & Vanclay F (eds) *Critical Landcare*, Centre for Rural Social Research Key Papers No. 5, Charles Sturt University, Wagga Wagga, pp 185–99.

Dempsey K (1992) *A Man's Town: Inequality Between Women and Men in Rural Australia*, OUP, Melbourne.

Dijk TA van (1993) 'Principles of critical discourse analysis', *Discourse and Society*, 4(2), pp 249–83.

Dunn P (1989) 'Rural Australia: are you standing in it?' *Rural Welfare Research Bulletin*, July(2), pp 12–13.

Ewing S (1997) '"Small is beautiful": the place of the case study in Landcare evaluation', in Lockie S & Vanclay F (eds) *Critical Landcare*, Centre for Rural Social Research Key Papers No. 5, Charles Sturt University, Wagga Wagga, pp 175–83.

Foucault M (1991) 'Governmentality', in G Burchell, C Gordon & P Miller (eds) *The Foucault Effect: Studies in Governmentality*, Harvester-Wheatsheaf, Hemel Hempstead, pp 87–104.

Gray I (1991) *Politics in Place: Social Power Relations in an Australian Country Town*, Cambridge University Press, Cambridge.

Hannigan J (1995) *Environmental Sociology: A Social Constructionist Perspective*, Routledge, London.

Haralambos M, Krieken R van, Smith P & Holborn M (1996) *Sociology: Themes and Perspectives*, Australian edition, Longman, Sydney.

Herbert-Cheshire L (2000, forthcoming) 'Changing people to change things: technologies of government and rural development', in G Lawrence, V Higgins & S Lockie (eds) *Environment, Society and Natural Resource Management: Theoretical Perspectives from Australasia and the Americas*, Edward Elgar, Cheltenham.

Higgins V (1999) 'Economic restructuring and neo-liberalism in Australian rural adjustment policy', in Burch D, Goss J & Lawrence G (eds) *Restructuring Global and Regional Agricultures: Transformation in Australasian Agri-food Economies and Spaces*, Ashgate, Aldershot, pp 131–43.

Lawrence G (1987) *Capitalism and the Countryside: The Rural Crisis in Australia*, Pluto Press, Sydney.

Lawrence G & Williams C (1990) 'The dynamics of decline: implications for social welfare delivery in rural Australia', in Cullen T, Dunn P and Lawrence G (eds) *Rural Health and Welfare in Australia*, Centre for Rural Welfare Research, Charles Sturt University, Wagga Wagga, pp 38–59.

Liepins R (1995) 'Women in agriculture: advocates for a gendered sustainable agriculture', *Australian Geographer*, 26(2), pp 118–26.

Liepins R (1998) 'Fields of action: Australian women's agricultural activism in the 1990s', *Rural Sociology*, 63(1), pp 128–56.

Lockie S (1997a) 'Chemical risk and the self-calculating farmer: diffuse chemical use in Australian broadacre farming systems', *Current Sociology*, 45(3), pp 81–97.

Lockie S (1997b) '"Beyond a 'good thing": political interests and the meaning of Landcare', in Lockie S & Vanclay F (eds) *Critical Landcare*, Centre for Rural Social Research Key Papers No. 5, Charles Sturt University, Wagga Wagga, pp 29–43.

Lockie S (1997c) 'Rural gender relations and Landcare', in Lockie S & Vanclay F (eds) *Critical Landcare*, Centre for Rural Social Research Key Papers No. 5, Charles Sturt University, Wagga Wagga, pp 71–82.

Lockie S (1998a) 'Environmental and social risks, and the construction of "best-practice" in Australian agriculture', *Agriculture and Human Values*, 15(3), pp 243–52.

Lockie S (1998b) 'Landcare in Australia: cultural transformation in the management of rural environments', *Culture and Agriculture*, 20(1), pp 21–9.

Lockie S (1999) 'The state, rural environments and globalisation: 'action at a distance' via the Australian Landcare Program', *Environment and Planning A*, 31(4), pp 597–611.

Lockie S, Mead A, Vanclay F & Butler B (1995) 'Factors encouraging the adoption of more sustainable cropping systems in south-east Australia: profit, sustainability, risk and stability', *Journal of Sustainable Agriculture*, 6(1), pp 61–79.

Long N (1992) 'From paradigm lost to paradigm regained? The case for an actor-oriented sociology of development', in Long N & Long A (eds) *Battlefields of Knowledge: The Interlocking of Theory and Practice in Social Research and Development*, Routledge, London, pp 16–43.

Madden B, Hayes G & Duggan K (2000) 'National investment in rural landscapes: An investment scenario for National Farmers' Federation and Australian Conservation Foundation with the assistance of Land and Water Resources Research and Development Corporation', ACF & NFF, Melbourne.

McHugh S (1996) *Cottoning On: Stories of Australian Cotton Growing*, Hale and Iremonger, Sydney.

Miller, P. and Rose, N. (1990) 'Governing economic life', *Economy and Society*, 19(1), pp 1–31.

Murdoch J & Ward N (1997) 'Governmentality and territoriality: the statistical manufacture of Britain's "national farm"', *Political Geography*, 16(4), pp 307–24.

Poiner G (1990) *The Good Old Rule: Gender and Other Power Relationships in a Rural Community*, Sydney University Press, Sydney.

Reeve I (forthcoming), 'Tiptoeing round the slumbering dragon: property rights and environmental discourse in rural Australia', in Lockie S & Bourke L (eds) *The Social and Environmental Transformation of Rural Australia*, Pluto Press, Sydney.

Rose, N. (1993) 'Government, authority and expertise in advanced liberalism', *Economy and Society*, 22(3), pp 283–99.

Share P (1995) 'Beyond "countrymindedness": representation in the post-rural era', in Share P (ed) *Communication and Culture in Rural Areas*, Centre for Rural Social Research, Wagga Wagga, pp 1–23.

Sher J & Rowe Sher, K (1994) 'Beyond conventional wisdom: rural development as if Australia's rural people really mattered', in McSwan D & McShane M (eds) *Issues Affecting Rural Communities*, Rural Education Research and Development Centre, James Cook University of North Queensland, pp 9–32.

Vanclay F & Lawrence G (1995) *The Environmental Imperative: Eco–social Concerns for Australian Agriculture*, CQU Press, Rockhampton.

Voyce M (1994) 'Testamentary freedom, patriarchy and inheritance of the family farm in Australia', *Sociologia Ruralis*, 34(1), pp 71–83.

Watson V (forthcoming) 'Native title, reconciliation and the politics of race', in Lockie S & Bourke L (eds) *The Social and Environmental Transformation of Rural Australia*, Pluto Press, Sydney.

Wild R (1974) *Bradstow: A Study of Status, Class and Power in a Small Australian Town*, Angus & Robertson, Sydney.

3

THE MYTHS OF MODERN AGRICULTURE: AUSTRALIAN RURAL PRODUCTION IN THE 21ST CENTURY

GEOFFREY LAWRENCE & IAN GRAY

Will the 'family farm' survive? What will be the future importance of Australian agriculture? These are not unimportant questions to those who live and work in the non-metropolitan regions. A number of studies of social change in Australian agriculture have indicated that many producers face a battle to survive under conditions of falling commodity prices and increasing input costs (Lawrence, 1987; Gray et al., 1993; Lawrence et al., 1996; Stehlik et al., 1998). Statistical representations of the 'average farmer' may provide a snapshot of overall trends in farm viability, but can also conceal more than they reveal. A cursory glance at Australia's farming systems indicates how difficult it is to compare an orchardist with a wheat farmer, or an irrigated cotton producer or a chicken grower. The extent to which it is possible to discern a single pattern of social change, or a 'single' image of 'the bush', from the diversity of forms is consequently constrained. How then is it possible to grasp what might be happening 'down on the farm'? What can be said is that in relation to image, two traditional stereotypes have predominated throughout the past hundred or so years.

CHANGING IMAGES OF THE RURAL PRODUCER

The first image is that of those who farm the land. Often on small-holdings, the farmer — the tiller of the soil — has been viewed through urban eyes as hard working, but struggling economically. Dependent on reliable weather patterns for the planting of crops — while making decisions in the context of a country with 'droughts and flooding rains' — there has been a certain pathos surrounding the farmer's activities. The 'cocky' image of *Dad and Dave* reveals not only the climatic vulnerability of those with limited capital and land, but also the 'country hick' notion of simple people involved in a simple lifestyle. Farmers are often said to be reliant upon the state for handouts, and are sometimes considered 'whingers' — people whose economic livelihood is often so fragile that they must continually rely upon subsidies (such as drought or flood relief) to remain in farming. Their plight is summed up in a phrase by the fictitious and ever-pessimistic 'Hanrahan' whose pat response to predictions of falling prices or drought or rain is the predictable 'we'll all be rooned!'

The 'grazier' image can be contrasted to that of the 'cocky'. Graziers have tended to own large tracts of land, have inherited family wealth from the heady days of high wool prices, often reside in stately homes, possess a good education, and have taken leadership roles in industry. Rather than undertaking farming — getting their hands dirty working tirelessly on small blocks of land — they graze animals. They have been viewed as the elite of the bush, sometimes handing over their properties to managers so that they may engage in politics, trade or other worldly affairs. As a consequence, their image is connected with privilege and status. Unlike the farmers, who formed their own Country (now National) Party largely in an attempt to extract subsidies to underwrite and protect their activities, many graziers have joined the ranks of the more 'free trade'-oriented Liberal Party as legitimate members of Australia's ruling class. These two stereotypes are increasingly inappropriate portrayals of Australian rural producers, on at least seven grounds. An appreciation of these failings is a primary point of departure for a wider discussion of restructuring processes within Australian farming.

THE MYTH OF THE GRAZIER

It is now acknowledged widely that Australia's grazier elite was constructed from the appropriation of Aboriginal lands, and that much of the hard work in building the fortunes of grazing families was actually undertaken by indigenous Australians, who were exploited under social relations of semi-feudal subjugation (Taylor, 1993). The so-called 'squatters' occupied lands that the early settlers chose to consider as empty. Their subsequent actions were to force Aboriginal peoples from these lands so that wealth could be created in the production of wool, sheep-meat and beef — commodities ultimately accepted by governments as desirable for trading relations with Britain. Aboriginal occupants were often killed in response to their opposition and resistance. Trenchant and widespread racist attitudes ensured that the killing of black men and the raping of women would allow perpetrators to go largely unpunished. In the case of rape, the state and church were to work together to 'solve' the problem of the so-called 'half-casts' by taking an estimated 100 000 children from their Aboriginal mothers to be raised in missions and as state wards (Taylor, 1993: 17). It is both ironic and sad that those Aboriginal people who, following the destruction of their tribal societies, were to create wealth for the graziers, remained at the opposite end of the social scale from the new land owners. Despite being the backbone of the industry for well over one and a half centuries, Aboriginal stockmen were sacked en masse once Indigenous Australians were granted rights to citizenship and equal pay in the late 1960s — something which created widespread social dislocation. Their repayment for years of loyal and dedicated service was forced expulsion from rural lands. The final indignity is the continuing opposition of much of the grazing fraternity to Native Title. This is despite the fact that Native Title 'rights' are not about establishing freehold title for indigenous peoples but providing more secure opportunities for the practice of traditional ceremonial and hunting–gathering activities (Taylor, 1993: 4).

THE EMERGENCE OF AGRICULTURAL DIVERSITY

As prices of bulk commodities have continued to face international competition, new 'niche' industries have grown to complement or replace them. The growth in new agricultural industries — including viticulture, Asian vegetables, native floriculture, aquaculture and a vast array of others — has ended the view that the Australian rural sector 'rides on the sheep's back'. With diversity has come a fracturing of the notion and image of farming. What does a tea tree oil grower, an intensive pig producer or an ostrich farmer have in common with a wheat or lamb producer? The answer is — very little. Furthermore, there are deepening divisions within particular industries. There is a polarisation between producers in industries such as wheat, wool and beef, where the top 20 per cent or so of producers are becoming increasingly responsible for profits (Lawrence, 1995). Consequently, the views, actions, internal management regimes and economic futures in any single industry can be quite varied, with the larger producers becoming increasingly larger, and the smaller either leaving the industry, or surviving by supplementing farm income with off-farm income.

THE IMPOVERISHMENT OF SOME AGRICULTURAL PRODUCERS

This leads to a related consideration — the general economic wellbeing of farmers and graziers. Both groups are facing substantial economic pressures to increase productivity in line with declining terms of trade for agricultural commodities. Quite significant sections of the farming and grazing industries are no longer commercially viable. And while governments might provide social security support as a form of rural welfare, they are no longer willing to underwrite prices or subsidise inputs. In the commodity boom times of the 1950s and 1960s, rural producers were viewed as being well ahead of wage workers in terms of income, but by the mid-1990s the reverse was true. The average total income of broadacre and dairy farms was approximately $27 300 in 1994–95, while that of the average household in Australia was $38 700 about this time (Garnaut & Lim-Applegate, 1998: 2). Robertson (1997) has reported that approximately 80 per cent of broadacre agriculture was unprofitable during the 1990s, an indication that climatic circumstances and structural pressures were causing major social dislocation.

DECLINING FARM INDEPENDENCE

The fourth ground on which the older images fail relates to 'independence'. It was once held that farmers and graziers had control over their labour power. They made investment decisions, and were free to select the right production mix and determine when to plant, fertilise, harvest, shear sheep, drench cattle, pump water, and so on. They employed labour at certain times during the year to help with production. Such independence was tied, in a class sense, to their being owners–controllers of the means of production. But what does 'ownership' mean in terms of increasing indebtedness? What is 'control' when to remain viable contracts must be signed which allow external business entities to regulate on-farm production? We will return to this issue when we discuss subsumption.

DECLINING POLITICAL INFLUENCE

The fifth ground for rejecting the traditional stereotypes of farming relates to political influence. Neither farmers nor graziers are now capable of influencing policy in the way that was possible in the last 100 or so years of export-oriented agriculture. The rise of One Nation as an anti-free trade party, and the disaffection of many country people with the Nationals, is symptomatic of a deeper crisis within Australian agriculture. In Australia today, sport adds more to GDP than wool or wheat. This reinforces the liminal nature of farming in a 'postmodern' or service economy.

CHANGING PERCEPTIONS IN URBAN AUSTRALIA

The sixth ground relates to the status of farmers in the eyes of the wider Australian community. Once, rural producers were viewed — by themselves and by outsiders — as carers of the land. The noble pioneers might have, as Dovers (1992) has remarked, 'remade' the Australian landscape into a southern version of England through the widespread clearing of trees, but this was in line with desires (sometimes demands) by the state for a secure trading base in primary products. The pioneers 'tamed' a harsh country and were praised for it. The farmers and graziers who followed were subsequently admired for their tenacity, for their ability to manage to produce in climatically variable conditions, and for contributing to wider national prosperity. There was virtually no concern for the rural producer's role in natural resource management, apart from applauding the hard physical work required to clear land, fence, and to make farming and grazing viable businesses. Today, it is recognised that the impact of agriculture on native plants and animals has been highest in the pastoral zone, and current farm investment in sustainable practices has been deemed 'inadequate' (SCARM, 1998: 1–2). Rural producers are now widely viewed as having largely failed the test of producing in a sustainable manner, and their prior claim to being 'stewards' of the soil has been discredited. They are viewed, instead, as having been directly involved in massive environmental degradation estimated to be costing Australia approximately $1.7 billion per annum (Price, 1998). In concert with their vulnerable economic position, the 'blame' for the degrading of resources has subsequently diminished their status. The attitudes of farm organisations to Native Title legislation and the identification of many producers as 'rednecks' in supporting One Nation are two other factors which have reduced the status of rural producers in the eyes of urban Australians.

CHALLENGES TO MASCULINE IMAGES OF FARMING

The seventh ground for rejecting the traditional stereotypes of farming is tied up with a masculine image of the bush — one that is no longer (if it ever was) indicative of social relations and economic production in the countryside. The 'cocky' and the 'grazier' were always *male* images which, in an homogenised form, found expression in the phrase 'man on the land'. As we will show below, the recent changes in Australian agriculture now challenge ways in which we conceive of the rural producer.

THE CHANGING STRUCTURE OF AUSTRALIAN AGRICULTURE

As most researchers who attempt to make sense of agricultural statistics agree, it is particularly difficult to identify in an unambiguous manner what is happening to Australia's agricultural population. Changes to statistical definitions hamper longitudinal analyses. Until the mid-1970s 'agricultural holdings' were defined as those over one hectare engaged in the creation of rural produce (apart from timber and fish). Income produced from the property was introduced as a criterion after this, and all farms which generated less than $1500 from agricultural activity, or which were less than 10 hectares, were excluded. Thereafter the 'threshold' income was raised — first to $2500 in 1981–82, then to $20 000 in 1986–87, and finally to $22 500 in 1991–92. As a consequence, many properties were progressively removed from the calculations. According to ABARE, the sudden and dramatic (24 per cent) decline in the number of establishments which occurred in one year in the mid-1980s was 'mainly a result of the sevenfold increase in threshold value' of the estimated value of agricultural operations which came into currency at that time (Garnaut & Lim-Applegate, 1998: 17). Caution is therefore needed in the use of statistics to demonstrate that restructuring is resulting in large-scale losses of producers from agriculture. Dramatic reductions in the numbers of producers in some years were simply a paper trick of bureaucrats.

Nonetheless, it is evident that widespread attrition of farmer numbers has occurred painfully (and with significant resistance) since the Second World War. The best approximation, for 1996–97, is that some 140 700 farm businesses operate in Australia. These supported 220 000 farm households, comprising some 630 000 people (Garnaut & Lim-Applegate, 1998: 3). Assuming the Australian population currently stands at about 19 million people, the farming population is about 3.3 per cent of the total Australian population. More detailed survey work has not been undertaken on the entire farming industry, but it has on the 'broadacre' industries (sheep, beef and cropping) operating in Australia. Representing about 65 per cent of all farming industries, the broadacre industries give a reasonable approximation of what is occurring in Australian farming. A 'snapshot' provided by ABARE (Garnaut & Lim-Applegate, 1998) for 1994–95 indicates:

- Farming remains family-based, with some 98 per cent of properties owned and operated by families.

- Farm numbers have fallen by 1.3 per cent (or by 2000 farms) per year since the mid-1950s. This is viewed as a response to economic pressures to expand size and output in the face of deteriorating terms of trade.

- Sixteen per cent of owner-managers (of which 97 per cent were men) in the sheep and beef industries had a university or college degree or diploma — more than double that recorded in other industries. Importantly, these people had less formal education than their spouses (indicating the generally high level of qualifications among women partners).

- The average age of owner–managers was 52 years.

- The farming population accounted for only 13 per cent of the total population of rural and remote Australia (where 'rural and remote' were considered as those areas outside the metropoles of 100 000 people or more).

- Farm businesses were dependent upon family labour (which totaled 85 per cent of all farm labour).

- While the average income (from all sources) was $26 800, only $9900 was derived from the farm business. In fact 37 per cent of farm businesses recorded a farm business loss in 1994–95.

- Income from off-farm wages, investments and social support payments accounted for about 63 per cent of total income. Some 45 per cent of families received social support payments worth on average $5100 during the drought years of 1994–95. The latter indicates the extent to which farming is supported by the state — albeit in a new form.

- Some 39 per cent of families earned income from off-farm work. Off-farm income was less important for large-scale operations. These operations have had higher productivity gains over the last 20 years than small or medium-sized properties, and have maintained positive rates of return, while small and medium properties have been unable to do so.

- The share of farm cash income increased with the size of the farm business — irrespective of the level of education of the owner-manager.

How might this cross-sectional evidence be interpreted?

AGRICULTURAL RESTRUCTURING: FEATURES AND FANTASIES

Much of Australian agriculture quite obviously remains in the hands of 'family' farmers. But what might an expression such as 'in the hands of' really mean? While still carried out extensively by families, farming is becoming ever more integrated into the market system. Farms are consequently taking on more of the characteristics of capitalist firms. Yet many of the important traditions of farming which remain — such as succession (as the younger generation takes on the occupation of farming) — are based, most usually, on patriarchal notions of inheritance. Then there is 'tradition'. Tradition seems to intervene in rational business logic. This occurs when a younger generation takes over the family property — in the face of economic forecasts which might logically lead to a decision to sell up and invest capital in the share or property markets. Emotional attachment to the land and the culture of agriculture are partial explanations for the continuation of family-based farming at a time when it has become economically marginalised. While farming and grazing might be continuing — are they ultimately surviving? The evidence to be presented below suggests they are not, at least in terms recognisable as the farming systems of the agrarian 'ideal'.

The term 'family farm' is generally taken to mean an operation which can be handled by the members of one family, possibly (although rarely now) with the assistance of a very small number of employees. Family members, meaning women and children, can be called upon to do farm work at times of seasonal or other need, if not throughout the year. It is this flexible supply of labour, along with a willingness to suffer periodic poverty, which has created the resilience of the family farm system. There are strong signs, however, that this resilience may no longer be sufficient. With family farms vastly dominant among agricultural enterprises (with only 2 per cent of farms said to be owned by companies — Garnaut & Lim-Applegate, 1998), it might follow that contemporary capitalism has provided a secure home for the rural petty bourgeoisie. The overall picture is a little more complicated. As indicated earlier, we need to appreciate that corporate involvement is growing in a number of rural industries. Corporate farms contribute some 6.5 per cent of broadacre and dairy production, and for industries like beef and cotton, the level of involvement is much greater (Martin, 1996). In some industries most production is corporate-based. For example, one company owns 80 per cent of Tasmania's area planted to hops (Miller, 1996: 72). When one looks at other countries, the possibility of an accelerated downward trend in family ownership looms. Family-operated farms produce only about half of Europe's agricultural output (Hill, 1993). There, family farming is more significant as myth than as lived reality.

The declining significance of family farming, while not so prominent in Australia, has attracted attention here as well as overseas. The earlier comments about the changing definitions of 'farm' notwithstanding, broad statistics appear to indicate that the actual number of farms in Australia has declined by just over 25 per cent in 25 years (Gleeson & Topp, 1997). Is it simply a matter of the larger, more business-oriented or corporate-owned farms surviving or increasing in number, while the smaller farms disappear? It was thought for some time that the middle-sized farms were the ones disappearing — with the smaller persevering through help from alternative sources of income. More recent Australian evidence suggests, however, that it is the smaller rather than medium-sized farms that are tending to disappear most rapidly (Lindsay & Gleeson, 1997). It should not be inferred that this necessarily indicates a kind of cleansing process through which the smaller operations are eliminated as the larger, more efficient, remain. We often hear of the supposedly inefficient 'one-farm-in-five' which is destined for oblivion (Stehlik et al., 1998). Davidson (1997) argues that small operators still persevere and expansion for the larger is problematic.

This perseverance turns our attention to the process of coping: its effects on people and its implications for the farming system. Gray et al (1993) found that coping strategies included:

- reducing expenditure on household needs as well as farm inputs and equipment;

- debt restructuring;

- working harder and increasing production;

- seeking alternative sources of income either on or off the farm;

- retraining for an alternative occupation;

- seeking government assistance either to retain the farm or dispose of it and establish elsewhere.

The final and least acceptable option for most is to seek structural adjustment funding to leave the industry. At a personal level, seeking education and skill-development, just talking it through with family and friends, and sometimes even just hoping, worrying, or increasing alcohol consumption, are coping strategies. Off-farm work is frequently adopted as a legitimate strategy to seek to balance the books, but this can destabilise the family relationships upon which the coping process depends (Gray & Lawrence, 1996). Hence, while people 'hang on' in agriculture, the means they are adopting to do so actually erodes the family relations they so desperately want to preserve. Off-farm work is becoming a very common practice. According to ABARE survey findings, 30 per cent of the total income of Australian broadacre farm families was derived from sources off the farm in 1994–95, with about one in three spouses of operators having off-farm employment (Garnaut, 1998). Each farm's prospects for off-farm earnings depend very much on the availability of employment in local rural labour markets, many of which suffer severe unemployment. The point being made here — as earlier in the chapter — is that part-time work is not a supplement, but a mainstay, for struggling rural families.

Off-farm work is only one form of 'pluriactivity' (the term used to describe the broadening of economic activity among farm operators). Farm production is being diversified. This can bring significant change to practices, such as that encountered by sugar cane growers establishing a wine industry among other new types of production (Hungerford, 1996). Farm tourism is another form of pluriactivity, but one that, like off-farm employment, offers much greater prospects to farm families in some areas, notably locations which have natural attractions for tourists. The more attractive areas are also more likely to offer employment opportunities to family members. Farm tourism, in particular, is moving farming away from its productive tradition, toward a form in which tradition is maintained only as performance. The notion that a growing number of rural producers derive income by acting out their roles as farmers, rather than for the physical products they grow, indicates the extent to which survival depends upon the adoption of a 'service' industry strategy. Such an attitude is evidenced in the words of the former National Party leader Tim Fischer, who told National Party colleagues: 'farming is becoming more and more a service industry ... if we are not addressing the issues affecting service industries, we are not addressing the issues affecting our constituents (*The Australian*, 17–18 April 1999). Pluriactivity might be seen to threaten the patriarchal basis of family farming, as women are taking on responsibilities for that non-agricultural part of farm operations which earn very significant incomes. This is occurring, probably on a small scale, with farm diversification, but has been long developing in terms of off-farm work.

We have pointed out that the image of the farmer as male is very misleading: farm work has also extensively been women's work — despite their apparent subjugation (Alston, 1998). In a recent survey by ABARE (Garnaut et al., 1999), it was revealed that farm men and women work a similar number of hours (about 60) per week. For women the 'mix' included domestic duties, childcare, community work, off-farm work, and on-farm work. Women averaged 19 hours per week in on-farm work and did the great bulk of the domestic duties and childcare (estimated together at 36 hours per week compared to men's five). There was, as expected, quite a strong division of labour for on-farm work, with women's 19 hours below half men's 51 hours per week. Some 33 per cent of women undertook off-farm employment, as did 23 per cent of men (Garnaut et al., 1999: 2). The participation rates of spouses (largely females) nearly doubled over 15 years — from 18 per cent in the early 1980s to 33 per cent in the mid 1990s.

Interestingly, the majority of women undertaking off-farm work entered managerial or professional occupations, while the main occupation for men working off the farm was in labouring positions. Not unexpectedly, women located in close proximity to regional centres had higher levels of off-farm income compared with those in more remote rural sites (Garnaut et al., 1999: 30). Commuting time was a major factor limiting engagement in off-farm work. As new service options — such as farm tourism — present themselves, we might predict that the role of women will become increasingly important to on-farm earnings. As service industries continue to outpace growth in agriculture — even in regional areas — so women again will be drawn into those industries.

Alston (1998: 197) has correctly argued that women's roles have been misrepresented as 'supplementary' to farm survival. Figures indicate that women generate 48 per cent of real farm income and make up 40 per cent of farm business partners. Despite this, only 8 per cent currently occupy rural industry leadership positions. This is mirrored in patriarchal inheritance patterns, where women are bequeathed only 5 per cent of farms (Alston, 1998: 198). Williams (1992) identifies the elements of women's 'invisibility' as including poor documentation of women's lives; marginalisation in terms of public profile; and disempowerment based on isolation. Things are, however, changing rapidly. According to Teather (1998), women's presence can no longer be construed 'invisible'. Women are now recognised in official statistics. They have increased their participation in farm politics, and they are involved in newly formed rural women's networks. Social attitudes continue to restrict women adopting a more involved role in rural affairs, but what cannot be denied is their success in 'forcing' such initiatives as the formation of rural women's units, various rural alliances, and government attention to women's issues (Grace & Lennie, 1998; Liepins, 1998). Despite such gains, there appears to be a significant gap between what farm women are doing, and what they would prefer to do. Their 'silence' acts to perpetuate continued exclusion (Alston, 1996; Alston & Wilkinson, 1998) — even in situations where women are well qualified professionals who might expect better 'status' in a rural location.

The problem for analysts is to predict the fate of farm patriarchy which, while still apparently pervasive, is under attack from the further depletion of the structural relations which underpin the image of the male farmer as one who supports family and community. As indicated above, farm women are entering former male preserves, like the management of boards and organisations. They now have a voice in rural politics and, at the farm level, are developing their own enterprises. While the public image of farming remains well and truly male, the role of women is becoming recognised by the public and government. The male 'myth' in farming appears to be eroding rapidly, even if there remain powerful instruments reasserting patriarchy both on farms and elsewhere.

The question of subsumption overarches many of these considerations relating to the disappearance or disintegration of farms, and exposure of the myths of farming. Subsumption refers to the process through which farms are becoming increasingly subservient to off-farm organisations — particularly those of large-scale capital. If it can be shown to be significant, subsumption could destroy the image of the independent farmer. The evidence which might support such a proposition, however, is not clear. In some industries farming is tied to processing and marketing by way of direct ownership or, more likely, contracts, and in such cases the proposition seems reasonable (Burch et al., 1992; Miller, 1996). In this case, farmers simply do what is required of them, on terms set by those to whom they supply. Importantly, this loss of autonomy can involve farmers forsaking their capacity to manage their farms as sustainably as they might wish. This can extend to pluriactive farms that are, for example, having their 'agendas' set by tour operators (Evans & Ilbery, 1992).

We should, however, consider the consequences of more subtle forms of subsumption than those apparent in intensive industries – such as chicken or vegetable production (Dixon, 1999; Lawrence, 1999). Broadacre farmers may relinquish control of their operations to financial institutions through indebtedness, or to agribusiness through marketing contracts, but the extent of this dependence can vary greatly (Lockie, 1998). Technological dependence may be a form of subsumption. Plant breeding rights, which under 1994 legislation can be controlled by agribusiness, is an example. Farmers are also dependent on being able to apply ever more sophisticated technology, including chemicals and seeds, as well as equipment. This gives agribusiness great influence over the practice of farming and renders the concept of 'self reliance' meaningless in every way except as mythology.

AGRICULTURAL RESTRUCTURING: MEANING AND SIGNIFICANCE

The importance of agricultural production to the nation's exports continues to be of significance. The relatively low cost of land has been a factor fuelling Australia's rural export economy. 'Adjustment' — with producers on properties either too small or economically marginal leaving agriculture, or increasing the scale of production through land acquisition — has been yet another. Agricultural structures have moved in line with overseas price regimes and this has meant that agriculture is, and has been, a dynamic industry in Australia. Rural producers and their representatives have been acutely aware of factors affecting supply and demand and they have sought to influence international policy through the World Trade Organisation and other bodies. Along with the trust in science to provide new innovations to increase agricultural productivity, there has been a strong element of 'faith in the market'. Producers have — particularly in the last three decades — been quite prepared to follow the lead of their economically 'dry' masters in the National Farmers Federation and National Party to seek overall economic advantage. What they have seen in return for their support has been the decline in domestic agricultural support in the face of continued protectionism abroad. A recent example of this has been the decision of the US to place restrictions on Australia's sheep meat imports (see Chapter 6). The result of a free market approach in Australia has been the development and maintenance of a 'productivist' model of agriculture which has come to characterise farming in countries such as the US, Canada and in many European nations (Marsden et al., 1993; Lawrence, 1995; Gray & Lawrence, forthcoming). This has linked agriculture to 'input' industries — the agribusinesses that supply fertilisers, insecticides, pesticides and seeds.

Farming is becoming progressively linked to the industrial food sector. Class relations are changing with control over the production process moving off-farm and entities like banks and food companies having a greater say in production. Through new relations with the farming sector and via distribution arrangements, transnational corporations (TNCs) are being influential in on-farm decision making. With farming being drawn progressively into various circuits of industrial and finance capital, rural producers are now increasingly 'bound' to the policies and strategies of overseas companies — many of which have no real interest in Australia's rural communities or environment. Since the 1980s such integration has accelerated — linked, as it has been, to the dismantling of tariff barriers and the removal of most subsidies. Farmers have begun to negotiate with the corporate food sector, which has reciprocated by issuing contracts to individual producers for the provision of specific commodities for particular local and international markets (Burch et al., 1992; Burch et al., 1996; Burch et al., 1999; Share et al., 1991). As suggested earlier, while most producers (in the broadacre industries) do not usually enter contracts with commercial processors, there is a definite move in the intensive beef industry, horticultural industries and some cropping industries (such as cotton, soybeans and canola) toward contract production (Lawrence, 1999). As Miller (1996: 207) has argued, the TNCs provide a crucial 'integration with the global economy and that in order to stay in business farmers have little choice but to join forces with international and large national firms'.

Not surprisingly, rural producers appear to approve of the corporate involvement in agriculture (Fulton & Clark, 1996). An important concern arises, however, in regard to future company policy regarding global sourcing. If Australian farmers become uncooperative or unwilling to produce in the manner desired by the company, farmers in alternative (off-shore) sites can be employed to fulfil the demands of the TNCs. This adds an external element of control over production — particularly in the negotiation of product price. It gives flexibility to the TNCs, while reducing it for the individual farmer, whose whole production strategy may be exclusively geared to long-term production of certain commodities for the company (Burch et al., 1992; Burch, forthcoming).

Bryant (1992) has linked the poor state of finances in farming with environmental degradation. With little 'spare' cash from farming in the early 1990s, sheep producers in South Australia were turning to grains. They were increasing cultivations via shorter rotations and ploughing extensively. Many wool producers were overstocking. This intensification occurred at a time when there was no money for rehabilitative land practices (such as better fencing and minimum tillage). There is now other evidence suggesting that producers in other regions are prepared to 'risk' soil loss in dry times by overstocking — contrary to their own better judgement (Stehlik et al., 1998). The hope is to remain in agriculture, but the effect is to further undermine the physical basis of future production.

As indicated, the closer links between farming and agribusiness have been interpreted by most agricultural sociologists as representing increased subsumption (Marsden et al., 1993; Bonanno et al., 1994; McMichael, 1994; Symes & Jansen, 1994). Levels of real subsumption (farm ownership by external capital) are very low, but formal subsumption (farm linkages with agribusiness for credit, inputs and processing) is becoming an increasingly important feature of on-farm production. That agri-chemicals and other off-farm inputs 'must' be purchased, and that such purchases are usually funded from bank or other borrowings, links farming to financial capital in a manner generally favourable to the latter organisations. One important outcome of subsumption is, then, that global finance is in a very strong position to influence the terms of production for Australian agriculture. It is here that contract farming — which Little and Watts (1994: 4) have argued is being generalised throughout the capitalist world economy — should be re-considered. Could 'subsumption' become the key to prosperity for producers? According to Rickson and Burch (1996: 173):

> Contracts are the key to company strategies for industrialising farm labour and regulating farmer relationships with their land, so that the biological uncertainties of growing plants and animals can be reduced … Contracts 'vertically coordinate' or subsume farmer land use decisions and behaviour into organisational management structures where farm land, effectively, becomes an organisational asset for as long as the farmer remains in the contract relationship.

There is some evidence, however, that in a world food marketplace which is 'greening', the corporate sector is attempting to convince more producers to farm sustainably (and organically) to give firms sourcing farm products a niche in the 'clean and green' export market (Burch et al., 1998). If this allows or requires producers to reduce their chemical and other inputs, this would be a victory for the 'output' side of agribusiness (the food industries) over the 'input' side of agribusiness (the agri-chemical corporations). The issue of whether there is any corporate greening in agriculture is one of immense interest in the determination of a sustainable future for commercial agriculture (Burch et al., 1998).

Another outcome of agricultural restructuring is the progressive erosion of farming culture — something which can be best described as 'detraditionalisation' (Gray, 1996; Gray & Lawrence, forthcoming). Farming systems based on traditional ways of thinking and ways of doing have been reproduced over many generations. Socialisation into the culture of agriculture provides for stability in the interpretation of what is acceptable and unacceptable in the ways the farm is operated, in family relations, and in community obligations. Today, structural changes are confronting values and lifestyle choices that have been part of farming tradition in Australia. Individualism is an example of one changing orientation in rural production. The dismantling of sections of farming, the movement of neighbours from the industry, and the necessity of off-farm work, are others which are altering — probably forever — rural 'tradition'. The stability of farm family relations is threatened by the constant battle to remain in agriculture in the face of economic decline within the industry. 'Culture' may only survive in the enactment of farming practices 'performed' in some regulated and contrived manner for urban Australians and overseas tourists looking for a quaint reminder of the past.

CONCLUSION

That Australian agriculture has undergone a period of quite significant change is not in question. The issues are: what have been the main features of change; and to what extent have such features led to new forms of social organisation in farming practice?

In this chapter we have indicated that the homogeneous image of the 'rural producer' or 'man on the land' is as flawed now as in past generations. We should note that there has always been an historic and important distinction between the 'farmer' and the 'grazier'. The former was identified with hard work, austerity and adversity; the latter with privilege and success. If there is any 'homogenisation', it is in the grazier having joined the farmer as a 'victim' of the policies of governments determined to pursue economic rationalism, and in having succumbed to the same forces of price decline which have destabilised 'family farming'.

There are at least seven grounds for rejecting the notion that the 'rural producer' is a person economically independent of high social status and of considerable political influence. The first is tied up with the 'myth' of the grazier. If we were to be historically accurate and racially unbiased, images of noble white pioneers would be replaced by those of black stockmen, who produced enormous wealth under conditions of quasi-feudalism. The second is that of the great diversity of production types — it is no longer appropriate to consider the 'farm' as something raising sheep or cattle, or growing wheat. It now grows ostriches, emus, or bamboo shoots for export. Third, rural production is no longer as important to Australia's future as it was three or four decades ago: it is just another industry struggling to survive in a world of globalised production relations. The fourth ground is that the majority of rural producers are tied to national and global capital in a manner that limits on-farm decision making. The fifth questions farmers' political influence. If the 'nose thumbing' of the Clinton administration in its 1999 decision to restrict the importation of Australian sheep meats to the US was not enough, the 'dry' line of Coalition parties about any reintroduction of support for the farming community provides a statement about the future of agriculture: don't expect the government to intervene to arrest the economic deterioration primary producers are facing. The sixth is that, in an era of ecologically sustainable development, the status rural producers once had as 'stewards' of the land has been replaced by an image of greed, rapaciousness and disregard for the environment. Finally, while males might undertake the majority of the physical on-farm duties, the image of agriculture as a masculine enterprise must be seriously questioned. Women's role in the social and economic reproduction of the family farm is now supported by statistics which show their extensive contributions, including the fact that their engagement in outside activities to supplement on-farm income actually keeps the farm viable. It is women's work, in the end, which sustains family farming throughout most of Australia.

Agricultural restructuring has been as disruptive as it has been pervasive. All sections of farming and grazing have had to weather the exposure to international markets in the context of the gradual withdrawal of state support. The effect has been to 'force' rural producers closer to the market via engagement with agri-food corporations, and via articulation with 'input' industries — including financial organisations. If one were to take the position of neo-classical economics in this regard, the conclusion might be drawn that primary producers have correctly 'read' the market signals and have modified their production to remain internationally competitive. They should be praised, in other words, for having adjusted quickly and with limited pain to the marketplace. In contrast, if one were to understand the situation from the position of critical sociology, the conclusion could be drawn that rural producers have been incorporated into circuits of global capital which promote the concentration and centralisation of capital, which more or less guarantee their continued subsumption to large-scale (and transnational) firms. As well, the latter interpretation would suggest that not only will their status continue to decline, but that — unless corporations become 'green' in both intention and practice — the environment will continue to suffer as a result of attempts by farmers and graziers to remain in agriculture at any cost. This is not to admonish farmers but to acknowledge that they are, at one and the same time, perpetrators and victims. Whether the move to gender equity in agriculture — where women not only share more fully in farm decision making, but also have influence over wider agricultural policy — provides a new trajectory in farming is yet to be determined. At this time of substantial change in Australian farming and grazing, innovative ideas — especially those that might lead to alternative and less environmentally damaging forms of production — are lamentably few. That is, in an era of burgeoning agricultural surpluses, continuing low prices, environmental degradation, and farmer stress and rural protest, new approaches to resource management, new ways of thinking about production, and new options for a sustainable future, remain in very short supply.

REFERENCES

Alston M (1996) 'Backs to the wall: Rural women make formidable activists', in Lawrence G, Lyons K & Momtaz S (eds) *Social Change in Rural Australia: Perspectives from the Social Sciences*, Rural Social and Economic Research Centre, Central Queensland University, Rockhampton, pp 77–84.

Alston M (1998) 'There are just no women out there: how the industry justifies the exclusion of women from agricultural leadership', *Rural Society* 8(3), pp 197–208.

Bonanno A, Busch L, Friedland W, Gouveia L & Mingione, E. (eds) (1994) *From Columbus to ConAgra: the Globalisation of Agriculture and Food*, University Press of Kansas, Kansas.

Bryant L (1992) 'Social aspects of the Farm Financial Crisis', in Lawrence G, Vanclay F & Furze B (eds) *Agriculture, Environment and Society: Contemporary Issues for Australia*, Macmillan, Melbourne, pp 157–72.

Burch D (forthcoming) *The Political Economy of Agri-food Restructuring, Report to the Government of Thailand*, Griffith University, Nathan.

Burch D, Rickson R & Annels R (1992) 'The growth of agribusiness: environmental and social implications of contract farming', in Lawrence G, Vanclay F & Furze B (eds) *Agriculture, Environment and Society: Contemporary Issues for Australia*, Macmillan, Melbourne, pp 259–79.

Burch D, Rickson R & Lawrence G (eds) (1996) *Globalization and Agri-food Restructuring: Perspectives from the Australasia Region*, Avebury, Ashgate.

Burch D, Lawrence G, Rickson R & Goss J (eds) (1998) *Australasian Food and Farming in a Globalised Economy: Recent Developments and Future Prospects*, Department of Geography and Environmental Science, Monash University, Melbourne.

Burch D, Goss J & Lawrence G. (eds) (1999) *Restructuring Global and Regional Agricultures: Transformations in Australasian Agri-food Economies and Spaces*, Ashgate, Aldershot.

Davidson A (1997) 'The dilemma of the middle: restructuring of the dairy industry in New South Wales', *Rural Society*, 7(2), pp 17–27.

Dixon J (1999) 'Reflexive accumulation and global restructuring: retailers and cultural processes in the Australian poultry industry', *Rural Sociology,* 64(2), pp 320–33.

Evans N & Ilbery B (1992) 'Farm-based accommodation and the restructuring of agriculture: evidence from three English counties', *Journal of Rural Studies,* 8(1), pp 85–96.

Fulton A & Clark R (1996) 'Farmer decision making under contract farming in northern Tasmania', in Burch D, Rickson R & Lawrence G (eds) *Globalization and Agri-food Restructuring: Perspectives from the Australasia Region,* Avebury, Ashgate, pp 219–38.

Garnaut J & Lim-Applegate H (1998) 'People in Farming', *ABARE Research Report,* 98(6), ABARE, Canberra.

Garnaut J, Rasheed C & Rodriguez G (1999) *Farmers at Work,* ABARE, Canberra.

Gleeson T & Topp V (1997) 'Broadacre farming today — forces for change', in *Agriculture, `Volume 2, Proceedings of the National Agricultural Outlook Conference,* ABARE, Canberra, pp 53–66.

Grace M & Lennie J (1998) 'Constructing and reconstructing rural women in Australia: the politics of change, diversity and identity', *Sociologia Ruralis,* 38(3), pp 351–70.

Gray I (1996) 'The detraditionalization of farming', in Burch D, Rickson R & Lawrence G (eds) *Globalization and Agri-food Restructuring: Perspectives from the Australasia Region,* Ashgate, Avebury, pp 91–106.

Gray I & Lawrence G (1996) 'Predictors of stress among Australian farmers', *Australian Journal of Social Issues,* 31(2), pp 173–89.

Gray I & Lawrence G (forthcoming) *Global Misfortune: Regional Australia in the New Millennium,* Cambridge University Press, Cambridge.

Gray I, Lawrence G & Dunn A (1993) *Coping with Change: Australian Farmers in the 1990s,* Centre for Rural Social Research, Charles Sturt University, Wagga Wagga.

Hill B (1993) 'The "myth" of the family farm: defining the family farm and assessing its importance in the European Community', *Journal of Rural Studies,* 9(4), pp 359–70.

Hungerford L (1996) 'Beyond sugar: diversification within the primary production sector in the Wide Bay–Burnett region', in Cryle D, Griffin G & Stehlik D (eds) *Futures for Central Queensland,* Rural Social and Economic Research Centre, Central Queensland University, Rockhampton, pp 27–30.

Lawrence G (1987) *Capitalism and the Countryside: The Rural Crisis in Australia,* Pluto, Sydney.

Lawrence G (1995) *Futures for Rural Australia: From Agricultural Productivism to Community Sustainability,* Rural Social and Economic Research Centre, Central Queensland University, Rockhampton.

Lawrence G (1999) 'Agri-food restructuring: a synthesis of recent Australian research', *Rural Sociology,* 64 (2), pp 186–202.

Lawrence G, Lyons K & Momtaz S (eds) (1996*) Social Change in Rural Australia,* Rural Social and Economic Research Centre, Central Queensland University, Rockhampton.

Liepins R (1998) 'Fields of action: Australian women's agricultural activism in the 1990s' *Rural Sociology,* 63(1), pp 128–56.

Lindsay R & Gleeson T (1997) 'Changing structure of farming in Australia', *ABARE Current Issues,* 4, ABARE, Canberra.

Little P & Watts M (eds) (1994) *Living Under Contract: Contract Farming and Agrarian Transformations in Sub-Saharan Africa,* University of Wisconsin Press, Madison.

Lockie S (1998) 'Is "Subsumption" still relevant? The question of control in Australian broadacre agriculture', *Rural Society* 7(3–4), pp 27–36.

Marsden T, Murdoch J, Lowe P, Munton R & Flynn A (1993) *Constructing the Countryside*, University College of London Press, London.

Martin P (1996) 'Ownership and management of broadacre and dairy farms', *Farm Surveys Report*, 1996, ABARE, Canberra, pp 46–7.

Miller L (1996) 'From contract farming and dependency to control by transnational capital: A case study in Tasmanian hops and agribusiness power', in Lawrence G, Lyons K & Momtaz S (eds) *Social Change in Rural Australia: Perspectives from the Social Sciences*, Rural Social and Economic Research Centre, Central Queensland University, Rockhampton, pp 64–76.

Price P (1998) 'Sustainability — what does it mean and how should it be applied in a regional context?', in Grimes J, Lawrence G & Stehlik D (eds) *Sustainable Futures: Towards a Catchment Management Strategy for the Central Queensland Region*, Institute for Sustainable Regional Development, Central Queensland University, Rockhampton, pp 15–27.

Rickson R & Burch D (1996) 'Contract farming in organisational agriculture: the effects upon farmers and the environment', in Burch D, Rickson R & Lawrence G (eds) *Globalization and Agri-food Restructuring: Perspectives from the Australasia Region*, Avebury, Ashgate, pp 173–202.

Robertson G (1997) 'Managing the environment for profit', *Outlook 97, Proceedings of the National Agricultural and Resources Outlook Conference*, ABARE, Canberra, pp 75–79.

Share P, Campbell H & Lawrence G (1991) 'The vertical and horizontal restructuring of rural regions: Australia and New Zealand', in Alston M (ed) *Family Farming: Australia and New Zealand*, Centre for Rural Social Research, Charles Sturt University, Wagga Wagga, pp 1–23.

Standing Committee on Agriculture and Resource Management (SCARM)(1998) *Sustainable Agriculture: Assessing Australia's Recent Performance*, CSIRO Publishing, Canberra.

Stehlik D, Gray I & Lawrence G (1998) *Australian Farm Families' Experience of Drought in the 1990s: A Sociological Investigation*, Rural Industries Research and Development Corporation, Canberra.

Symes D & Jansen A (1994) *Agricultural Restructuring and Rural Change in Europe*, Agricultural University, Wageningen.

Taylor M (1993) *Bludgers in Grass Castles: Native Title and the Unpaid Debts of the Pastoral Industry*, Resistance Books, Chippendale.

Teather E (1992) 'Remote rural women's ideologies, spaces and networks: the example of the Countrywomen's Association of New South Wales, 1922–1992', *Australian and New Zealand Journal of Sociology*, 28(3), pp 369–90.

Williams (1992) *The Invisible Farmer: A Report on Australian Farm Women*, Department of Primary Industries and Energy, Canberra.

4

THE RESTRUCTURING OF AUSTRALIA'S RURAL COMMUNITIES

MATTHEW TONTS

Over the past three decades, Australia's rural communities have experienced profound economic and social changes. Many of these changes are directly associated with the upheaval being experienced in agriculture. Problems such as declining farm incomes, farm amalgamation and enlargement, and the outmigration of the agricultural population are seriously undermining the economic and social viability of many small rural towns which service the agricultural sector. These towns have tended to experience a contraction of local economic activity, rising unemployment, depopulation, and the breakdown of local social institutions and networks (Smailes, 1995). More recently, these changes have been exacerbated by a general shift away from government policies based on socio-spatial equity, towards those that emphasise economic efficiency. The subsequent reforms in public policy have seen the withdrawal of many services which are essential to both the identity and survival of country towns, such as the local school or post office, on the grounds that their provision cannot be justified in narrow economic terms. Needless to say, the impact of such changes on the wellbeing of rural people has received considerable attention (see, for example, Black et al., 2000). There is, however, evidence to suggest that not all country towns are experiencing decline. Commentators have noted the success of local community initiatives in reviving local economies and reversing demographic contraction and social decay (Sorensen & Epps, 1996).

The purpose of this chapter is to examine the recent social and economic changes affecting Australia's rural communities. The chapter is divided into four main parts. The first section provides an overview of the nature of economic and political restructuring, and how these processes influence patterns of rural development. The second presents an overview of the demographic changes affecting Australia's rural communities, highlighting the socio-spatial dimensions of restructuring. The third section examines recent changes in public service provision and the concomitant impacts on rural communities. The final section reviews the prospects for local development initiatives as a means of overcoming decline, deprivation and socio-economic marginalisation.

ECONOMIC AND POLITICAL RESTRUCTURING

The term restructuring is commonly used to characterise major shifts in the economic trajectories and political strategies of advanced nations following the end of the postwar boom in the 1970s (Marsden et al., 1993). The onset of these processes of restructuring is usually attributed to a series of major structural changes in the world economy during the late 1960s and early 1970s, such as the collapse of the Bretton Woods agreement in 1971 and the 1973 oil shock (Dicken, 1992). These changes severely undermined the prosperity of Western nations, and contributed to falling demand for goods and services, rising unemployment and spiralling levels of public and private debt (Forster, 1995). At the same time, many trans-national firms were shifting their operations into the low wage countries of South-East Asia and Latin America, thereby contributing to problems of deindustrialisation in Western cities and regions (Fagan & Webber, 1994).

In response to these problems, many Western governments, including Australia's, began to turn away from traditional postwar policies based on economic protectionism and the welfare state, in favour of approaches which emphasised minimal government intervention in the economy (Walmsley, 1993). In Australia these neo-liberal policies contributed to, inter alia, the deregulation of the banking and finance sectors, the floating of the dollar, a reduction in the level of protection for Australian industries, the reduction of business and income tax, and the privatisation of public goods and services. The widely held belief was that such reforms would improve Australia's economic competitiveness and productivity, thereby restoring profits, economic growth and socio-economic wellbeing.

At more regional and local levels, the term 'restructuring' has also been used to describe the impacts of, and responses to, these broader economic and political changes (Fagan & Webber, 1994). While much of this literature has focused on restructuring in cities, and in particular on the changes experienced in urban labour markets and industrial areas, there is also an increasing body of research on non-metropolitan restructuring (see, for example, Burch et al., 1999). As the previous chapter pointed out, economic and political restructuring have contributed to radical changes in the characteristics and wellbeing of Australia's farm population. There has also been widespread concern about the impact of restructuring in rural communities. In many of the country towns which have traditionally existed to service the farming industry, population losses associated with agricultural restructuring have reduced the demand for services, eroded local employment opportunities and contributed to further outmigration.

These problems have been accompanied by changes in the nature of public sector institutions. Increasingly, the delivery of public services and infrastructure has become driven by market forces, rather than social and economic needs (Stilwell, 1994). The subsequent reduction in financial assistance for public services and infrastructure have had a disproportionate impact on rural areas (Furuseth, 1998). While there is evidence to suggest that there are serious social and economic consequences associated with these changes (Tonts & Jones, 1997), many politicians, public servants and commentators argue that they are simply unfortunate side effects in the drive for national competitiveness and productivity (see Pusey, 1991).

There is also another, more positive, dimension to economic and political restructuring in rural areas. Improvements in transport and communications technology, together with changes in the organisation of production, have contributed to a shifting spatial division of labour within Australia. The newer growth sectors in the economy, such as tourism and services, have different locational requirements to older industrial enterprises, and this has contributed to changing patterns of economic activity and employment. For example, the growth of the tourism sector has created new economic opportunities for coastal and other scenic rural environments (Butler et al., 1998). A general rise in the level of affluence has given further impetus to this growth, since many urban residents now have the ability to act on preferences for rural or semi-rural life-styles (Greive & Tonts, 1996). The outcome has been population growth on the fringes of Australia's metropolitan areas and in coastal and other scenic rural regions (see Maher & Stimson, 1994).

There is also evidence to suggest that, as part of the process of economic restructuring, private capital has become increasingly mobile (Massey, 1995). Improvements in transport and communications technology enable private firms to rapidly relocate their operations to areas most conducive to profit maximisation (Peck & Tickell, 1994). As a consequence, rural communities have become actively involved in domestic and international competition to attract or maintain capital investments and industries (Furuseth, 1998). This has led to a less predictable process of rural development, although much of the evidence suggests that coastal and peri-urban regions tend to perform better than inland areas in this pattern of inter-spatial competition. Thus, one of the dangers is that uneven levels of prosperity and development between places and regions are being exacerbated, with declining rural areas often marginalised by wealthier and politically stronger areas (Furuseth, 1998).

THE RURAL DEMOGRAPHIC DIVIDE

One of the ongoing concerns for rural Australia has been the decline of small country towns, particularly in regions heavily dependent on the agricultural sector (McKenzie, 1994). The problem of population decline in rural Australia is not new, and has generally been linked to a combination of farm mechanisation, farm enlargement and improvements in transport technology (Bolton, 1963). Since the 1970s, this decline has been exacerbated by restructuring in the agricultural sector (Productivity Commission, 1999a). Table 4.1 provides a summary of the population change experienced in rural communities with between 200 and 20 000 residents for the period 1991–96. From this, it is evident that nearly 40 per cent of Australia's rural settlements experienced a decrease in population. This confirms Sorensen's (1993) assertion that decline is predominantly a small town phenomenon, with around 92 per cent of declining settlements having resident populations of less than 5000 (see also Davies et al., 1998).

While this pattern of decline represents a long-term trend, it is also important to recognise that small towns are capable of growth. Table 4.1 shows that over 60 per cent of Australia's rural communities are expanding. Most of the growing towns (54.6 per cent of all towns) have fewer than 5000 residents. It is also interesting to note that 66.4 per cent (91 of 137) settlements with populations between 5000 and 20 000 grew between 1991 and 1996. This lends support to the argument of Beer et al (1994) that many of Australia's regional centres are experiencing a demographic and economic revival (see also Maher & Stimson, 1994).

TABLE 4.1
NUMBER OF SETTLEMENTS BY POPULATION CHANGE IN
AUSTRALIA'S RURAL SETTLEMENTS, 1991–96

% change in population	Population size of rural settlements				Totals
	≤999	1 000–4 999	5 000–9 999	10 000–19 999	
Growth %					
≥10	240	147	31	12	**430**
0<10	251	174	24	24	**473**
Growth total	**491**	**321**	**55**	**36**	**903**
Decline %					
0<-10	278	143	27	13	**461**
≥-10	84	34	5	1	**124**
Decline total	**362**	**177**	**32**	**14**	**585**
All towns	**853**	**498**	**87**	**50**	**1488**

SOURCE ABS, 1998.

Significantly, much of the population growth in rural Australia has been spatially selective, with the location of the settlement in its regional context more important than broad national economic and demographic trends (Lewis, 1998). Rural growth tends to be restricted to metropolitan commuter belts or to coastal and other scenic regions. For example, much of coastal Victoria, New South Wales and Queensland grew rapidly during the 1980s and 1990s (Haberkorn et al., 1999; Essex & Brown, 1997). The areas around most of the country's major capital cities also experienced considerable growth during this period (Maher & Stimson, 1994). By contrast, depopulation was the defining feature of Australia's inland agricultural regions (Productivity Commission, 1999a).

Nowhere are these trends more evident than in Western Australia. Figure 4.1 illustrates the spatial distribution of population change in local government areas (LGAs) in the south-west of Western Australia between the 1991 and 1996 censuses. From these data, it is evident that most of the population growth was concentrated along the coast or in the region surrounding the Perth metropolitan area. Further inland, in the State's wheat–sheep belt, the trend was one of almost universal decline. In the eastern parts of the State's south-west, the development of mining and, to a lesser extent, tourism contributed to population growth between 1991 and 1996.

FIGURE 4.1
POPULATION CHANGE IN SOUTH-WEST OF WESTERN AUSTRALIA,
1991–97

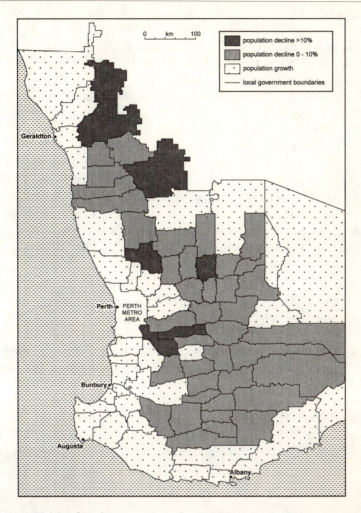

Not surprisingly, the pattern of population growth in coastal and metropolitan fringe LGAs is reflected in the changes experienced in the State's rural settlements. The evidence presented in Table 4.2 shows that, of the 59 Western Australian settlements located in the coastal zone or metropolitan fringe, only ten, or 17 per cent, recorded decline between 1991 and 1996. Recent reports by the Productivity Commission (1999a) and the Bureau of Rural Sciences (Haberkorn et al., 1999) demonstrate that these trends are not restricted to Western Australia. In Victoria, New South Wales, Queensland and South Australia the major-ity of growing towns are located in coastal and metropolitan fringe areas. Indeed, Davies et al. (1998) found a direct relationship between the commercial viability of Victorian country towns and their proximity to the Melbourne metropolitan area or coastal regions. On the other hand, it is clear that settlements located in the more remote inland parts of Australia are likely to be characterised by demographic and economic decline (see Productivity Commission, 1999a). In the case of Western Australia, more than half of all inland settlements experienced a decrease in population between 1991 and 1996. The majority of these were located in agricultural regions (Table 4.2).

The decline of these settlements is largely the result of the ongoing changes in the agricultural sector, such as falling incomes, farm amalgamation and the shrinking farm labour force. Fewer farmers and farm workers, together with lower incomes, means less spending in country towns. Thus, businesses in agricultural service settlements are not only disadvantaged because of the falling population, but also as a result of the reduction in spending by the remaining farmers, particularly during times of economic stress. The associated negative multipliers have eroded local employment opportunities, undermined the viability of many country businesses and contributed to further decline in rural communities (Sorensen, 1993).

TABLE 4.2
POPULATION CHANGE IN WESTERN AUSTRALIAN RURAL
SETTLEMENTS BY LOCATION, 1991–96

% change	Population size				Totals
	≤999	1 000–4 999	5 000–9 999	10 000–19 999	
Settlements in the coastal zone or Perth commuter belt					
≥10	13	10	3	1	27
0<10	9	10	1	2	22
0<-10	3	0	2	0	5
≥-10	3	2	0	0	5
Totals	28	22	6	3	59
Inland settlements					
≥10	8	3	0	0	11
0<10	20	11	2	0	33
0<-10	23	8	1	0	32
≥-10	6	5	1	1	13
Totals	57	27	4	1	89

SOURCE ABS, 1998.

From Table 4.2 it is also evident that decline is not uniform and that a number of inland towns experienced an increase in population between 1991 and 1996. While some of this growth can be explained by the development of new mining ventures in remote parts of the State, there is also evidence that at least some towns in the wheat–sheep belt have recently reversed long-term patterns of decline (Tonts, 1996). Such changes are also evident in other states. Case studies in New South Wales (Hudson, 1989), Queensland (Wildman et al., 1990) and Victoria (Cahill, 1995) have revealed that some small country towns have the capacity, at least in the short term, to revitalise their local economies and stimulate population growth — a theme given greater attention later in this chapter.

Alongside these broad population shifts, there are a number of other important demographic changes affecting Australia's rural communities. The majority of people leaving declining country towns are aged between 15 and 35 years (Hugo, 1994). This section of the population tends to leave rural areas because of the lack of employment and educational opportunities, and the greater lifestyle options available elsewhere (Montague, 1978; Rolley & Humphreys, 1993). For rural communities, though, this young adult population is vital in terms of providing a pool of marriage partners, maintaining birthrates and, eventually, reproducing the school age groups. There is also evidence to suggest that this younger population cohort tends to generate economic growth through higher levels of spending than some other sections of rural communities (Hudson 1986; see Chapter 5). Furthermore, the loss of this section of the population, together with the retention of older age cohorts, can contribute to a distorted age profile, with significant consequences for local social interaction and community sustainability. The younger age groups are important in maintaining local social institutions and organisations, such as sporting teams and voluntary organisations, and in contributing to new and fresh ideas for rural communities (Black et al., 2000).

Of further significance for rural communities has been the ageing of the population. Throughout much of rural Australia, the population over the age of 65 years has increased steadily. In part, this is a direct result of the greying of the national population, but it has also been fuelled by a growing number of retirees migrating to rural environments. Several case studies have revealed that factors such as the lower cost of living in rural areas, together with perceived lifestyle benefits, have prompted many urban retirees to move not only to coastal and scenic areas, but also to some inland country towns (Smailes & Hugo, 1985; Greive & Tonts, 1996). There is also evidence to suggest that many towns are retaining a high proportion of their retirees, when previously they might have migrated to urban or coastal regions (Black et al., 2000). The reasons for this appear to be fourfold. Firstly, rising real estate values in coastal and metropolitan regions has made purchasing housing in these areas less affordable to many rural retirees. Secondly, negative images of urban life, such as crime, violence and congestion, have contributed to some retirees remaining in country towns (Hudson, 1986). Thirdly, with the economic difficulties besetting agriculture, many farmers have retired to local towns and continue to help out on the family farm. This reduces labour costs and, in some cases, allows other family members to seek off-farm income. Finally, as Greble (1979) points out, there is a natural reluctance on the part of many retirees to leave rural areas and lose touch with networks of family and friends.

While a growing elderly population can help to stabilise rural communities, it is important to recognise some of the consequences associated with the greying of rural Australia. One of the most important issues is that of service provision. The low incomes, poor health and restricted mobility of many elderly rural residents makes them particularly vulnerable to reforms in the provision of services and facilities (Black et al., 2000). Thus, catering for the needs of an older population presents an important challenge to governments and communities as they attempt to provide services on an efficient and equitable basis.

RURAL SERVICE PROVISION

Australia has a long tradition of public sector intervention in support of economic and social development in rural areas. It is a tradition that became established largely in response to the difficult conditions faced by pioneer farmers and settlers. Throughout much of rural Australia, governments promoted agricultural development through various forms of development inducements, such as land grants, cheap credit and, most importantly, the construction of railway networks (Glynn, 1975). Alongside these initiatives, State governments also provided facilities such as schools, hospitals, courthouses and police stations on a generous per capita basis, since it was widely held that a scarcity of such services would act as a disincentive to rural development and prosperity (Greble, 1979). A similar approach pervaded Commonwealth policy, with the government providing post offices and, later, telecommunications services throughout rural Australia (Powell, 1988). Federal and State governments also provided funding for the provision of social infrastructure, such as meeting halls, sporting facilities and local libraries.

Initially, the social support given to rural areas tended to be driven by economic development goals. By the late 1960s and early 1970s, however, government policy had become increasingly concerned with social equity issues (Powell, 1988). Despite the continuing constraints of distance, isolation and limited financial resources, particular attention was paid to ensuring that inequalities between urban and rural populations were minimised. During this period, governments increased spending on some rural services (particularly health and education) and initiated a number of welfare measures which targeted disadvantaged sections of the rural population. Federal and State governments also pursued equity goals through public monopolies, which have the capacity to subsidise loss-making rural services from more profitable urban and metropolitan services. Thus, monopolies such as Australia Post and Telstra (formerly Telecom) cross-subsidised their rural services and helped to temper extreme disparities between urban and rural postal and telecommunications costs, which would have otherwise disadvantaged rural people (Holmes, 1988). Other public services, such as education, health and police, are centrally administered and funded for similar reasons.

For Australia's rural communities, these approaches to rural service provision not only ensured a reasonable level of wellbeing, they made an important contribution to the economic and social viability of local communities. Local purchasing and spending by public services generates significant income for rural communities and can act as a partial counter to economic difficulties experienced in the private sector. Public sector employment is usually stable and has the capacity to inject new residents who can often bring fresh ideas and dynamic leadership to rural communities (Sorensen & Epps, 1996). The services themselves also provide an important social role within rural communities. Small rural schools, for example, not only provide education, but retain young people in local communities, help to avert problems caused by lengthy travel for students, and provide a centre for activities such as sport, voting and community meetings.

RURAL SERVICE REFORMS

The rise of neo-liberal politics in Australia during the early 1980s ushered in a series of radical reforms of the public sector. The downturn in the national economy was accompanied by policies which emphasised lower taxes and a reduction in public spending (Stilwell, 1994). This shift was accompanied by a hardening of social attitudes and a general backlash against policies based on redistribution and social equity. Increasingly, Commonwealth, State and local governments opted for market-led solutions in deciding how to best allocate and deliver the limited resources available for public services and infrastructure. Such an approach has been criticised on the grounds that it results in a lower social wage, a reduction in the level of cross-subsidised services, a deterioration in the quality of public infrastructure, and the provision of many public services on a user-pays basis, with rural and remote dwellers frequently paying more than metropolitan residents (Webber & Crooks, 1996; Stilwell, 1994; Taylor, 1991). Despite this, governments throughout Australia have tended to eschew the goals of social equity in favour of greater 'economic rationality' in the delivery of public services and infrastructure. This approach has been characterised by three strategies:

1   the privatisation of public services and infrastructure,

2   the withdrawal or rationalisation of public services and infrastructure,

3   the devolution of responsibility for service provision to the local government level (Furuseth, 1998; Tonts & Jones, 1997).

PRIVATISATION

The first of these strategies, privatisation, has been embraced enthusiastically by policy makers. Notable examples of privatisation have occurred in the banking, communications and transport sectors. In the banking sector, the selling-off of publicly owned banks, such as the Commonwealth Bank, has had a significant impact on Australia's rural communities. While the Commonwealth Bank and the various State banks were provided throughout much of rural Australia on a cross-subsidised basis, following privatisation governments had less capacity to regulate the nature and extent of the services provided by these former public assets. In the pursuit of profits, the former publicly owned banks rationalised or closed many smaller cross-subsidised rural branches (see Chapter 9). Recent research has indicated that, following bank closures, residents and businesses experience difficulties accessing credit, exhibit a decreased propensity to save and are more likely to shop or conduct business in neighbouring towns that retain full banking services (Ralston, 1999). Consequently, towns that have experienced bank branch closures are likely to suffer from contracting local economies, further service withdrawal and depopulation.

The privatisation of public monopolies in the communications sector has also impacted on rural communities. Australia Post, for example, has recently closed unprofitable post offices or replaced them with smaller private agencies (Share, 1993). Furthermore, the partial privatisation of Telstra has resulted in increasing concerns over the continued provision of cross-subsidised telecommunications services in rural areas. As a recent federal government report has argued (IPAC, 1997), access to comprehensive and affordable telecommunications is essential if rural areas are to overcome the problems of distance and isolation, and if rural communities are to integrate into a global economy dominated by newly emerging information technologies.

A similar set of policy actions has involved the outsourcing, or contracting-out of functions previously undertaken within the public sector. In many country hospitals, for example, 'non-core' services, such as cleaning, catering, gardening and general maintenance, have recently been contracted out to private firms in an attempt to reduce costs. The rationale for such changes is that, if non-core services are open to tender from private firms, the cost of providing them will be reduced through market competition. For the employees of these hospitals, outsourcing has resulted in considerable uncertainty and, in some cases, job losses, since the contracts to provide the services are often won by mobile metropolitan-based firms. The eventual outcome for rural communities is a contraction of employment opportunities and further outmigration (Evatt Foundation, 1996: 217).

Similar changes have occurred in the transport sector. In 1995, for example, the Western Australian rail service, Westrail, decided to contract out the maintenance of rural railway lines. Previously, such work was undertaken by Westrail employees based in country towns. Not surprisingly, most of the contracts were awarded to large firms based in Perth, thereby reducing rural employment opportunities. This problem is compounded by the demographic characteristics of the Westrail employees being laid off, the majority of whom were unskilled men over the age of 50. According to a recent report by the Productivity Commission (1999b), these former railway workers have less than a 44 per cent chance of finding local work within 12 months of being made redundant, thus exacerbating the problem of outmigration from country towns (see also Industry Commission, 1996).

RATIONALISATION

The shift towards the market-led allocation of resources has also resulted in the rationalisation and withdrawal of many public services from small and declining rural communities. In rural areas with low and often declining population thresholds, the pursuit of economic efficiency goals has resulted in the downgrading or closure of many basic public services, including schools and hospitals. This is despite the lower health, educational and welfare status of rural people (Black et al., 2000).

Increasingly, public services and the employment and development that they generate are being concentrated into larger regional centres (Jones & Alexander, 1998). While such centralisation might be seen as an efficient market response that enables operating, administrative and overhead costs to be reduced, the social and economic costs borne by rural people are often ignored. For example, the closure of small country hospitals lengthens patients' travelling time, thereby increasing the costs associated with receiving health care. Such changes also have a disproportionate impact on the less mobile members of the community, particularly young people and the aged.

The withdrawal of public services can have other socio-economic impacts in rural communities. In addition to the loss of local employment, the closure of public services, particularly schools and hospitals, can also have a significant psychological impact on rural communities, often signalling the 'death' of a town (McKenzie, 1994). Some commentators have argued that such changes can lead to a sense of deprivation among the remaining rural residents and contribute to further outmigration (Lawrence, 1987). Furthermore, the loss of services can act as a disincentive for potential new residents and industries, thus acting as a barrier to population and economic growth.

It is also likely that the ongoing rhetoric of economic rationalism and the constant spectre of service withdrawal might be as damaging to the viability of rural communities as actual service closures. The Western Australian government, for example, recently released a statement on the closure of small country schools which was widely reported in the rural press (Tonts & Jones, 1997). While the report did not commit the government to school closures, the uncertainty created amongst rural communities with schools targeted as possibilities for closure was probably quite damaging. Such speculation about the future of local schools can undermine the confidence of potential new residents, and can even result in local parents sending their children to more secure schools in larger towns (McGinness, 1996). Thus, the speculation about service closures in rural areas might lead to further stagnation and decline, thereby contributing to actual service withdrawal.

There have, however, been a number of government programs which have attempted to mitigate the impacts of service withdrawal from country towns. For example, schemes have been introduced which provide financial assistance to rural residents needing to travel to metropolitan areas for specialist health care. Governments also provide assistance to financially disadvantaged rural students who need to leave their communities in the pursuit of secondary and tertiary education (McGinness, 1996). Another way that governments have attempted to improve rural service delivery is by consolidating similar or overlapping services. An example of this is the Multi-Purpose Services (MPS) scheme, which has attempted to improve both the economic efficiency and the standard of health care in rural areas. This program, which is jointly funded by the Commonwealth and various State governments, has attempted to integrate and consolidate rural health care services in rural communities which are not able to justify (financially) their existing health care services on a 'stand alone' basis. The MPS scheme usually brings together a traditional country hospital with a number of allied health services, such as Home and Community Care, geriatric health care, and social work and counselling. By pooling financial and other resources, the MPS enables previously separate health care programs to share accommodation, infrastructure and administration costs, thereby increasing economies of scale and operating efficiencies. Thus, while the establishment of Multi-Purpose Services are 'economically rational' in that they attempt to maximise economic efficiency and minimise costs, the benefit of such a scheme is that it does not necessarily result in the wholesale withdrawal of smaller health services from rural areas. On the contrary, by improving cost efficiencies, services are being consolidated and maintained.

DEVOLUTION

Devolution is another strategy that governments have used in their pursuit of economic efficiency in service delivery. Increasingly, small and often declining local governments are being handed the responsibility for delivering services and infrastructure previously provided by State and federal governments. Thus, in many parts of rural Australia, local governments, often with populations below 1000, and some below 500, are now providing (or at least facilitating) services such as geriatric health care, public housing, and telecommunications infrastructure. The rationale for such a shift is that local authorities are more attuned to local needs than centralised governments. There is also an argument that local governments are better managers of limited financial resources, and are therefore more capable of making difficult policy and spending decisions (Furuseth, 1998).

Despite the economic rationality of devolution, there are a number of potential problems in shifting the responsibility for the delivery of basic and essential services down the administrative hierarchy. While there is little doubt that the provision of services by local governments can be successful and responsive, achieving a uniform level of service delivery across rural regions can be difficult following devolution. Decisions about which services will be provided where and to what extent are generally made by the individual local authorities and often depend upon the support of those in positions of political power (Gray, 1991). As such, there is a danger that some services which might be accepted as essential in some areas will not be provided by all local governments. This increases the likelihood of social inequalities between rural communities.

Local governments also face funding constraints in the provision of public services. While local governments° have been burdened with increasing responsibilities for community wellbeing, there has been a gradual reduction in financial assistance for local authorities from both the State and federal governments. Between the mid-1980s and the mid-1990s, the level of local government grants per-capita declined in real terms by around 17 per cent (Park, 1996). As a result, many rural local governments do not have a large enough revenue base to generate the funding required to provide essential services and infrastructure. In rural Western Australia, for example, local government rates and charges contribute only 46 per cent of all revenue, and with steady population decline affecting many agricultural areas, the revenue generated from local sources is likely to continue to diminish (Park, 1996).

One of the responses to this has been the widespread amalgamation of small, 'inefficient' local governments in declining rural areas. According to proponents of amalgamation, larger local governments means increased economies of scale and a capacity to provide services on a more efficient and sustainable basis (Vince, 1997). While local government amalgamation has the potential to offer substantial cost savings in many declining rural areas, the wider economic and social benefits are not so clear. Merging local governments can be a severe blow to the local sense of identity and has the potential to erode community social sustainability (Rentschler, 1997). This was confirmed by Jones (1993), who found that very few small inland towns which are not the headquarters for local government are capable of remaining economically or socially viable in the long term. In the process of amalgamation, towns which become the headquarters for local government tend to benefit from the centralisation of spending and employment, and are in a stronger political and economic position than the nearby non-shire headquarters towns as a consequence. Those towns which lose local government headquarters usually suffer a concomitant loss of economic activity, population and social interaction. In this respect, local government amalgamation has the potential to exacerbate patterns of uneven economic and social development in rural Australia.

REVITALISING LOCAL COMMUNITIES

Earlier in this chapter it was noted that economic and population decline are not necessarily characteristic of all rural communities in agricultural regions. While there are no simple solutions to the problem of decline, many rural communities have begun to pursue various survival and revitalisation strategies (see Sorensen & Epps, 1996; Moon, 1991; Wildman et al., 1990; Tonts, 1996). This response has been encouraged by the State and Commonwealth governments who, in line with the principles of economic rationalism, have become increasingly reluctant to engage in proactive economic development strategies in rural (and other) areas. Such an approach is consistent with neo-liberal calls for greater self-reliance and voluntarism as alternatives to social redistribution (Badcock, 1997). Thus, the approach of Commonwealth and State governments over recent years has been to simply provide guidance to communities attempting to help themselves (Wheatbelt Development Commission, 1999).

At the heart of most rural revitalisation projects is the use of local people and resources in solving local problems. This requires the active participation of local residents in community governance and decision making (Etzioni, 1993). In rural Australia, the forum for such an approach is usually local government. Through this tier of government, a town's civic and business leadership can identify local needs, formulate development strategies, galvanise community support, and raise capital and resources (Sorensen, 1993). On its own, however, local government is unlikely to be successful in promoting economic and social revitalisation. Voluntary skills, labour and resources, often provided by the local business sector, are critical in ensuring the success of revitalisation projects.

Rural communities throughout Australia have engaged in a variety of local development and revitalisation projects. These have included main street beautification and rejuvenation, local rate subsidies for new industries, the provision of free land for new industries and households, and the development and promotion of local tourism and recreation ventures (Wildman et al., 1990; Cahill, 1995; Sorensen & Epps, 1996; Tonts, 1996). Although the projects undertaken are usually small in scale and limited in scope, their impact in some country towns has been positive and has prompted further entrepreneurial development in some cases. Furthermore, when local projects contribute to the diversification of the local economic base, they can help shield rural communities from the periodic difficulties which affect the agricultural sector.

While economic development projects tend to dominate the literature on rural revitalisation, social and environmental projects can be equally significant. These might include the provision of sporting and recreational facilities, the organisation of cultural events, and ecological rehabilitation schemes. For Murray and Dunn (1996), such projects are just as important as economic revitalisation strategies, since they not only improve the local quality of life, but also provide a sense of community involvement and achievement. Murray and Dunn also note that economic development without broader social development can be exploitative and divisive, but when pursued alongside social, cultural and environmental objectives it can enhance community wellbeing.

It is important to recognise, however, that there are a number of potential problems with the current focus on local development and revitalisation. Firstly, the establishment of successful local strategies depends upon leadership, initiative and the availability of resources to develop (Sorensen, 1993). Communities without these attributes face the prospect of continued decline. Not surprisingly, one of the major constraints facing rural communities is the lack of financial resources available for local development, since State and Commonwealth governments rarely provide direct assistance for rejuvenation projects.

Secondly, not all projects will lead to the revitalisation of local economic and social systems. Many communities that have attempted to pursue local development strategies have been unsuccessful due to a lack of community motivation, poor leadership, or simply bad luck. Thirdly, although some local revitalisation strategies have the capacity to be successful, changes in macroeconomic conditions or circumstances can radically alter local economic conditions and undermine the viability of community projects (Chisholm, 1995). Finally, it is difficult to see how local development strategies can be successful if they are formulated in the context of a zero-sum competition with other communities targeting the same potential markets and investors. The outcome of this competition tends to be a pattern of uneven spatial development, since communities with stronger leadership, greater economic and physical resources and certain locational advantages tend to win at the expense of neighbouring communities (Tonts & Jones, 1996).

Averting such problems will not be easy in the current economic rationalist policy environment. The potential benefits of approaches to local development are unlikely to be realised without a greater degree of support from the higher tiers of government. Most obviously, local strategies require at least some degree of financial assistance, and the contribution that rural communities can make to local revitalisation is ultimately circumscribed by the availability of finance (Murray & Dunn, 1996). It is also important for governments to recognise that a vibrant rural society is unlikely to be achieved by encouraging communities to compete for resources, markets and investors. In the pursuit of economic and social revitalisation, rural communities should be encouraged to collaborate and cooperate on a wider regional basis. As such, rural development demands not just a local, but also a regional and national focus — something that is the responsibility of the State and Commonwealth governments. Without such a commitment, local strategies are likely to be short-lived and will probably achieve only limited success.

CONCLUSION

The challenges facing Australia's rural communities are serious. In many cases, ongoing processes of economic restructuring have contributed to declining local trade, depopulation and the deterioration of local social institutions and interaction. Alongside these trends, rural communities have been directly affected by the emergence of economic rationalism in Australian public policy. Under such policies, the unfettered intrusion of international economic pressures into highly specialised rural economies is contributing to considerable local economic and social turmoil. This has been exacerbated by reforms in the delivery of public services and infrastructure, which have resulted in increasing levels of social dislocation and marginalisation in many rural areas. There is, however, evidence that rural communities need not be passive recipients of negative economic, social or political pressures. Many rural communities have reversed long-term patterns of decline using local knowledge, skills and ingenuity. Nevertheless, it is also important to recognise the limitations of local strategies. It has become increasingly evident that without support from the higher tiers of government, local development initiatives can result in a highly ephemeral and uneven pattern of rural development.

While governments have become increasingly aware of the limitations of economic rationalism and a minimalist approach to dealing with rural social and economic affairs, it is also evident that they are not about to embrace any radical alternatives. Indeed, a recent federal government report argued that the only means of delivering a viable future for rural communities is to remain committed to a program of economic reform (see Anderson & MacDonald, 1999: 1). This is despite the mounting evidence to the contrary. While there is little doubt that economic efficiency and competitiveness are worthwhile goals, an increasing number of commentators, both in Australia (Stilwell, 1994; Walter, 1996) and overseas (Giddens, 1998), have begun to call for policy approaches which provide a better balance between the values of economic liberty, self-help and social justice and equity. The evidence presented in this chapter suggests that these calls are justified.

REFERENCES

Anderson J & MacDonald I (1999) *Regional Australia: Meeting the Challenges*, Commonwealth of Australia, Canberra.

Australian Bureau of Statistics (ABS) (1998) 'Census of Population and Housing, 1996' (various catalogues).

Badcock B (1997) 'Recently observed polarising tendencies and Australian cities', *Australian Geographical Studies*, 25, pp 243–59.

Black A, Duff J, Saggers S & Baines, P (2000) *Rural Communities and Rural Social Issues: Priorities for Research*, Rural Industries Research and Development Corporation, Canberra.

Bolton GC (1963) 'Australian country towns', *Hemisphere*, 7, pp 13–18.

Burch D, Goss J & Lawrence G (eds) (1999) *Restructuring Global and Regional Agricultures: Transformations in Australasian Agri-food Economies and Spaces*, Ashgate, Aldershot.

Butler R, Hall CM & Jenkins J (eds)(1998) *Tourism and Recreation in Rural Areas*, John Wiley and Sons, Chichester.

Cahill G (1995) *Growing Your Own Community: Successful Adjustment Strategies for Rural Communities*, Rural Industries Research and Development Corporation, Municipal Association of Victoria and Agriculture Victoria, Melbourne.

Chisholm DA (1995) 'Maintaining a sustainable economic base in rural towns: a case study of Leeton', *Australian Geographer*, 26, pp 156–63.

Davies WKD, Townshend I & Ng L (1998) 'The survival of commercial hierarchies: rural service centres in western Victoria, Australia', *Tijdschrift voor Economische en Sociale Geografie*, 89, pp 264–78.

Dicken P (1992) *Global Shift: The Internationalization of Economic Activity* (second edition), Paul Chapman, London.

Essex SJ & Brown GP (1997) 'The emergence of post-suburban landscapes on the north coast of New South Wales: A case study of contested space', *International Journal of Urban and Regional Research*, 21, pp 259–85.

Etzioni A (1993) *The Spirit of Community: Rights, Responsibilities and the Communitarian Agenda*, Crown Publishers, New York.

Evatt Foundation (1996) *The State of Australia*, Evatt Foundation, Sydney.

Fagan RH & Webber MJ (1994) *Global Restructuring: The Australian Experience*, OUP, Melbourne.

Forster CA (1995) *Australian Cities: Continuity and Change*, OUP, Melbourne.

Furuseth O (1998) 'Service provision and social deprivation', in Ilbery B (ed) *The Geography of Rural Change*, Longman, Harlow, pp 233–56.

Giddens A (1998) *The Third Way: The Renewal of Social Democracy*, Polity Press, Cambridge.

Glynn S (1975) *Government Policy and Agricultural Development: A Study of the Role of Government in the Development of the Western Australia Wheatbelt, 1900–1930*, University of Western Australia Press, Nedlands.

Gray I (1991) *Politics in Place: Social Power Relations in an Australian Country Town*, Cambridge University Press, Melbourne.

Greble WE (1979) *A Bold Yeomanry: Social Change in a Wheat Belt District*, Creative Press, Perth.

Greive S & Tonts M (1996) 'Regulation, land development and the contested countryside: reflections on Bridgetown, Western Australia', *New Zealand Geographer*, 52, pp 87–92.

Haberkorn G, Hugo G, Fisher M & Aylward R (1999) *Country Matters: Social Atlas of Rural and Regional Australia*, Bureau of Rural Sciences, Department of Agriculture, Fisheries and Forestry, Canberra.

Holmes JH (1988) 'Private disinvestment and public investment in Australia's pastoral zone: policy issues', *Geoforum*, 19, pp 307–22.

Hudson PB (1986) *Processes of Adaptation in a Changing Rural Environment: A Comparison of Four Rural Communities in New England, NSW*, unpublished PhD thesis, Macquarie University, Sydney.

Hudson PB (1989) 'Change and Adaptation in Four Rural Communities in New England, NSW', *Australian Geographer*, 20, pp 54–64.

Hugo GJ (1994) 'The turnaround in Australia: some first observations from the 1991 census', *Australian Geographer*, 25, pp 1–17.

Industry Commission (1996) *Competitive Tendering and Contracting Out by Public Sector Agencies*, Commonwealth of Australia, Canberra.

Information Policy Advisory Council (IPAC)(1997) *Rural&regional.au/forall: Report of the Working Party Investigating the Development of Online Infrastructure and Services Development in Regional and Rural Australia*, AGPS, Canberra.

Jones R (1993) 'Country town survival: some Anglo–Australian comparisons', in Wilson MR (ed) *Proceedings of the Prairie Division, Canadian Association of Geographers*, Department of Geography, University of Saskatchewan, Saskatoon, pp 1–19.

Jones R & Alexander I (1998) 'Remote living: the case of Esperance, Western

Australia', in Bowler IR, Bryant CR & Huigen PPP (eds) *Dimensions of Sustainable Rural Systems*, Netherlands Geographical Studies No. 244, University of Utrecht, Utrecht, pp 195–204.

Lawrence G (1987) *Capitalism and the Countryside: The Rural Crisis in Australia*, Pluto Press, Sydney.

Lewis G (1998) 'Rural migration and demographic change', in Ilbery B (ed) *The Geography of Rural Change*, Longman, Harlow, pp 131–60.

Maher CA & Stimson RJ (1994) *Regional Population Growth in Australia*, AGPS, Canberra.

Marsden T, Murdoch J, Lowe P, Munton R & Flynn A (1993) *Constructing the Countryside*, University College London Press, London.

Massey D (1995) *Spatial Divisions of Labour: Social Structures and the Geography of Production* (second edition), Macmillan, London.

McGinness M (1996) 'Social issues for rural and remote Australia', in Burdon A (ed) *Australian Rural Policy Papers, 1990–95*, AGPS, Canberra, pp 199–264.

McKenzie F (1994) 'Population decline in non-metropolitan Australia: impacts and policy implications', *Urban Policy and Research*, 12, pp 253–63.

Montague MM (1978) *Internal Migration and an Australian Rural Community*, unpublished PhD thesis, University of Queensland, Brisbane.

Moon J (1991) 'From local economic initiatives to marriages a la mode?; Western Australia and Tasmania in comparative perspective', *Australian Journal of Political Science*, 26, pp 63–78.

Murray M & Dunn L (1996) *Revitalizing Rural America: A Perspective on Collaboration and Community*, John Wiley, Chichester.

Park H (Chairman)(1996) *Advancing Local Government in Western Australia: The Report of the Local Government Structural Reform Committee*, Government Printer, Perth.

Peck J & Tickell A (1994) 'Jungle law breaks out: neoliberalism and global-local disorder', *Area*, 26, pp 317–26.

Powell JM (1988) *The Historical Geography of Australia: The Restive Fringe*, Cambridge University Press, Cambridge.

Productivity Commission (1999a) *Impact of Competition Policy Reforms on Rural and Regional Australia*, AusInfo, Canberra.

Productivity Commission (1999b) *Progress in Rail Reform* (Draft Report), AusInfo, Canberra.

Pusey M (1991) *Economic Rationalism in Canberra: A Nation-Building State Changes Its Mind*, Cambridge University Press, Cambridge.

Ralston D (1999) *Banking in the Bush: The Transition in Financial Services*, Centre for Australian Financial Institutions, University of Southern Queensland, Toowoomba.

Rentschler R (1997) 'Community and cultural participation', in Dollery B & Marshall N (eds) *Australian Local Government: Reform and Renewal*, Macmillan, Melbourne, pp 125–50.

Rolley F & Humphreys JS (1993) 'Rural welfare: The human face of Australia's countryside', in Sorensen AD & Epps R (eds) *Prospects and Policies for Rural Australia*, Longman Cheshire, Melbourne, pp 241–57.

Share P (1993) 'Telecommunications and rural and remote Australia', *Rural Society*, 3, pp 22–6.

Smailes PJ (1995) 'The enigma of social sustainability in rural Australia', *Australian Geographer*, 26, pp 140–49.

Smailes PJ & Hugo GJ (1985) 'A process view of the turnaround: an Australian rural case study', *Journal of Rural Studies*, 1, pp 31–44.

Sorensen A (1993) 'The future of the country town: strategies for local economic development', in Sorensen A & Epps R (eds) *Prospects and Policies for Rural Australia*, Longman Cheshire, Melbourne, pp 274–89.

Sorensen A & Epps R (1993) 'An overview of economy and society', in Sorensen A & Epps R (eds) *Prospects and Policies for Rural Australia*, Longman Cheshire, Melbourne, pp 7–31.

Sorensen A & Epps R (1996) 'Community leadership and local development: dimensions of leadership in four central Queensland towns', *Journal of Rural Studies*, 12, pp 113–25.

Stilwell F (1994) 'Economic rationalism, cities and regions', *Australian Journal of Regional Studies*, 7, pp 54–65.

Taylor M. (1991) 'Economic restructuring and regional change in Australia', *Australian Geographical Studies*, 29, pp 255–67.

Tonts M (1996) 'Economic restructuring and small town adjustment: evidence from the Western Australian Central Wheatbelt', *Rural Society*, 6, pp 24–33.

Tonts M & Jones R (1996) 'Rural restructuring and uneven development in the Western Australian wheatbelt', in Lawrence G, Lyons K & Momtaz S (eds) *Social Change in Rural Australia*, Rural Social and Economic Research Centre, Central Queensland University, Rockhampton, pp 139–53.

Tonts M & Jones R (1997) 'From state paternalism to neo-liberalism in Australian rural policy: perspectives from the Western Australian wheatbelt', *Space and Polity*, 1, pp 171–90.

Vince A (1997) 'Amalgamations', in Dollery B & Marshall N (eds) *Australian Local Government: Reform and Renewal*, Macmillan, Melbourne, pp 151–71.

Walmsley DJ (1993) 'The policy environment', in Sorensen AD & Epps R (eds) *Prospects and Policies for Rural Australia*, Longman Cheshire, Melbourne, pp 32–56.

Walter J (1996) *Tunnel Vision: The Failure of Political Imagination*, Allen & Unwin, Sydney.

Webber M & Crooks W (eds)(1996) *Putting the People Last: Government, Services and Rights in Victoria*, Hyland House, Melbourne.

Wheatbelt Development Commission (1999) *Annual Report, 1998–99*, Government Printer, Perth.

Wildman P, Moore R, Baker G & Wadley D (1990) 'Push from the bush: revitalisation strategies for smaller rural towns', *Urban Policy and Research*, 8, pp 51–59.

5

WHERE DO PEOPLE FIT IN THE RURAL EQUATION?

FIONA HASLAM McKENZIE

Farming has been a key industry in the history of Australia over the past 200 years and has been pivotal in shaping Australian nationhood. Until the mid-1950s, agriculture contributed 85–90 per cent of the country's export earnings, although this has now declined to about 30 per cent (Alston, 1995). Furthermore, rural Australia and 'the bush' have been central to the invention of national identity. The image of 'the bush' had a certain romance that the suburban reality did not engender, so although Australia has always been highly urbanised, the rural idyll has been a persistent influence. It is therefore of national significance to report on trends on depopulation, the tenuous economic situation of many farmers and the stultification of some communities in contemporary rural Australia.

Australia is no exception to the worldwide pattern of declining regional areas, and these trends have coincided with an international shift to neo-liberal policies since the 1970s. Prior to this, governments tried to ensure that people in rural and remote regions enjoyed a similar standard of services to those living in the cities. However, by the mid-1980s, policies to protect farmers from global market trends were regarded as not in the long-term interests of farmers, and in any case were becoming difficult to maintain in a small economy. Consequently, governments at both State and federal levels have been committed to micro-economic reform and less intervention. They have rationalised infrastructure provision and cannot justify to the voting majority (usually urban based), large scale expenditure to small rural communities. The federal government is no longer prepared to protect Australian farmers with tariffs and levies. Deregulation, the removal of protection and the rapid integration of the country into the global economy have been seen as the only mechanisms that could maintain prosperity and quality of life.

Restructuring associated with deregulation and the opening of Australian markets to international competition has had a substantial impact on regions (see Chapter 6). As a consequence, the business of farming is in a state of almost continuous change. There has been increasing capitalisation of agriculture and technological advances have led to major shifts in the way the business of farming is conducted. Australian agricultural producers, usually family farmers, have been required to expand and develop skills in a wide range of areas. The pressure to achieve economies of scale and efficiencies has caused farms to become bigger, producing more with less labour. Alongside these patterns, communities are becoming progressively smaller. These changes have been painful because the fundamental economic restructuring has also challenged traditional social values.

This chapter provides an insight to the often overlooked social and environmental outcomes of the restructuring of rural and regional Australia. It explores the implications of the changes at a human level and examines the interrelations between economic outcomes and their impact upon the environment and the social fabric of rural society. The chapter draws extensively on the results of a research project funded by the Rural Industries Research and Development Corporation (RIRDC) into conditions in the Western Australian Central Wheatbelt, that commenced late in 1997 (Haslam McKenzie, 1999). In the Central Wheatbelt, broadacre farms vary in size but they average 2500 hectares (ABS, 1997). The RIRDC study focused on three statistical divisions (Hotham, Lakes and Campion) that together comprise approximately half the area of the Central Wheatbelt (Figure 5.1). Although focusing on farm people and their experience of economic and government policy changes, field research undertaken for the project revealed that town based participants who are not directly involved with farming had similar concerns about their own and their community's future.

THE CENTRAL WHEATBELT OF WESTERN AUSTRALIA

Western Australia contributes a significant proportion of Australian agricultural exports. In 1996 the State contributed 24.5 per cent of Australian agricultural exports, producing 40.6 per cent of the nation's wheat and 25.3 per cent of its wool (ABS, 1997). Unlike the eastern States, however, Western Australia has few regional centres and a small rural population scattered over a large geographic area. In the Wheatbelt, in 1996 there were only eight rural urban centres with more than 2500 people. Only one of these eight had more than 7000 people (Geraldton). The Wheatbelt has limited industrial diversity, meaning that the regional economy is heavily influenced by the health of the agricultural sector. Farm enterprises in the three divisions of Lakes, Campion and Hotham are recognised for generating a significant proportion of Western Australia's wheat quota as well as producing high quality fine merino wool and a variety of other grains, including barley, oats, lupins and pulse grains (Table 5.1).

FIGURE 5.1
LOCATION OF LAKES, CAMPION AND HOTHAM STATISTICAL
DIVISIONS

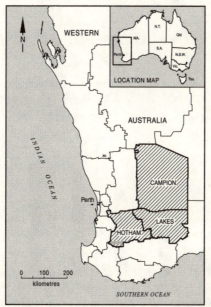

SOURCE ABS, 1996

TABLE 5.1
WHEAT AND WOOL PRODUCTION OF LAKES, CAMPION AND
HOTHAM, 1995–96

| | Wheat for grain | | Shorn & on-skin wool | |
	($'000)	%	($'000)	%
Campion	411 969.4	22.74	39 435.7	6.40
Hotham	120 792.5	6.67	98 604.6	15.99
Lakes	262 117.6	14.47	41 421.9	6.72
Total	794 879.5	43.87	179 462.2	29.10
West Australia	1811 958.6	100.00	616 621.7	100.00

SOURCE ABS, 1997.

There is evidence (Haslam McKenzie, 1998) that the number of family farming enterprises in Western Australia has approximately halved in the last 35 years as the cost price-squeeze has forced many from the sector and rural regions. Even though the number of farms has decreased, the area being farmed has not changed (ABS, 1997, 1992–3, 1989–90, 1996). ABS census data for 1961–96 shows that Campion, Lakes and Hotham are the most severely depopulated regions in the West Australian sheep–wheat belt (ABS, 1961, 1971, 1981, 1991, 1996). Furthermore, the depopulation trend is not occurring evenly between the genders. The number of women in the three agricultural divisions has decreased although, as shown in Figure 5.2, the number of women has decreased at a slower rate than that of men.

FIGURE 5.2
POPULATION CHANGE BY GENDER, HOTHAM, LAKES AND CAMPION, 1961–96

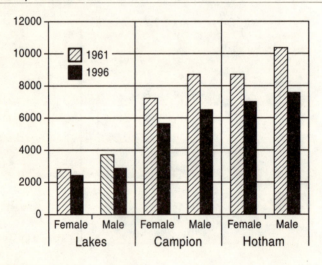

SOURCE ABS, 1961, 1996.

This depopulation trend has occurred against a backdrop of a declining farm labour force generally throughout Australia, particularly for men. It is difficult to accurately ascertain the changes in female participation rates in the agricultural sector because census statistics have not always been gathered in a way to properly account for farm women and their work.[1] Nonetheless, ABS and anecdotal evidence suggest that the increase in the number of women working on farms has escalated in the last 15 years. ABARE data from the AAGIS survey of broadacre and dairy farms found that in 1993–94 approximately 40 per cent of all business partners were women. This was supported in a survey of agricultural women undertaken throughout Western Australia in June 1997 (Haslam McKenzie, 1997).

INFRASTRUCTURE AND SERVICES

Media reports and other anecdotal evidence have suggested that centralisation and the closing of services is impacting on the profitability and efficacy of farm enterprises. The provision of government infrastructure, such as railway, postal, health and education services, as well as corporate services such as banking, have been referred to as crucial for the survival of a viable rural Australia (see Chapters 4 & 9; Tonts, 1996; Jones & Tonts, 1995; Vanclay & Lawrence, 1995; Taylor, 1991). Accordingly, a key goal of the RIRDC research project (mentioned above) was to find out what happens to people and communities when these services are withdrawn or severely pared.

Questionnaires were sent to 2000 farm enterprises, which were randomly selected from the local government electoral roles. The response rate to the questionnaires was 22 per cent. Unfortunately the timing of the mail out coincided with an early harvest, and so follow-up reminders were not feasible as farmers were completely focused on that important task. Mail questionnaires were followed by face-to-face interviews with 68 respondents from throughout the Central Wheatbelt. The interviews were conducted in a semi-formal structure, in line with the framework of the mailed questionnaire. Focus groups were also held in four key regional locations. In most situations, the interviewees were keen to discuss both personal and business issues. Sensitive issues such as farm succession, disposable income, marital issues and mental health were discussed willingly by most interviewees, to the extent that very often it was difficult to complete the interview within the agreed time.

A significant proportion of the questionnaire was devoted to assessing the effects of diminishing infrastructure provision, and the centralisation or the closure of services. Health, particularly mental health, and education resources were the services most research participants of all ages were particularly concerned about. Through their written responses and the interviews, participants showed how mental health and educational issues impact on the immediate community and the region generally, as well as on the efficiency of rural enterprises. A diminution of services can have a crucial impact on the sense of community which, it is argued, is critical for the social sustenance of people. Ignoring people's social needs can influence the business viability of some enterprises, with wide counter-productive outcomes.

RATIONALISATION OF HEALTH SERVICES

Most interviewees acknowledged the difficulties of maintaining health and medical services in the Central Wheatbelt given the dispersed population and government policies of micro-economic reform, but a number raised questions of equity. One respondent ('J') from Lakes felt very angry about the intermittent medical services, the unreliability of services and the lack of choice given regional dwellers compared to urban dwellers:

> Just get this straight. Out here we earn a hard buck but we are good for Australia. I mean, our crops are pretty useful for the Australian export dollar. But hey, we are human too, we get sick sometimes and we need a quack [doctor], no, we deserve better than a quack. I don't like some of the people that get shoved out here, I want a choice just like you fat cats in the city. If I want to pick and choose who my family goes to, I have got to go to Perth, four hours away. I know the argument is that a doctor does swing by here every other week, but listen, I can't be guaranteed to get sick on that day.

While most respondents reported that general health services were within an hour's drive, this does not capture the very real difficulty and frustration many communities experience in accessing services. As the 'K' family in Lakes explained, the inconvenience of living on a farm, straddled between several basic health services, can be frustrating and wasteful of time and resources:

> When [baby] needed some antibiotics and the Corrigin guy [doctor] didn't have them, we drove to Narrogin to get the script filled. So, we went 50 kilometres to see the doctor, and 150 kilometres to get a script filled and 100 kilometres home, all in a day with a three week old sick baby.

Obstetric services are not generally available outside the larger centres such as Perth, Albany, Geraldton and Kalgoorlie, none of which are situated in the Central Wheatbelt. Merredin (Campion) has a well-equipped hospital, but it has not been able to maintain reliable full-time anaesthetist services so full-time obstetric services ceased in mid-1997. The lack of more sophisticated support facilities and the relatively small numbers of potential patients are factors that discourage doctors from establishing or taking over a rural medical practice. Several interviewees spoke of the inconvenience and cost of staying in Perth to have their babies, particularly when there are other children to be cared for. Not only is accommodation and travel expensive, but being away from the business for several days at a time is inefficient, inconvenient and potentially costly if other labour has to be employed, or essential tasks are left undone. Similarly, sick babies or children are regularly transferred from smaller hospitals to larger, far away ones to receive specialised treatment. When a mother usually accompanies her child, she is separated from her family, perhaps other children, and her support networks. This experience can be both expensive and traumatic.

Suicide and general mental health issues were not highlighted in the questionnaire, yet many questionnaire returns (28 per cent) made mention of one or both issues. Mental health issues were a recurring concern in each of the information gathering instruments. Overall, 19 per cent of all respondents perceived that there was a need for a dedicated mental health service and the responses were evenly spread across all three statistical divisions. It is well known that young males living in rural and remote areas have a significantly higher rate of suicide than those in urban areas. The Commonwealth Department of Health and Family Services' *Youth Suicide Monograph* (1997: 3) acknowledges major variations among rural communities, with small, remote and inland communities at highest risk.

A few interviewees were prepared to speak of their own experiences of mental illness, but more were concerned about how the various expressions of mental health were impacting upon their families and communities generally. Many respondents indicated that mental health encompassed unresolved family issues and sustained stress that were having a direct impact on the economic viability of some enterprises. Several interviewees indicated that, although they didn't have significant financial worries, they had difficulty coping with community expectations of being a successful farmer while also trying to balance a family life. During the interview process, one community was still coming to terms with a recent male youth suicide, seven months after another male had suicided in a neighbouring community. These events were mentioned over and over again, sometimes in communities far from the grieving community, and regardless of whether the interviewee actually knew the families closely involved. As communities shrink, the social net is cast wider, and as a consequence events have a far-reaching impact.

EDUCATION

The study showed that education is a high priority for most families and the availability of what is deemed an acceptable education can influence the way parents operate their business and how they live their lives. It was found that the availability of secondary and to a lesser extent tertiary education has the potential to influence the cropping program, the intensity of farming, the acquisition of off-farm income, and even the temporary splitting of families while extra income is sought.

The availability of higher education (senior high school and TAFE) had impacted on the disposable income of 19 per cent of all respondents to the questionnaire. The closure of a local school had meant that parents had to drive their children further each day to catch transport to school, and children were travelling longer. 'K' from Hotham described the quandary some families face and the impact on the general community when facilities close:

It is disastrous. It is a roundabout route and it is actually about one and half hours on the bus there as well as back which I would never consider. If you want them to do any good you are wasting your time. If they had a straight route over there it would probably only be three-quarters of an hour. [It's a] huge impact when the high school closes because you lose the teachers, the kids are leaving now when they are 12. How many will come back? No farming families would catch that bus because the buses that come from the outside areas wouldn't meet with the other bus in time, unless you left home at crack of ... The school closing has had a big effect.

For most, there was the expectation that if the children were to be educated privately, the wife would have to fund it with off-farm income. In their report, *Missed Opportunities: Harnessing the Potential of Women in Agriculture*, Elix and Lambert (1998) identify women as increasingly contributing to farm enterprises through their off-farm earnings: from 24–68 per cent of farm cash income since 1984. This off-farm income is critical to the ongoing viability of some farm enterprises, as well as meeting family needs. Relying on women to generate off-farm income introduces a new set of problems. Many farms cannot afford the additional labour costs of outside wage workers, and in any case it is often not possible to find a paid worker, or a combination of paid workers, who can perform the multi-dimensional and interrelated functions of the typical farm wife.

For some families, funding education through off-farm work while living on the farm has been either not viable or not the preferred choice. As population and services dwindle, parents have demonstrated that they are willing to change their lifestyle, live separately, leave their community and commute long distances for their children to get the education they deem suitable. Four families that were interviewed had made major changes to the way they live their lives, farm their enterprise, or both. The wives and children had left the farm and rented or bought accommodation in Perth in order that the children can be educated privately. The husbands–fathers of these families commute to the city and the wives and children visit the farm only on school holidays or during particularly busy farm times. These families conceded that rural infrastructure will continue to retract if more families follow their example. Attaining an education at tertiary and, sometimes, secondary level are the times when the next generation leaves the community, sometimes permanently. Many parents feel their family unit is broken up prematurely; as one respondent from Campion suggests: 'if children need to go to Perth for work and education, family ties are broken, it is difficult to keep the family together'.

It was also found that the location of a child's school would often influence where the family shops, socialises and does business, so the closure of a school has a significant impact upon a community. It appeared that the local school means more to a small community than simply a place to educate children; it is a meeting place and central focus for the energy of the community. When a school closes, quite often the rest of the town dies with it. 'J' in Hotham recounted her husband's experience:

> In [husband's] schooling life there was a school at Harrismith, that closed and the children all came up here to our school. There isn't much left there now. The pub closed soon after and everyone went elsewhere to shop, wherever their kids were. It's the same now, all over.

SOCIAL AND COMMUNITY ISSUES: DOES A SENSE OF COMMUNITY MATTER?

A large number of participants in this research project have increased the land-size of their farm enterprise in order to achieve economies of scale and sufficient return on investment. Many of the same farmers expressed regret and concern about the dwindling rural population and the shrivelling of a sense of community. With little prompting, many conceded that a farm enterprise 'buying out' another farm enterprise translates to fewer children in the school, fewer teachers in the community, fewer customers for the local community, and so the cycle continues. This supports Lawrence and William's (1990: 40) claim that 'a more productive agriculture is coming to mean less productive and viable rural communities'. This trend seems cumulative (McKenzie, 1994; Lawrence & Williams, 1990), and becomes self-sustaining as it leads to service diminution and subsequently more out migration.

The social and cultural aspects of restructuring have affected social institutions such as community repertory clubs, sporting clubs and service organisations. Most respondents and interviewees were loathe to overtly describe their town as 'dying', but it was obvious that many felt their town was struggling to remain socially, if not economically, viable. In the focus groups, residents were asked if it should be accepted that some towns be allowed to die, given the historical reasons for the location of towns and the current mobility of population. This caused a great deal of emotive discussion. It was suggested that the three large regional centres were a long distance from many farm enterprises, and that the time to travel to access services in these centres was time away from productive work and therefore a significant cost. Also, an attractive feature of rural life is a sense of community that has the potential to enhance the environment and the satisfaction of the individuals within that environment. Focus groups mentioned the importance of keeping older people in the community, and unless there are services to help maintain them, they will drift away to other centres. Older citizens are valued for their voluntary contributions around the district and their business.

Maintaining the younger generation was seen by some as a very important goal for local communities. If events and occasional entertainment are provided for younger people in the district, it is hoped they will be encouraged to stay. Few communities in this region had been able to provide facilities for youth entertainment, apart from hotels. In most towns children congregate at hotels, even though legally they are not able to imbibe alcohol. Children go to the hotel because it is where parents and friends congregate. Most interviewees agreed that underage drinking was no more a problem in the bush than the city, but that pubs are sometimes the scene of unacceptable behaviour, and that children are often exposed to it at an early age in the bush, because pubs are often the only regular social gathering place in some communities. Sport was the only other option most towns had to offer as a community activity, although sporting teams struggle for numbers as communities shrink. If one town's club or team amalgamates with that of another town, hotel, food and other entertainment outlets inevitably suffer in the town which loses its organisation.

Community activities are an avenue for establishing the friendships and social support that sustain individuals when services are not available. A regularly cited example was childcare, particularly for women:

> I don't have family here and I need childcare from time to time. That sense of community is important because I know people who can help me out with the kids or by just being my friend. You need a town as a focus.

and:

> We [the town] have a crèche once a week, on Tuesdays, so everything is organised on Tuesdays. It can be really hard if you are trying to organise something and they are trying to utilise the crèche. You can have four or five things happening on Tuesday, which is bad because you don't get a lot of support for any of them. It also affects the businesses in town, because everyone comes in on one day, so all the groceries and vegies have to be here by Monday or they just sit on the shelf and wilt.

Maintenance of the sense of community often falls to civic-minded citizens who are prepared to give their time and energy. Nonetheless, community involvement comes at a cost to individuals, families and businesses. Anecdotal evidence suggests that as economic margins narrow for some farm enterprises, farmers and their families spend less time contributing to their community and being actively involved in sporting teams, service organisations and recreational clubs. The author of this study was keen to ascertain whether the increased demands of farming and financial pressures influenced participation in community activities. It appears that the participation of respondents whose disposable income had increased or remained the same during the last ten years was more likely to be influenced by the financial health of their enterprise. Of respondents whose disposable income had decreased in the last ten years, however, about the same numbers reported they were influenced by the financial health of their enterprise, as were not. The results are shown in Figure 5.3.

FIGURE 5.3
COMMUNITY PARTICIPATION BY CHANGE OF DISPOSABLE INCOME

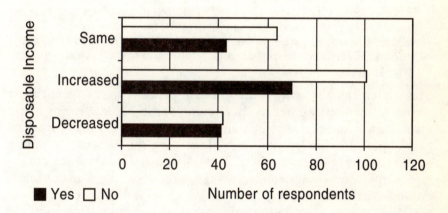

SOURCE Author's survey results.

In particular, focus groups discussed the relationship between farm enterprises' disposable income and community involvement. Many participants suggested they would forego some business requirements in order that family members continue to participate in some community and social activities. The question was asked by one focus group: 'Is farming a means to an end and shouldn't that end be a certain quality of life?' The issue of 'community' is central to rural peoples' lives. According to the 1997 *Farm Weekly Rural Women's Survey* (Haslam McKenzie, 1997) — a survey of approximately 1000 respondents conducted throughout Western Australia — the single biggest problem for rural women was 'isolation'. Sixty-three per cent of respondents indicated that isolation was a major concern. Many respondents qualified this statement by explaining their sense of isolation: it was not necessarily physical isolation, but also psychological, emotional and cultural isolation. A number of women interviewed for the RIRDC project also discussed the problem of isolation. According to a young married woman at Bruce Rock in Campion:

> I felt I didn't know anyone, and that everyone was checking me out. I was lonely. I spent a lot of time on the phone and then I started going to Perth more and more, even when I was needed here at seeding time. My husband and his family couldn't understand it and then were furious when they had to employ someone. Their anger just made it all worse. It improved a lot when I started playing tennis in town and went to craft.

A sense of community also mattered a great deal for participants such as 'S', a young woman who had married into an established farming family:

> If there had not been a community here when I married I think I would have walked away. People who have lived here all their lives don't understand. For a young newly married girl, it is all new; a new husband, a new house, a new family who probably own the house, a new industry, a new culture. If I had not been able to go to the local town, how else would I have recognised myself as me?

This statement underlines the difficulties newcomers, particularly young women, encounter in small communities. Aside from the human cost of isolation, there is an economic cost. Conservative data based upon *Missed Opportunities: Harnessing the Potential of Women in Agriculture* (Elix & Lambert, 1998) calculated that women constitute 32 per cent of agricultural workers and make up a major client group for agencies and organisations which serve the agricultural sector. Women have skills and priorities that mirror and complement the skills brought by men. They have taken on an increasingly broad range of farm activities and increasingly fill the requirement for flexible farm labour in response to the highly variable climatic and economic circumstances on farms. A National Farmer's Federation study (Kilpatrick, 1996) argues that greater use of labour-saving technologies enable women to do previously extremely strenuous tasks, whereas greater emphasis on keeping good financial records and farm management planning has also allowed women to employ a greater range of skills on-farm. Many farm women, however, are unpaid for the work they do, or as one woman joked, they are 'the unpaid employed'. ABS statistics cited by the National Farmers' Federation (1995) show that the number of 'employers', 'own account workers' and 'employees' have all dropped dramatically since the mid-1980s; however, the accounted contribution of family labour has increased significantly. Many women who belong to a multi-generation farm enterprise complain they rarely see the income attributed to them for business purposes. 'L' at Lakes felt that she, like many other daughters-in-law, were always seen as a financial 'threat', even after 12 years of marriage. By discounting her tangible contribution, it minimised the bargaining power she might have for personal expenditure:

INTERVIEWER: What work do you do on the farm?

L: Quite a lot now the kids are in school. I drive tractors and trucks when required, do a lot of the sheep work, I'm a good sheep dog and last year I did a couple of kilometres of fencing with a young work experience kid, so I do my bit.

INTERVIEWER: Are you paid?

L: Well, no, not formally. My husband gets a wage from the family partnership but it's the same as when I was housebound with babies. That's how it works for most young marrieds.

INTERVIEWER: How do you feel about that?

L: Don't start me. I don't bring it up any more because it makes life tough for [husband] with his parents, and they are my kid's grandparents. But put it this way, because I just 'help out' and don't have a say, I can't put in my two bobs worth for my new bathroom or those other things which would make living here really nice. A bathroom doesn't earn its keep on a farm so it's not a priority.

The research project found that farm succession issues have enormous potential to undermine enterprise sustainability. Due to its 'private' nature, succession has been largely overlooked in much previous rural research. The RIRDC project demonstrates how persistent and insidious the outcomes of poor farm business planning are when succession is ignored. Many farmers fail to appreciate the parallels between a commercial corporate organisation and a commercial broadacre farm, and particularly the parallel in that its financial partners and human resources are crucial to its continued viability. Familial relationships and the close proximity of several families on a farm make discussion of the issues awkward, and for many they are ignored. The farm succession issue showed itself to be a poisoned challis, which few families seem able to escape, and has broad ramifications for communities and even industries.

Of the 68 on-farm interviews conducted for this research project, 51 had been through a traumatic farm succession, and 36 admitted the process had been extremely expensive. A respondent from Hotham suggested: 'For last 12 years we have tried to split a family farm between two brothers. The liquidator and his lawyer have been useless and we have lost a lot of money over this and we are [still] not yet independent and none of us are happy. It is very sad.' Of the 51 families, 14 had not had a family reconciliation. Not one interviewee could think of, or remember, a family enterprise where there were multiple married family partners who were all happy with the business farm succession arrangements, equity and future plans. Those who have endured the process and whose relationships and enterprise have survived, such as 'M' in Lakes, are sought after by community groups and individuals to share their experiences and insights for achieving successful outcomes for all participants:

> Look, it is an issue that is tearing country WA apart. The need for farm and succession planning. People come to us now and say 'how did you do it?' They saw us all going through the pain. Our family went to a farm succession seminar in early 1990, [and my] husband's parents came reluctantly. When we got someone in to help us they [parents] sat at the table and wouldn't say a word. It was hard because they wouldn't acknowledge the need for succession planning.

Many participants explained that while the succession was being worked out, co-operation and farming efficiency was compromised. 'I' from Campion explained a not uncommon scenario:

> Oh God it was awful, and the farm really suffered. We were spending money on lawyers and accountants which meant we didn't plant trees, attend field days when we should have, we held off on the fencing program and I think we are still paying for that in erosion and inefficient paddock sizes. I think both families felt the other was gossiping so I stopped shopping in town and that set off a whole lot of bad feeling in the community. In the end, the farm borrowed money at a rate that wasn't sensible, to buy us all out from each other, but we all just wanted to be separate, almost at any cost. It's ghastly.

Sometimes the farm does not survive the succession process and the costs are enormous. The usual scenario is that the farm is broken up and sold (usually to neighbours), and the family often breaks down irrevocably. The community often loses a family or families, the school is smaller and may lose a teacher or other resources, and local businesses lose more custom. So the cycle continues.

CONCLUSION

Research shows that economic strategies are less likely to have success if social and community needs are ignored (Tonts & Jones, 1996; Lawrence, Share, & Campbell, 1992; Jones & Tonts, 1995). While agricultural and economic restructuring have been called for, in the Central Wheatbelt there have been some painful social costs which have impacted negatively on large and small enterprises. Even profitable farms and businesses are experiencing social issues that undermine their efficacy and economic returns.

It is also increasingly being acknowledged that the contribution to the agricultural sector by women has not been sufficiently recognised (Teather, 1996; Teather & Franklin, 1994; Liepins, 1996; Alston, 1995). The data and information reported here indicates that women bear the brunt when social services in rural communities are reduced. Isolation and limited support for women are consistent reasons for them wanting to leave a rural situation. All participants in the study have admitted that rural regions and agricultural industries can ill afford a drain of women. Similarly, the youth drain is a real concern for the continuing viability of the community services that remain. Regions that are losing population or employment because of a perceived lack of good business opportunities, lose capital and potential entrepreneurs and therefore vibrancy and optimism, continuing the cycle of pessimism and devaluation.

Local initiatives and strategic economic development are limited by the processes of government policy (Hubley, 1997) that do not necessarily understand or even recognise the spatial and locational development of rural social and regional development, nor the differences between regions. Many in the Central Wheatbelt region of Western Australia are concerned about the balance of government policy concerning economic, social and environmental issues, and the perceived lack of understanding of regional issues. The increasing pressure on rural communities to meet their own needs requires voluntary labour and time to be given by citizens who therefore compromise their own enterprise. There are consistent complaints that businesses can no longer afford that benevolence, and consequently the sense of community is further threatened. Rural and regional Australia is increasingly exposed to issues that threaten social sustainability. This tearing of the social fabric has economic and environmental consequences. The future of small towns and rural communities is dependent upon the regeneration of a socio-economic fabric through the restoration of a sense of community and place.

NOTE

1 Up until the last census women were not formally counted as rural workers. Ironically, just before some Australian women became among the first in the world to get the vote more than 100 years ago, the government decided to officially 'hide' the fact that women laboured in agriculture, fearful that this would send the wrong message 'home' to England about the industry's viability in Australia (Lake, 1987). When formulating census categories, government officials decided not to classify farmer's wives as engaged in agriculture because of the shame it would bring on a progressive, developing country like Australia to admit that 'women were in the habit of working in the fields as they are in some of the older countries of the world' (Lake, 1987: 179). For these reasons it is difficult to properly ascertain the number of women working on farm enterprises in the 20th century.

REFERENCES

Alston M (1995) *Women on the Land: The Hidden Heart of Australia*, UNSW Press, Sydney.

Australian Bureau of Statistics (ABS) (1996) *Census of Population and Housing*, (Cat. No 2015.5), ABS, Canberra.

Australian Bureau of Statistics (1961) *Census of Commonwealth of Australia*, (Table 10), ABS, Canberra.

Australian Bureau of Statistics (1971) *Census of Population and Housing*, (Reference 2.89.5), ABS, Canberra.

Australian Bureau of Statistics (1981) *Census of Population and Housing*, (Cat. No. 2405.0), ABS, Canberra.

Australian Bureau of Statistics (1989–90), *Agricultural Land Use and Selected Inputs: Western Australia*, (Cat. 7411.5), ABS, Canberra.

Australian Bureau of Statistics (1991) *Census Counts for Small Areas: Western Australia*, (Cat. No. 2730.5), Canberra.

Australian Bureau of Statistics (1992–93), *Agricultural Land Use and Selected Inputs: Western Australia*, (Cat. No. 7411.5) ABS, Canberra.

Australian Bureau of Statistics (1997) *AgStats*, (Cat. No. 7115.0), ABS, Canberra.

Commonwealth Department of Health and Family Services (1997) *Youth Suicide Monograph*, AGPS, Canberra.

Elix J & Lambert J (1998) *Missed Opportunities – Harnessing the Potential of Women in Australian Agriculture*, Rural Industries Research and Development Corporation and Commonwealth Department of Primary Industries and Energy, Canberra.

Ferguson J. & Simpson R (1995) 'The Australian rural labour market', *A National Farmers' Federation Research Paper*, 9 (November).

Haslam McKenzie F (1997) *The Farm Weekly Women's Survey*, Small to Medium Enterprise Research Centre, Edith Cowan University, Churchlands.

Haslam McKenzie F (1998) 'Statistical boundaries: A means by which the realities of rural decline in the Western Australian Wheatbelt have been hidden', in Staples M & Millmow A (eds) *Studies in Australian Rural Economic Development*, Centre for Rural Social Research, Charles Sturt University, Wagga Wagga, pp 41–50.

Haslam McKenzie F (1999) *The Impact of Declining Infrastructure in Rural Western Australia*, Rural Industries Research and Development Corporation, Canberra.

Hubley G (1997) 'Enhancing the capacity of a region through communication', Paper presented at the Internationalising Communities Conference, Toowoomba.

Jones R & Tonts M (1995) 'Rural restructuring and social sustainability: Some reflections on the Western Australian wheatbelt', *Australian Geographer*, 26(2), pp 133–40.

Kilpatrick S (1996) 'Change, training and farm profitability', *A National Farmers' Federation Research Paper*, 10 (November).

Lake M (1987) *The Limits of Hope*, Oxford University Press, Melbourne.

Lawrence G (1996) 'Rural Australia: Insights and Issues from Contemporary Political Economy', in Lawrence G, Lyons K & Momtaz S (eds) *Social Change in Rural Australia*, Rural Social and Economic Research Centre, Central Queensland University, Rockhampton, pp 332–49.

Lawrence G, Share P & Campbell H (1992) 'The Restructuring of Agriculture and Rural Society: Evidence from Australia and New Zealand', *Australian Journal of Political Economy*, 30, pp 1–23.

Lawrence G, Vanclay F & Furze B (eds) (1992) *Agriculture, Environment and Society: Contemporary Issues for Australia*, Macmillan, Melbourne.

Lawrence G & Williams C (1990) 'The Dynamics of Decline: Implications for Social Welfare in Rural Australia', in Cullen T, Dunn P & Lawrence G (eds) *Rural Health and Welfare in Australia*, Centre for Rural Welfare Research, Charles Sturt University, Wagga Wagga, pp 38–59.

Liepins R (1996) 'Women with broad vision: The women in agriculture movement and its use of environmental discourse to promote rural sustainability', *Environment and Planning A*, 30, pp 1179–96.

McKenzie F (1994) *Regional Depopulation Decline: Impacts and Policy Implications*, AGPS, Canberra.

National Farmers' Federation (1996) *Beating the Trend — A Path to Rural Prosperity, The National Farmers' Federation Strategy*, National Farmers' Federation, Canberra.

Taylor M (1991) 'Economic restructuring and regional change in Australia', *Australian Geographical Studies*, 29(2), pp 255–67.

Teather E (1996) 'Rural Women's self-concepts and aspirations as members of selected voluntary organisations in New Zealand, Australia and Canada', *New Zealand Geographer*, 52(2), pp 35–45.

Teather E & Franklin M-A (1994) 'Signposts for rural women in the 1990s', in Franklin M-A, Short L & Teather E (eds) *Country Women at the Crossroads: Perspectives on the Lives of Rural Australian Women in the 1990s*, University of New England Press, Armidale, pp 3–10.

Tonts M & Jones R (1996) 'Rural restructuring and uneven development in the Western Australia Wheatbelt', in Lawrence G, Lyons K & Momtaz S (eds) *Social Change in Rural Australia, Rural*, Social and Economic Research Centre, Central Queensland University, Rockhampton, pp 139–53.

Vanclay F & Lawrence G (1995). 'The restructuring of agriculture: Environmental and social implications', in Vanclay F & Lawrence G (eds) *The Environmental Imperative: Eco-social Concerns for Australian Agriculture*, Central Queensland University Press, Rockhampton, pp 3–19.

6
NEGOTIATING THE TWO-EDGED SWORD OF AGRICULTURAL TRADE LIBERALISATION: TRADE POLICY AND ITS PROTECTIONIST DISCONTENTS

BILL PRITCHARD

In July 1999, the Prime Minister, John Howard, visited Washington for a round of discussions with US leaders, including President Clinton. At the top of the Prime Minister's agenda — at least in terms of the media coverage of his visit — was the issue of Australian lamb. One week prior to Howard's visit, the Clinton administration imposed tariff restrictions to the detriment of Australian exporters. A 9 per cent tariff was imposed on 'in-quota' lamb imports of 32 000 metric tonnes, with a prohibitive 40 per cent tariff on imports over and above this quota. The Australian government had been lobbying for an increase in the US quota, and for a zero tariff. This decision sparked a flurry of media releases in Australia, with Trade Minister Tim Fischer calling the decision a 'regrettable cave-in to protectionist pressures' within America. Two days after the US announcement, the Australian and New Zealand governments initiated action in the World Trade Organisation seeking to overturn the decision. At a more local level, the trade dispute quickly moved into the realm of nationalistic folklore: within a week, the industry's promotional body, Meat and Livestock Australia, began a marketing campaign based on the slogan: 'The Americans put tariffs on our lamb. We recommend rosemary and garlic.'

The 1999 lamb dispute exemplified and reinforced a set of dominant discourses about the position of Australian agriculture in the world trading system. Australian (and New Zealand) lamb producers were positioned within the media as holding the high moral ground in battling against a corrupted regime of world trade. The American position was understood as being driven by sectional and political interests that were anathema to economic logic. It seemed that Australian and New Zealand producers were being punished for their efficiency, with widespread negative implications for the economic health of these nations. A month before his visit to the US and on the day that he sealed the deal with the Australian Democrats to introduce a goods and services tax, Prime Minister Howard told journalists that 'so long as the Yanks bought some more lamb', the Australian economy's prospects were bright.

This episode highlights a pre-eminent theme in debate about Australia's rural economy: that is as economically efficient producers, the economic prospects of Australian farmers are crucially dependent on the operation of external markets. The economic salvation of rural Australia, so this argument goes, hinges on actions taken outside of Australia in bilateral and multilateral fora concerning trade liberalisation. In material terms it is difficult to disagree with the broad contours of this argument. Access to markets and the extent of agricultural subsidisation by competitor nations impact directly on the income earning potential of the Australian farm sector. At the same time, for Australia to argue for trade liberalisation elsewhere in the world it has had to implement a program of trade reform internally. Australian farmers are expected to be competitive without a reliance on government support. This manifests trade liberalisation as a two-edged sword, with attendant controversy.

Rural producers have greeted this two-edged sword of trade policy with varied levels of acceptance and contestation. There is generally unambiguous support for Australian government attempts to prise open foreign markets and reduce the agricultural subsidies paid by Australia's competitors, but local tariff reductions and the dismantling of statutory marketing arrangements has proved highly contentious. Rural disquiet on these issues gathered steam in the second half of the 1990s, following high-profile trade disputes concerning oranges, pork, chicken and salmon, which in turn encouraged One Nation to make trade policy a plank of its 1998 federal election campaign.

One Nation's entry into the trade policy debate exposed an extent of discontent in rural Australia concerning the free trade orthodoxy — the assumption that free trade is in the interests of the Australian economy, and certainly in the interests of Australian primary producers. In the construction of this debate, One Nation positioned itself as the champion of rural producers left isolated and exposed by the government's supposed doctrinal insistence on the merits of free trade. According to the Hansonite argument, Australia's free trade stance naively subjugated the nation's commercial interests to meeting the purities of neo-liberal economic theory. The main proponents of the free trade orthodoxy were said to be the 'ivory-tower' economic theorists who populated institutions such as the Productivity Commission (PC) and the Australian Bureau of Agricultural and Resource Economics (ABARE). Additionally, One Nation suggested that the National Farmers' Federation (NFF) and the federal National Party had become detached from the real concerns of farming communities, and thus represented a so-called 'rural aristocracy' (Wahlquist, 1999).

Inevitably, the debate on agricultural trade policy reflects a deeper and more complex set of circumstances than either the Hansonites or mainstream economists have been willing to accept. The substantive argument here is that the Australian government's advocacy of trade liberalisation has been constructed politically in ways that have belittled critical debate on the magnitude and distribution of benefits and costs from these policies. Consequently, concern for the losers from trade policy has been marginalised. In the key institutions of power in the Australian government, negative consequences of Australia's embrace of agricultural trade liberalisation have been either ignored or hastily dismissed. There has been a distinctive arrogance in the way mainstream economists generally have dealt with these issues, which in turn has fuelled the scepticism of many in rural Australia over the merits of agricultural trade liberalisation. These failings have led directly to the situation in which One Nation's populist mantras could pretend to represent a legitimate trade policy alternative for Australian agriculture.

THE CONSTRUCTION AND IMPLEMENTATION OF AUSTRALIA'S TRADE ORTHODOXY

In the 1970s an intellectual sea change occurred within the economics profession. This transformation involved the revival of classic economic theory, and the adoption of new theories concerning 'public choice' (Quiggin, 1996: 65). These theories found an active expression in the Fraser Coalition government from about 1980 onwards, and formed a key intellectual philosophy for the Hawke Labor government elected in 1983. Through the 1980s Australia's trade policies were restructured in line with these theories. The Hawke government wound back tariff and quota protection as part of a broad project to restructure the Australian economy in line with neo-liberal arguments relating to internationalisation and market efficiency. Within the key institutions of Australian public policy around this time, there was a coalescence of opinion that saw the aggressive promotion of free trade as being fundamentally important to Australia's future competitiveness. This project climaxed in 1991 with the announcement of a timetable for the removal of remaining tariffs and quotas throughout the economy.

Agriculture played a pivotal role throughout the 1980s debate on free trade. As the sector's peak lobby group, the NFF took an assertive stance within the debate. Under the reigns of Ian McLachlan and his successor Rick Farley, the NFF was positioned as the champion of free trade. Assistance to the rural sector was traded-off in return for support for ongoing tariff and quota reform elsewhere in the economy (Halpin & Martin, 1999: 79). Politically, this represented a fundamental shift from the 'national development' model that was at the heart of rural politics in the 1960s and 1970s. The NFF strategy was aligned closely with key institutions in the Canberra bureaucracy. The status of agriculture was central to the broader free trade debate in the economy. The Bureau of Agricultural Economics (BAE) and its successor ABARE took a leading role in national economic debates. Leading advocates of agricultural trade liberalisation, such as the former adviser to Prime Minister Hawke and Ambassador to China, Ross Garnaut, gained national prominence as a result of these processes. The 1987 abolition of the Department of Trade, to make way for the Department of Foreign Affairs and Trade, marks a decisive moment in the shift towards a multilateral trade policy based on the promotion of free trade. Through the merger of these Departments, bilateral trade advocacy was subsumed within wider multilateralist diplomatic agendas (Jones, 1994).

The strength of the free trade orthodoxy within the key institutions of the Australian government created the context in which Australia assumed a leading international role in the push for agricultural trade liberalisation during the Uruguay Round of the General Agreements of Tariffs and Trade (GATT) (1986–94). At the commencement of these negotiations, Australia joined with other agricultural exporter nations to form the Cairns Group, a negotiating bloc that had the ambition of putting pressure on the United States and European Union.[1] Though Australia was officially just one member of the Cairns Group, it provided the driving agenda for the Group's positions. Administrative support for the Group was provided through the Australian consular mission in Geneva (Oxley, 1999). Econometric modelling and advice was largely generated by Australian institutions, notably ABARE. Whereas Australia's activism in the Cairns Group may be explained in part by various geopolitical concerns of the late 1980s (Ravenhill, 1994), it fundamentally derived from the dominance of the prevailing trade orthodoxy in Canberra.[2]

THE ECONOMIC IMPACTS OF AUSTRALIA'S FREE TRADE POSITION: NATIONAL INCOME EFFECTS

Australia's aggressive promotion of agricultural trade liberalisation is premised on the argument that the adoption of these policies will generate significant net gains to national income. Since the onset of the

Uruguay Round in 1986 there have been numerous econometric studies in Australia attempting to provide estimates of the size of these benefits, and these have been routinely reported at industry conferences with subsequent dissemination by the media. Less visible, however, has been critical debate over the assumptions of this modelling, or any attempt to place the numerical estimates of net benefits in any qualitative context.

Economic arguments that agricultural trade liberalisation will generate strong national income gains for Australia can be traced to Ricardo's (1817) theory of comparative advantage (Pomfret, 1995). As augmented by the Heckscher–Ohlin theorem, the theory suggests that a country's comparative advantages lie in commodities that most intensively use the resources in which the country is relatively well endowed. In Australia's case, these arguments point to the potential for generating significant national income gains through free trade policies that encourage capital and labour to flow to the agricultural and resource sectors where Australia has abundant natural advantages.

Various estimates have been made of the potential net addition to national income arising from these policies. According to econometric modelling by Murtough, Zheng and Vanzetti (1994) cited by the Bureau of Industry Economics (1995: 61–62), the trade liberalisation outcomes of the Uruguay Round are anticipated to raise Australia's annual net exports of agriculture and processed foods by US$1.64 billion. Given that Australian agricultural and processed food turnover was approximately $A57 billion (roughly US$40 billion at prevailing exchange rates) at the time this research was undertaken, the Uruguay Round could be estimated as encouraging an increase in annual output for these sectors of between 3.5 and 4 per cent.[3] In all likelihood these estimates overstate any positive impacts of the Agreement, because they assume situations where factors of production move effortlessly between sectors of the economy (cf. Quiggin, 1996: 137–39). The fact that the BIE reports this econometric modelling with only marginal acknowledgment of its underlying assumptions highlights the tendency within the trade orthodoxy to 'write the story of trade liberalisation' in a partialised and politicised manner.

Such boosterism is a common characteristic of the discursive strategies deployed by proponents of trade liberalisation. Media discussion of the Uruguay Round of the GATT, and especially its Agreement on Agriculture, was often cloaked within simplified assertions of substantial global net economic benefits. Interrogation of the outcomes from these negotiations reveals an alternative picture. The entire economic outcome from seven years of negotiations in the GATT, estimated at US$274 billion spread over nine years, represents less than 1 per cent of world GDP. These gains are 'so small that they are within rounding error — no one will ever know whether they really existed or not' (Thurow, 1996: 132). The fact that developed nations receive two-thirds of these benefits and that the world's poorest region, Sub-Saharan Africa, is forecast to lose income from the Agreement tends to be conveniently overlooked in most reporting and analysis (Coote & Le Quesne, 1996: 194).

Notwithstanding these shortcomings in the analysis and reporting of trade liberalisation, protectionism in Australia's would-be export markets undeniably inhibits export opportunities. Some six years after the signing of the Uruguay Round Agreement on Agriculture, a significant bureaucratic superstructure remains in place dedicated to channelling support payments to European and North American farmers. In 1998, the EU Common Agricultural Policy (CAP) fed $A75 billion of support funds to the European farming sector. These payments impact directly on the export opportunities of Australian farmers. They assist the price-competitiveness of EU food exports and encourage the dumping of surplus product on world markets, with deleterious implications for world commodity prices. The dominant Australian media discourse regarding these farm subsidies dutifully reflects both the arguments of the trade orthodoxy and the vested interests of those Australian farmers who would benefit from freer world agricultural trade. Typically, European agriculture is represented as hopelessly inefficient and bureaucratically corrupted. It is 'subsidy wonderland' (Fullerton, 1999) where, according to the Australian Trade Minister, farming is in danger of being reduced to 'a Disneyland amusement park role' because of the ways EU farm support payments recognise the amenity, lifestyle, environmental and cultural significance of farming (Truss, 1999).

Consistent with criticisms of subsidies elsewhere in the world, proponents of Australia's trade orthodoxy have also targeted local mechanisms to manage agricultural markets. Australia's ability to propose trade liberalisation internationally has been argued to be dependent upon the extent to which its own 'house is in order'. Statutory marketing authorities and similar institutions have been subjected to intense scrutiny since the late 1980s, and especially since the advent of national competition policy in 1995. In the case of statutory marketing authorities, the advocates of free trade generally have used econometric modelling to argue that the removal of such 'interventions' will contribute to freer movement of factors of production with accompanying economic benefits. Detailed marketing studies and ex-post analyses of deregulated sectors have shown the general applicability of these arguments to be limited.

Arguments concerning the merits of wheat deregulation, for example, have fallen foul of marketing studies showing that an abolition of single-desk selling by the Australian Wheat Board would reduce the returns to export wheat growers by US$2 per tonne (Pritchard, 1996). In industry sectors such as egg marketing, deregulation has produced extremely mixed outcomes and it is not clear that consumers have bene-fited (New South Wales Legislative Assembly, 1997: 79). Even in the case of the dairy sector, an industry where recent deregulation has been associated with improved industry efficiency and the capture of new export markets, the story is more complex than economists are general-ly prepared to accept.[4] Detailed analysis of the ways deregulatory argu-ments are constructed by economists reveals their reliance on simplistic assumptions about market behaviour and resource allocation (Pritchard, 1999). In general, economists neglect ex-post analyses of policies in favour of ex-ante modelling so these issues (particularly those suggest-ing mixed results) do not receive the policy attention they deserve.

THE ECONOMIC IMPACTS OF AUSTRALIA'S FREE TRADE POSITION: DISTRIBUTIONAL EFFECTS AND THE REPRE-SENTATION OF THE 'NATIONAL INTEREST'

In addition to doubts over the legitimacy of net national income esti-mates arising from free trade, questions exist concerning the distribu-tional impacts of these policies. According to the theory of comparative advantage, Australia should receive net income benefits from allowing economic resources to flow to primary industries. Although the prin-ciples of comparative advantage indicate that net national benefits can be generated from the pursuit of free trade, the realisation of those gains is contingent upon the distributional flow of trade benefits through the economy. In agriculture's case, the benefits of free trade increasingly are being captured by larger farm enterprises and globally mobile agribusiness traders with the scale and scope to take advantage of shifts in factor prices. These tendencies suggest an intriguing sting in the tail of agricultural trade liberalisation.

In general, advocates of the trade orthodoxy give little attention to these distributional issues. When they do, their perspectives tend to be condescending. In general, the economists who advance arguments about the potential net national benefits from free trade take the view that any distributional impacts arising from these policies are the matter for 'political' interests to resolve (Galbraith, 1987). This stance repre-sents the promotion of economics as a positivist science removed from normative social science, in effect absolving economists from the social and political implications of the policies they promote. It is underpinned by an exclusionary definition of costs and benefits, so that consideration is given to only those factors that can be quantified in monetary terms. The ethical values embedded within these approaches tend to conflate human values to market outcomes, facilitating the creation of policy silences on questions of equality, community and quality of life.

The separation of arguments concerning national income from arguments concerning the distribution of benefits (and losses) arising from these policies is reflected in economic discourse dealing with the 'national interest'. Economists tend to suggest that free trade policies are in the 'national interest' because ex-ante modelled evidence suggests that they generate beneficial impacts for net national income. This represents a discursive tactic within economics to conflate the 'national interest' with (relatively narrowly constituted) forecasts of net income.[5] This is important because it strikes at the heart of recent scepticism in rural Australia over trade policy. Economists' predilections for seeking to represent the 'national interest', coupled with their generally limited and dismissive attitude towards researching the distributional impacts of free trade, have damaged the perceived legitimacy of their arguments within many sectors of rural Australia. This has helped fuel grassroots support for protectionist stances by One Nation and others.

This predilection to appropriate and speak for the 'national interest' permeates economics discourse from textbooks to policy statements. An influential Australian textbook on international trade theory, for example, suggests:

> In principle, if there are net benefits, then the losers could be compensated by the gainers, but such redistribution is likely to be opposed by the gainers and to be difficult to implement in any case. This is important because the losers from any policy change will oppose it, and if they are sufficiently powerful they might prevent the pursuit of policies which are in the national interest. [Pomfret, 1995: 14]

This quotation is instructive because it acknowledges a major shortcoming in economists' models of trade (that is, it is unlikely that the gainers will compensate the losers), but it interprets this as a problem for policy, not a problem for theory. The implicit conclusion of this quotation is that real world concerns of potential losers from trade policies need to be ignored in the pursuit of the national interest. This argument is also heard in policy corridors. In a presentation to the 1999 'Outlook' conference by the Department of Foreign Affairs and Trade, for instance, the farming community is implored to support the government's position, lest the 'credibility' of this position be tarnished:

> If we are going to move the negotiations forward, we will need to generate and sustain enthusiasm for liberalisation where there is fertile ground, and bring home the disadvantages of continued distortion and protection. But we will also need to bring with us the whole of the Australian agriculture sector as well — to fail to do so could expose our credibility in the negotiations to attack from those who seek to slow or halt reform. [McKinnon, 1999: 70]

Again, any real world concerns of the Australian rural sector need to be ignored for the broader goal of the 'national interest'. Two general conclusions can be drawn from the thinking characterised by the above quotations. First, the narrowness in which the 'national interest' is constructed corresponds to an intellectual dishonesty whereby economists pretend to speak on behalf of issues that demand a wider mandate. Second, to the extent that these arguments treat theoretical concerns as having superior legitimacy to the grounded implications of those concerns, they represent sloppy intellectual practice.

A further implication of these constructions of the 'national interest' concerns the way that they animate a further set of discourses relating to farm failure and farm success. The implicit condescension in economists' treatment of the 'national interest' reflects a positional transformation of success and failure within a deregulated economy. Effectively, the removal of 'market interventions' by government amounts to a privatisation of market experiences so that commercial success and failure become framed not as issues of public policy, but as issues of individual responsibility (Halpin & Martin, 1999: 93). With trade policy reforms, as with other policy shifts (national competition policy, drought assistance etc.), farmers are expected to adapt and change. Hence, farm financial crises and the overall reduction in farm numbers are understood and represented by advocates of the trade orthodoxy as the products of inefficiency or poor business planning by farmers, rather than the systematic outcomes of public policy stances. Consequently, there has been a qualitative shift in government policy discourse, so that issues of 'adding value' and 'supply chain management' have been given heightened profile (Department of Primary Industries and Energy, 1998).

REACTIONS TO THE TRADE ORTHODOXY

Faced with rural disquiet over trade policy, and One Nation's interventions in the debate, in 1996 the federal Minister for Primary Industries and Resources commissioned a parliamentary inquiry into the impacts of free trade on Australian agriculture (House of Representatives Standing Committee on Primary Industries, Resources and Rural Affairs, [HRSCPIRRA] 1998). From the outset, the HRSCPIRRA inquiry was laden with the duty to work within the orthodox ideological perspective on trade. The committee's terms of reference asked for an inquiry into 'the benefits' — not the 'impacts' — of trade liberalisation, and 'how the momentum for trade reform can be maintained'. For parties supportive of trade liberalisation, such as the NFF, Australian Wheat Board, the meat and livestock industries and federal government agencies, these terms of reference were not problematic. In the main, submissions from these parties detailed growth forecasts from the implementation of trade liberalisation, as suggested by the results of econometric modelling.

These prejudicial terms of reference did not silence the evidence of many rural producers sceptical of the trade orthodoxy, and led to one member of the committee (independent MP, Peter Andren) to submit a minority dissenting report. Submissions from these parties provide an important historical record of the contested negotiation of the trade orthodoxy in rural Australia.

Concerns over Australia's agricultural trade policies were clothed in discourse emphasising the inconsistencies between the stances of the Australian government and those of competitor nations. These inconsistencies were alleged for both tariff and non-tariff barriers. For example, the Australian Chicken Growers' Council asked why Australia imposes a zero tariff on chicken meat when a tariff of 9 per cent is allowable under multilateral trade obligations. The Council's greatest concern, however, was voiced in respect of Australia's supposed willingness to abide by the letter of the Agreement on Agriculture, when other nations used a combination of tactics to avoid their commitments. Of particular concern to the council were the so-called 'green box' provisions of the Agreement, empowering jurisdictions to impose various non-tariff restrictions as legitimate policy aspirations.[6] Focusing on the inconsistencies between the applications of 'green box' measures by Australia and its competitors, the council submitted:

> As a direct result of Australia's trade policies our industry is now being thrown to the wolves of the highly corrupt international poultry trade by agreements to remove our quarantine barriers and to allow tariff free imports of poultry meat into Australia for the first time in over 30 years. Not only is this decision irresponsible and foolhardy from the avian disease aspect (with its potentially devastating environmental consequences) but it totally fails to recognise the realities of the world trade in poultry meat. [HRSCPIRRA Submissions, 1997: 3]

The issue of quarantine was also raised by the Pork Council of Australia. Although accepting the broad principles of the Uruguay Round Agreements on Technical Barriers to Trade and Sanitary and Phyto–Sanitary Measures (the SPS Agreements), the council suggested that the Australian government was overly enthusiastic in its desire to facilitate pork imports: 'a balanced approach is required, where the integrity of Australia's quarantine status is maintained and an effective policy is in place to facilitate adjustment by domestic industries' (HRSCPIRRA Submissions, 1997: 42). The council asserted that although Australian governments have provided some assistance for industrial restructuring in line with tariff reductions (for instance, in the textiles, clothing and footwear industries), there was no adequate provision within existing policy for the provision of assistance due to changes in quarantine regulations. According to the council: 'at present, the quarantine policy framework is essentially disconnected from the rural policy framework' (HRSCPIRRA Submissions, 1997: 45).

The Australian Apple and Pear Growers' Association (AAPGA) voiced similar concerns over the social and economic implications of opening Australian markets as part of tariff reform and adherence to the SPS Agreements:

> There is no doubt of the longer term benefits of reform to Australia's agricultural exporting industries and Australia must be seeking to maximise these benefits. However, to some extent both the immediate and longer term practical benefits of the GATT agreement to Australia's agricultural industries have been overstated. Typically improvements have been incremental, hard won and the result of considerable effort by the agencies and industries involved. A harder edged approach is needed when assessing the expected benefits and weighing these up against opportunities to open Australia's agricultural markets to imports. *The potential economic and social damage of unrestrained agricultural imports to our market has not been the subject of a detailed assessment. It is essential that this assessment is performed.* (emphasis added) [HRSCPIRRA Submissions, 1997: 262]

The issues raised by the AAPGA bring into focus the distributional implications of agricultural trade liberalisation. Whereas the concern of the AAPGA rests with the question of who will be hurt from increased import penetration, of equal interest is the question of who actually gains from increased export access. The Australian beef sector provides a case where improved export market access has been associated with rapid corporate restructuring that has incorporated much of the local industry within vertically coordinated chains organised by offshore interests (Ufkes, 1993; Snell, 1996). The HRSCPIRRA inquiry was alerted by the Queensland government to some of the potential implications of this industrial transformation:

> a significant portion of slaughtering capacity in Australia is owned or controlled by foreign-owned companies (estimated at around 44 percent for the 25 largest meat processors), while there is also a significant degree of concentration of ownership / of export-certified abattoirs. Both of these factors are of concern to Queensland cattle producers as it is not clear what portion of incremental gains from the expanded sales of beef on the export market will actually flow through to the producing sector as opposed to being paid out in dividends to processor shareholders and transfer payments (ie. repatriation of profits offshore to parent companies in the US and Japan). The issue or threat here is that Japanese companies, for example, could transfer price beef at the Australian cost of production to its [sic] Japanese affiliates and then keep all the profits in the Japanese marketing chain. [HRSCPIRRA Submissions, 1997: 195]

As with the issues raised by the AAPGA, these concerns have not been the subject of any detailed assessment, despite their obvious relevance to the wider Australian trade policy debate.

In general, the final report of the HRSCPIRRA inquiry failed to make recommendations in line with the arguments of industry organisations that questioned Australia's trade policies. Instead, the HRSCPIRRA report sought to blame the messenger for opposition to the trade orthodoxy. The broad tenor of the inquiry's recommendations was to develop better communication mechanisms informing rural Australia of the merits of free trade. Recommendations included: more research by ABARE into the benefits of free trade; the development of materials to be used in schools explaining the benefits of trade liberalisation; the construction of public awareness campaigns at the regional level; and increased use of regional television as a medium to 'sell' the benefits of free trade.

These recommendations would sit well with economists trained in public choice theory, who would interpret industry concerns with trade policy merely as self-interested attempts to capture economic rents. But such offhand categorisations reinforce suggestions that those advancing the trade orthodoxy are relatively uninterested in the distributional implications of the policies they promote. As highlighted by a recent analysis of the effects of national competition policy reforms on rural industries, the abilities of the farm sector to adjust to shifts in market conditions are not as neat as economists sometimes assume (Purcell & Beard, 1999). Whilst opponents of reform at times may be engaged in rent-seeking activities, it is intellectually dishonest to fail to acknowledge their legitimate concerns. In particular, the imposition of trade liberalisation may lead to extensive restructuring costs as industry participants adjust to increased import penetration, and assessing these costs should be a legitimate goal of public policy. Moreover, it seems reasonable to suggest that benefits from export market access may not flow to Australian producers, but rather be captured by other players within internationalised commodity chains. The failure to seriously consider these (and other related) issues reflects arrogant self-confidence within the trade orthodoxy that has only served to garner mistrust of Australia's trade policies in rural Australia.

CONCLUSION

On balance, a freer global environment for agricultural trade generates net income gains to the Australian farm and food processing sectors; however, the imposition of this regime also has substantial distributional implications within Australia that are not yet fully understood. In general, Australian governments and others advancing the trade orthodoxy have overstated the former and tended to disregard the latter. The political implications of this have been to create the preconditions where populist trade policy prescriptions can flourish.

Attempts to paper over the distributional impacts of trade policy, as evidenced in the HRSCPIRRA report's recommendations of 'better communication' of the benefits of free trade, are nothing more than window dressing. If Australian policy makers wish to earn the support of rural Australia, the full social and regional policy implications of Australia's advocacy of agricultural trade liberalisation need to be debated frankly. Farm financial failure and an overall concentration of farm output within fewer farm enterprises needs to be understood as a systemic outcome of policy. The distribution of the benefits from trade need to be examined from the perspective of critical political economy, rather than the suffocating models of orthodox economics with assumptions of free resource mobility. To advocate free trade in agriculture is to advocate a massive restructuring of the Australian rural economy with likely fundamental shifts in the political economy of power and control in Australian farming. If Australian governments are prepared to confront these issues, they will nip in the bud the spectre of a protectionist rebellion within rural Australia based on trade populism.

By the second half of 1999 there was some evidence that the Howard government was taking these issues more seriously. The Dairy Industry Package announced in September 1999 proposed $1.8 billion structural adjustment for dairy farmers affected by these policy changes. Dairy farmers wishing to leave the industry will be offered $45 000 in adjustment assistance. The chief executive of Bonlac Foods, the nation's largest dairy processor, called the package: 'a model of how to balance equity, efficiency and adjustment considerations while effecting major change in a rural industry' (Scanlon, 1999: 17). Although the passage of these arrangements was criticised by many dairy farmers and some State governments, nonetheless they reflect a commitment by the Australian government to acknowledge the distributional reality of rural restructuring. The fact that federal Cabinet agreed to these measures shortly after the electoral demise of the Kennett government in Victoria — a political event widely interpreted as being caused partly by a rural voter backlash — is emblematic of the rural policy reality currently facing Australian governments. The extent to which it marks a sea change in rural policy, as opposed to a knee-jerk reaction to electoral shifts, is a key issue for the trajectory of Australian agriculture in the 21st century.

NOTES

1 Countries of the Cairns Group were: Australia; New Zealand; Uruguay; Brazil; Argentina; Thailand; Hungary; Fiji; Chile.

2 To some, Australia's activism in the Cairns Group was explained by geo-political concerns of the Australian government over the prospect in the late 1980s that the world's economy would collapse into continental trading blocs based around the EU and NAFTA, to which Australia would be excluded. By promoting unilateral trade liberalisation, the Australian government was attempting to avert the negative consequences of such developments.

3 Because of the significant seasonal volatility of agricultural output and of the US–Australia exchange rate, these figures are presented as approximate only. Incidentally, this same research suggests that the negative impacts of the Uruguay Round on Australian manufacturing and service industries will more than offset any positive impacts on agricultural, food and resource industries, thereby reducing national net exports by US$4.7 billion.

4 Dairy is an exceptional case of regulation and deregulation because of the inordinate complexity of previous regulatory devices. The shift to a simpler regulatory regime has been one factor assisting the recent strong performance of this sector, but other factors are equally significant. Amongst these factors are improvements to industry productivity arising from capital investment, and the sound management of dairy cooperatives since the late 1980s. Elsewhere I argue that management agency within dairy cooperatives has been a critical reason for the industry's success in Australia (Pritchard, 1996).

5 It also contradicts the general philosophical tenet of positivist economics; that economists provide value-free advice that elected officials use to represent the 'national interest'.

6 Legitimate 'green box' measures include subsidisation for farm income insurance and support, for public stockholding of food for food security and domestic food aid, for regional assistance, and for marketing and promotional purposes.

REFERENCES

Bureau of Industry Economics (1995) *Potential Gains to Australia from APEC: Open Regionalism and the Bogor Declaration,* AGPS, Canberra.

Coote B & Le Quesne C (1996) *The Trade Trap: Poverty and the Global Commodity Markets,* Oxfam, Oxford.

Department of Primary Industries and Energy (1998) *Chains of Success: Case Studies on International and Australian Food Businesses Cooperating to Compete in the Global Market,* AGPS, Canberra.

Fullerton T (1999) 'The Common Agricultural Policy', *Landline,* ABC television broadcast 22 August (transcript available at: *http://www.abc.net.au/landline/1220899.html*).

Galbraith JK (1987) *A History of Economics: The Past as the Present,* Hamilton, London.

Halpin D & Martin P (1999) 'Representing and managing farmers' interests in Australia', *Sociologia Ruralis* 39(1), pp 78–99.

House of Representatives Standing Committee on Primary Industries, Resources and Rural Affairs (1997) *Submissions,* Parliament of the Commonwealth of Australia, Canberra.

House of Representatives Standing Committee on Primary Industries, Resources and Rural Affairs (1998) *Adjusting to Agricultural Trade Reform: Australia No Longer Down Under,* Parliament of the Commonwealth of Australia, Canberra.

Jones E (1994) 'Bureaucratic politics and economic policy: The evolution of trade policy in the 1970s and 1980s', *Working Papers in Economics, Department of Economics*, University of Sydney, No. 212.

McKinnon A (1999) 'WTO negotiations: why Australian agriculture must strongly support trade liberalising reform', *Outlook '99*, pp 65–70.

Murtough G, Zheng S, & Vanzetti D (1994) 'APEC trade liberalisation post-Uruguay Round: a general equilibrium analysis', Paper presented at the Conference of Economists, Gold Coast International Hotel, 25–28 September.

New South Wales Legislative Assembly (1997) *Debates*, 25 November, Vol 15, pp 79–81, NSW Government, Sydney.

Oxley A (1999) 'History of the group — lessons for the future', in Oxley A (ed) *Liberalising World Trade in Agriculture: Strategies for Cairns Group Countries in the WTO*, Rural Industries Research and Development Corporation, Canberra, pp 3–12.

Pomfret R (ed) (1995) *Australia's Trade Policies*, OUP, Melbourne.

Pritchard B (1999) 'National competition policy in action: The politics of agricultural deregulation and the Murrumbidgee Irrigation Area Wine Grapes Marketing Board', *Rural Society* 9(2), pp 421–43.

Pritchard W (1996) 'Shifts in food regimes and the place of producer co-operatives: Insights from the Australian and United States dairy industries', *Environment and Planning A*, 28, pp 857–75.

Purcell T & Beard R (1999) 'National competition policy and its effects on rural Australia: a comparative analysis of three industries', Paper presented at the 43rd Annual Agricultural and Resource Economics Society Conference, Christchurch, 20–22 January.

Quiggin J (1996) *Great Expectations: Microeconomic Reform and Australia*, Allen & Unwin, Sydney.

Ravenhill J (1994) 'Foreign Affairs and Trade', in Brett J, Gillespie J & Goot M (eds) *Developments in Australian Politics*, Macmillan, Melbourne, pp 299–321.

Scanlon P (1999) 'Brighter future for dairy farmers', *Sydney Morning Herald*, 13 October, p 17.

Snell D (1996) 'Graziers, butchers, boners and the internationalisation of Australian beef production', *Culture and Agriculture*, 18(1), pp 23–25.

Thurow L (1996) *The Future of Capitalism*, Allen and Unwin, Sydney.

Truss W (1999) 'QUINT Ministers agree to urgency of WTO Agriculture Round', Media Release AFFA99/50WT, 5 October.

Ufkes F (1993) 'Trade liberalization, agro-food politics and the globalization of agri-culture', *Political Geography*, 12(3), pp 215–31.

Wahlquist A (1999) 'Demographic and social changes in Australia', Paper presented to the Regional Australia Summit (27 October), Parliament House, Canberra.

7

ENVIRONMENTAL AND ABORIGINAL ISSUES: THE EMERGENCE OF NEW TENSIONS IN RURAL AND REGIONAL POLITICS

PHIL McMANUS & GLENN ALBRECHT

Many people in rural and regional Australia are challenged by the emergence of environmental and Aboriginal issues on the national agenda. Why is this so? This chapter explores the development of environmental and Aboriginal issues in the Australian political context. In doing so, it is understood that rural producers, environmentalists and indigenous people are not homogenous blocs, and that future directions in rural and regional Australia depend on interactions both within and between the various institutions and actors representing rural indigenous and environmental issues. The chapter concentrates on the attitudes of rural producers to environmental issues and examines specific cases of environmental politics involving indigenous people.

The chapter begins with an overview of changes in Australian agriculture. It identifies the disparity between farmers' and environmentalists' perceptions of land, nature and issues of ecological sustainability. These perceptions are then compared with One Nation's positions

The section on indigenous Australians highlights differences between groups who support continuity with traditional links to their land and those who support western-style development as a desirable and inevitable part of the future. Mining companies, particularly in the gold and uranium industries, have forged ties with some Aboriginal groups as part of regional employment, education and health strategies. These new partnerships, in addition to independent investments in rural and regional economies by indigenous people, mark a new era of development. Indigenous economic contributions to rural and regional

Australia are significant and will increase into the foreseeable future. Aboriginal support is often seen as a precondition of, and is sometimes a legislative requirement for, development in remote areas. This is a real change from the processes of exploitation of the people and their land that has characterised much of the history of non-indigenous settlement and the creation of rural economies in Australia (see Broome, 1994; Reynolds, 1989: 1996).

The chapter concludes that, while environmental and Aboriginal issues have similarities, they are not inherently linked. The heterogeneity of views held by Aboriginal people, environmentalists and rural industry means that the negotiation of outcomes in rural and regional Australia is complex because the lines of alliance and conflict become increasingly blurred as the inherent tensions within economic development, self-reliance and ecological sustainability come to the surface.

CHANGES IN THE PHYSICAL, CULTURAL AND POLITICAL LANDSCAPES OF RURAL AND REGIONAL AUSTRALIA

The ecological impacts of agricultural and pastoral practices, combined with changing environmental awareness, a reassessment of the history of contact with indigenous cultures, technological change and a long-term decline in the terms of trade (see Chapters 3 & 6), have progressively undermined the position of established interests in rural and regional Australia. This fall from the perceived 'good old days' of high rural employment and the expansion of transport and financial services (see Chapter 9), leads to a sense of vulnerability about the future (see Chapter 4).

The concern about the decline of rural and regional Australia has been reflected in numerous studies and reports. Unfortunately, people living in these parts of Australia do not see the situation improving. For instance, a historically important report in 1990 on the future of country towns in Western Australia saw the increasing primacy of Perth and the consistent decline in population between 1976–81 and 1981–86 for the Upper Great Southern and Midlands regions of the State (Country Shires Councils' Association and Country Urban Councils' Association Working Party, 1990). A recent report using slightly different regional boundaries predicted that, although population will not decline in rural regions of rapidly growing States such as Western Australia and Queensland, the worst employment prospects in the period 1998–2004 were in the Midlands and Central region of Western Australia and Central Queensland (National Institute of Economic and Industry Research, 1998). This recent report does not consider the fortunes of individual towns within these regions (see Chapter 4).

Factors which may further the sense of loss, environmental and Aboriginal issues for example, are often viewed with distrust and resentment. While many farmers in Australia face financial pressure to maximise production, they are farming in areas that have low and unreliable rainfall. To this environmental limitation are added concerns about their right to clear land for more production, plus issues of salinisation, erosion, 'pest' control, loss of biodiversity and global climate change.

Many farmers are aware of environmental concerns. This is partly reflected in the number of agricultural producers participating in Landcare groups. Landcare originated in Victoria in 1986 and emerged as a national program in 1989 due to the joint efforts of the Australian Conservation Foundation and the National Farmers Federation (Lockie, 1995; Martin, 1995). It focused on concerns about the environment in rural and regional Australia. Lockie and Vanclay (1997) claimed there were 2500 Landcare groups in 1996, representing 30 per cent of commercial farming operations in Australia. As Davenport (1997) noted, however, this meant 70 per cent of farmers were not in Landcare groups. Recent data puts the number of Landcare groups at 4500, but still only covering a third of Australian commercial farming operations (AFFA, 1999). As Bailey (1997: 133) recognised, however, 'every farmer in Australia could be a member of a Landcare group and every stream and river bank fenced off … but ecologically sustainable development or sustainable resource management could still be a long way off'. The release of findings for the Murray Darling Basin Ministerial Council's salinity audit in October 1999 showed salt affected areas as 'the biggest man-made [sic] disaster in Australian history' (Murphy & Woodford, 1999: 3). Despite Landcare's apparent 'success', environmental degradation in Australia is still occurring, and in cases such as the clearing of vegetation in Queensland, it has accelerated.

Despite the ability of some farmers to work with some environmentalists through programs such as Landcare, the gulf between the two broad groups is very wide. The political affinities of the two groups appear to be distinct. While the party representing many environmentalists' interests — the Greens — poll well in some regional areas of Australia, these are often coastal locations based on lifestyle (for example, the south-west of Western Australia and the north coast of New South Wales) or diverse regional cities such as Newcastle. Traditionally, support in rural communities has gone to the National Party (formerly the Country Party), which has often ensured a rural representation in the governing coalition and has helped define the parameters of 'environmental issues' in rural and regional Australia. Until recently, the Liberal Party and National Party did not compete against each other in 'three-way contests' with the Australian Labor Party (and other candidates). The growing awareness of voting power among residents of rural and regional Australia has challenged the established parties. In places such as Queensland this protest vote has favoured One Nation. In the southern States of Australia it has favoured independent candidates. In the 1999 Victorian election, one victorious candidate ran on a single environmental issue: restoring the flow of the Snowy River.

Many environmentalists, politicians and agricultural producers are concerned about the changing physical conditions of the planet, Australia, its regions and localities. Environmentalists who hold a strong view of ecologically sustainable development would argue that a key issue in regional areas is the recognition of the physical, climatic and ecological limits and parameters within which all forms of human development must operate. In addition to this overarching issue is the recognition in countries such as Australia of prior Aboriginal occupancy, and the new, legally supported claims that indigenous Australians have on traditional land (Mabo, Wik) and its flora and fauna (*Yanner vs Eaton*). Reconciliation of the past injustices perpetrated on indigenous people — including the issues of genocide, stolen land and stolen generations — is now on the political agenda of all major parties.

The issues outlined above amount to a context that has never been seen before in Australia. Environmental and Aboriginal claims set limits on Western-style development that have previously been ignored, suppressed and temporarily 'solved' with state-sanctioned force, legal 'fictions' and technology. Part of the frustration in rural Australia is that these internal factors, along with globalisation, are now 'out of their control'. Politicians have no 'solutions' to these problems — despite the attempts of One Nation to implement policies from a time when tariffs solved economic problems, the environment was not an issue, subsidies were given to rural producers and Aboriginal people could be legally subjugated. As seen in studies presented below, however, there is not always consensus between and within environmentalist, Aboriginal, rural producer and political groups. While this situation remains, environmental and Aboriginal issues will continue to generate conflict in rural and regional Australia.

ATTITUDES TO SUSTAINABILITY IN RURAL AND REGIONAL AUSTRALIA

Environmentalists often argue that rural producers are a part of the problem rather than, as rural producers see themselves, part of the solution. Studies of rural producers' attitudes in Australia have revealed discrepancies between the beliefs of these two groups. Macleod and Taylor (1994) investigated the perceptions of beef producers and research scientists to potentially unsustainable land management practices in Queensland.

Over 73 per cent of beef producers and over 82 per cent of research scientists either agreed or strongly agreed that the knowledge currently existed to devise sustainable systems of grazing land management. However, approximately 51 per cent of beef producers believed that this knowledge was possessed by experienced beef producers, in contrast to over 65 per cent of research scientists who believed their group possessed the required knowledge (Macleod & Taylor, 1994).

Why is there such a disparity in the beliefs between rural producers, research scientists, environmentalists and, as demonstrated by Harrison et al. (1998), local residents? Macleod and Taylor (1994) found a marked difference between the research scientists (3.3 per cent) and beef producers (25.4 per cent) who thought that current grazing practices were sustainable. Assuming that these responses were given with integrity, there is a clear difference in the perception of the existence of a problem. Further, the scale of the problem is perceived differently. Macleod and Taylor (1994) identified that grazing land degradation was seen as a national problem by almost 40 per cent of research scientists, but only 30 per cent of beef producers saw the problem as being of a national scale. Research scientists also tended to see the problem at the scale of whole properties (39.3 per cent) compared to individual paddocks (10.7 per cent). In contrast, only 20 per cent of beef producers saw land degradation at the scale of whole properties, but 38.3 per cent of them saw it at the scale of paddocks (Macleod & Taylor, 1994).

The findings of a study by the Rural Needs Research Unit of the University of Newcastle Research Associates Limited (TUNRA, 1997) complement the work done in Queensland by Macleod and Taylor (1994). In times of drought, for example, other producers (25 per cent) and extension officers from NSW Agriculture (16 per cent) were considered the most important sources of information on property management. This is similar to the emphasis on experienced beef producers (although the proportion is significantly lower) in Macleod and Taylor (1994). The TUNRA (1997) study also highlighted key points on which primary producers and environmentalists disagree. For example, all of the eight focus groups in the TUNRA study of rural NSW beef and sheep producers defined 'sustainability' in economic rather than ecological terms. A complementary postal survey of 4000 rural producers asked about the importance of environmental protection measures to the sustainability of their property, and 43.9 per cent of rural producers said that the most important consideration was to maintain and improve soil fertility. The other significant issues for rural producers were controlling noxious and woody weeds, minimising soil loss and, controlling animal pests (TUNRA, 1997).

The factors that environmentalists are likely to rank more highly, such as reducing the use of fertilisers, fossil fuel, herbicides and pesticides, and using alternative fertilisers, were ranked the least important by rural producers. On a scale of one (useless) to five (very important), with three being 'not sure', the mean score for reducing the use of fertilisers and fossil fuels was below three. By way of contrast, maintaining soil fertility and controlling noxious and woody weeds scored means of 4.47 and 4.43 respectively (TUNRA, 1997). The TUNRA study highlighted regional variations in New South Wales, but also noted that there was a consensus throughout the State that improving soil fertility, controlling weeds and minimising soil loss were the most important environmental issues for beef and sheep producers (TUNRA, 1997).

In answer to the question of what 'threats' existed to the long-term viability of each respondent to remain as a rural producer, depressed markets rated as the major concern. This response was ranked as the most important by 44.7 per cent of respondents. Excessive bureaucracy (20.1 per cent) and water allocation policy (12.1 per cent) followed. Environmental issues such as government controls on land clearing (8.8 per cent), endangered species legislation (4.6 per cent) and the possibility of their property being incorporated into a national park (1.2 per cent) were not seen as significant threats (TUNRA, 1997). Importantly, native title claims (6.0 per cent State-wide and only 10.9 per cent in the pastoral leaseholders in the Western Lands Division) did not rate highly as concerns, despite the political climate being stoked by the Mabo and Wik decisions in the High Court.

The overwhelming focus on economic survival and economic sustainability in rural Australia is understandable in a period when global influences on market prices were paramount. The preoccupation with economic issues also opened a political window of opportunity to be filled by a party prepared to offer policies focused on arresting the 'demise of the bush' through subsidies, public campaigns to buy Australian made produce and low interest loans for farmers. In addition, the preoccupation presented the opportunity to capitalise by promising that potential impediments to a revival of the bush, such as environmental issues, Aboriginal land rights and excessive bureaucracy, would be removed from the political landscape. These groups and issues provide convenient targets to blame for economic circumstances in lieu of any alternative acceptable explanation.

HANSONISM AND THE ENVIRONMENT

The emergence of Pauline Hanson's One Nation was based upon the party's clearly stated support for primary industries such as agriculture, fishing, mining and forestry. In Australia, an alternative to the established political parties or the more environmentally focused smaller parties does not have to produce an environmental policy in order to gain votes in rural areas. Pauline Hanson's One Nation does not have a separate environmental policy at either the Queensland State level or the national level, although one of the six goals that define its platform is 'to cap population for environmental reasons' (One Nation, 1999a). The clearest environmental statement may be found in the Queensland policies under the Primary Industries Policy. Under the sub-heading 'environment' it is stated that:

> One Nation supports sustainable land use practices and achievable measures to repair past environmental damage. Department of Primary Industries research and extensive functions will be deployed to ensure that maximum long-term, sustainable production levels are achieved. [One Nation, 1999b: 3]

These brief statements demonstrate similarities between the One Nation understanding of sustainability and the understanding of sustainability expressed by rural producers in the TUNRA (1997) survey. The term 'sustainable' is connected both to land use and production levels within the one policy. There are no policies such as reducing fossil fuel use or reducing herbicide use which could antagonise any potential rural supporters. Other commitments, such as lobbying the federal government on diesel rebates for farm usage, are likely to be strongly supported by rural producers and opposed by environmentalists.

By focusing on the economic issues that corresponded with producers' concerns, Pauline Hanson's One Nation hit a receptive audience in rural Australia. By ignoring or downplaying genuine environmental issues, it was possible for One Nation not to lose votes in a political context where environmental issues were always going to be placed behind economic survival. From the perspective of ecological sustainability, however, the One Nation approach failed to address important issues such as biodiversity loss, soil erosion, increasing salinisation, water allocations, reducing fertiliser, pesticide and herbicide applications and the Greenhouse implications of the use of fossil fuels.

INDIGENOUS CONCERNS, DEVELOPMENT AND THE ENVIRONMENT

THE NATIONAL CONTEXT

Although environmental and indigenous issues are sometimes linked in media discussion of rural and regional Australia, the relative importance of these issues in the emergence of Pauline Hanson's One Nation Party differs markedly. We will now explore the other 'intruder' in the established politics of rural and regional Australia — the emergence of Aboriginal issues on the national agenda.

The first major intrusion in the rural and regional landscape involving Aboriginal people was the overturning of the doctrine of terra nullius by the Mabo High Court judgement in 1992. Terra nullius, literally meaning 'land belonging to no one', had been used to justify the appropriation of Aboriginal land since 1788 (Butt & Eagleson, 1993). Australia was the last of Britain's former colonies to recognise a form of native title to land. The key aspect of the Mabo decision was that where Aboriginal people could demonstrate a continuous connection with their land, native title had not been removed by any action taken by the Crown.

In order to bring the Mabo decision into the structure of statutory law, the *Native Title Act 1993* came into being. This law provided a framework and process whereby claims by Aboriginal people for native title could be assessed. As a consequence of Mabo, many wild statements were made by pressure groups and reported in the popular media about Aboriginal people taking land away from non-Aboriginal Australian settlers (including their back yards). The reality was that claims to native title were most likely to succeed only on vacant crown land and where Aboriginal people still practised a traditional lifestyle. The very idea that Aboriginal people had rights to land by virtue of the highest court in the land and entrenched in law, however, was enough to create a climate of fear among rural land holders and mining companies.

The fear of challenges to development based on unclear land tenure was realised with the Wik decision of the High Court (1996). This decision established that native title was not necessarily extinguished by the possession of pastoral and mining leases. Given that pastoral leases cover large tracts of the largely undeveloped parts of northern Australia, it is likely that native title claims could be successful in a large number of these cases. As a consequence of this greater 'uncertainty' with regard to mining and pastoral leases, the Commonwealth government decided to amend the *Native Title Act* to clarify the situation for all 'stakeholders'. The Prime Minister, John Howard, inflamed the issue by holding up a map of Australia on national television that purported to show just how much of Australia was at risk of a native title claim due to the Wik decision.

The 10 Point Plan was produced by the Howard government to amend the *Native Title Act* in the light of the Wik judgement. With the support of the independent senators (Harradine and Colston), the amendments were passed in July 1998. The amended law, larger and more complicated than ever, is now in place and the job of assessing native title claims continues.

Adding to this climate of legal change, a recent decision of the High Court (October 1999) in *Yanner versus Eaton* decided in favour of Murrandoo Yanner, a Gangalidda Aboriginal man from north Queensland, who had been prosecuted under the now outdated *Queensland Fauna Conservation Act 1974* for killing and eating two crocodiles between 31 October and 1 December 1994. Yanner had already come into public prominence in that year for his outspoken opposition to the multi-billion dollar Century Zinc mine in the Gulf country and his criticism of both Aboriginal and non-Aboriginal leaders who supported the mine.

The High Court decided that the federal *Native Title Act 1993*, which protected 'bush tucker' rights on land held under native title, over-rode the State law under which Yanner was prosecuted. Some conservationists expressed concern that the judgement would see native title rights conflict with conservation of native fauna, especially rare and endangered species (Hutton & Connors, 1999: 252). Aboriginal leaders have countered that, in traditional Aboriginal law, hunting could only take place within clan boundaries and that there were carefully defined limitations on what animals, and how many, could be taken.

The legal precedents in the Mabo, Wik and Yanner cases have transformed relationships between Aborigines and the other major groups in rural and regional Australia. Pastoralists and miners now have a legally based constraint on what they can do on land that has, or might have, a valid claim to native title by an Aboriginal clan. Beyond the legal constraints, corporations and industry groups have adopted policies, guiding principles and employee training programmes to develop positive relations with Aboriginal communities living in or near areas designated for exploration or production (Wand, 1996; Wells, 1996; Howitt, 1998). Similarly, conservationists can no longer ignore Aboriginal people and their presence in the Australian landscape. In 1993, the Australian Conservation Foundation, Greenpeace Australia, The Wilderness Society, the Australian Greens and the Australian Democrats adopted a common position on Aboriginal ownership of land and, among other things, claims under native title legislation (Hutton & Connors, 1999).

One outcome of these shifts is that Aborigines are now in a much stronger position to negotiate benefits for their own communities. This strength is derived from ownership of the land and from the natural resources present on or under their land. While this has resulted in royalty sharing with mining companies and regional agreements, this new strength has also been a catalyst for a reaction to what is described as the 'Aboriginal Industry' by politicians of various persuasions. None has been more forthright than Pauline Hanson.

HANSON AND ABORIGINAL ISSUES

Pauline Hanson's maiden speech to the federal parliament on 10 September 1996 amplified her previously stated view that Aboriginal people had received more benefits than non-Aboriginals. In her speech she claimed:

Apart from the $40 million spent so far since Mabo on native title claims, the government has made available $1 billion for Aboriginals and Torres Strait Islanders as compensation for land they cannot claim under native title. Bear in mind that the $40 million spent so far in native title has gone into the pockets of grateful lawyers and consultants. Not one native title has been granted as I speak. The majority of Aboriginals do not want handouts because they realise that welfare is killing them ... Those who feed off the Aboriginal industry do not want to see things changed. [House of Representatives (Commonwealth), 1996: 3860–61]

A recent development in the relationship between Pauline Hanson's One Nation and Aborigines has been the case of Peter David, a non-Aborigine used car salesperson in Perth who was adopted by a Noongar elder. At the time of writing, David is the controversial editor of a newspaper called the *Aboriginal*, the publication of which is funded by a Japanese business person. The distribution arm for the paper includes One Nation branches. This is highly controversial and divisive in the Noongar community in Perth (ABC, 1999).

The above situation can be seen to reflect the opportunism of Pauline Hanson's One Nation. This opportunism was previously demonstrated when the publication of Tim Flannery's *The Future Eaters* (1994) produced a public debate about the relationship between Aboriginal people and the natural environment, land management themes and population issues in Australia. These issues were taken up by many sectors of Australian society, including the emerging One Nation and other players in rural and regional contexts. Flannery presented the thesis that an optimum population for Australia was 6–12 million on the basis of the very low productivity of our soils and extremes of climatic variability (drought and flood) (Flannery, 1994: 368–69). While Flannery has flatly rejected restricting immigration based on racial origins, his views have been pushed in this direction by One Nation and other groups in their advocacy of restricting immigration from Asian countries. As Hanson herself put it in her maiden speech: 'I believe we are in danger of being swamped by Asians' (House of Representatives (Commonwealth), 1996: 3862)

CONCEPTIONS OF WILDERNESS AND COUNTRY

Another important issue that Flannery tackled in *The Future Eaters* was the idea, firmly entrenched in the environmental movement in Australia during the 1970s and 1980s, that unoccupied land was to be thought of as 'wilderness'. Flannery saw this view as the environmental equivalent to the doctrine of *terra nullius* which conveniently removed Aboriginal occupation of Australia from the environmental landscape. Flannery was one of the first to make it clear in popular books and television documentaries that: '... the entire continent has been actively and extensively managed for 60 000 years by its Aboriginal occupants. To leave it untouched will be to create something new, and less diverse, than that which went before' (Flannery, 1994: 379).

Aboriginal writers on environmental issues such as Marcia Langton (1998) have highlighted the divide between wilderness-based conservation in Australia and Aboriginal perspectives on the land. The failure of the early conservation movement to acknowledge prior Aboriginal occupancy and management of the land and the influence of colonisation established a divide between some indigenous interests and some interests within the environmental movement. The strongly anthropocentric character of Aboriginal perspectives on the environment contrasts with the ecocentric views of the wilderness-based conservation movement. The Aboriginal and Torres Strait Islander Commission's (ATSIC) view of wilderness as land 'without its songs and ceremonies' (in Langton 1998, 19) clearly highlights the intense link between humans and the physical environment (also see Rose, 1995). Conversely, Aboriginal definitions of 'country' must acknowledge the songs and ceremonies associated with the cultural maintenance of a particular piece of land (Rose 1996).

The agreement between Flannery and Langton ends at this point. The type of impact Aboriginal people have had on the environment has been a hotly debated issue. Flannery's thesis has been interpreted as suggesting that the early Aboriginal people were environmental vandals who rearranged components of the ecosystem to suit their own interests. As part of their version of non-sustainable 'future eating', Aboriginal people were thought to be a major cause of the extinction of the megafauna by 'blitzkrieg' hunting and changes to the established vegetation regimes by increasing the fire frequency. According to Flannery, only after a period (40–60 000 years ago) of destructive future eating did Aborigines develop conservation of the resources needed to sustain themselves over the long term. Flannery argues that, for at least the last 40 000, years Aboriginal culture became of necessity a 'conserver culture' based on the careful management of resources. This argument collapses the dichotomy of 'the Noble Savage in harmony with the environment and the modern Aborigine who poses the threat of extinction to rare and endangered species by virtue of wearing shoes, driving a Toyota and hunting with guns' (Langton, 1996: 17). It does so, however, by removing the one area where traditional Aboriginal people had been viewed positively by Europeans; that is, as the original 'environmentalists' who were good stewards of 'country'.

Flannery-type arguments about the true nature of pre-1788 vegetation have also been used to defend increased fire frequencies and further clearing of semi-arid and marginal agricultural land. In Queensland, for example, in the latter half of 1999 the rates of land clearing have been described as among the highest in the world and have been defended by farmers with the argument that 'woodland was more open when it was burnt by Aborigines, but had now "thickened" to the point where it had to be "pulled" to make it suitable for cattle' (Roberts, 1999: 38). Similar arguments have been used to increase the fire frequency in national parks and State forests to reduce the impact of wildfires. Such strategies have pitted fire-based land managers against conservationists.

NATIVE TITLE AND SUSTAINABILITY ISSUES

Indigenous people have reacted to native title and other changes to the national and regional policy framework in a number of different ways. One reaction was for Aboriginal people to see their new found autonomy as the basis for a new legal and economic independence from the shackles and constraints imposed on them by past Commonwealth, State and Territory governments. Another was to use this new independence to reject western-style development and reassert the value and authority of traditional Aboriginal culture, as seen in the 'outstation movement' in remote Australia. Within different groups of Aboriginal people in the Northern Territory, such as the Jawoyn, and the Mirrar, we can see both types of reaction in relation to the mining industry and the potential it has to assist indigenous people achieve their own goals.

Indigenous people and mining

Opposition by Mirrar people to uranium mining has been led by female activists and traditional owners such as Jacqui Katona and Yvonne Margarula. The Mirrar, supported by green activists, unsuccessfully tried to stop the extension of uranium mining in the Kakadu National Park at Jabiluka mine during 1998–99. Not all Aboriginal people oppose uranium mining, however. In West Arnhemland, Aboriginal people have joint ventures and exploration licences with established mining companies to exploit commercially viable deposits of uranium and other ore bodies. The Nadjinem Aboriginal Corporation, West Arnhem Corporation, Yok Aboriginal Corporation and Warrga Aboriginal Corporation hold 2 per cent interests in exploration leases. The Northern Aboriginal Investment Corporation and Bongoi Aboriginal Corporation hold 10 per cent shares in exploration licences (Scott, 1998).

The Jawoyn Association have a long history of involvement with mining and other commercial activities such as tourism. The Jawoyn became nationally well known in the late 1980s when they attempted to prevent BHP from mining gold, platinum and palladium at Coronation Hill (also mined for uranium from 1957–1964) adjacent to the Kakadu National Park. The cabinet of the Hawke Labor government agreed on June 19 1991 not to allow mining to proceed, and on 21 June the government proclaimed that Coronation Hill would be incorporated into the national park (Toyne, 1994). A major part of the Jawoyn argument to stop mining was the assertion that the country was a sacred site connected to other major sites within what they called the 'sickness country', a recognition of the rich uranium deposits in the area. The creator of sickness country, 'Bula', lies dormant under the ground and will be disturbed by mining. Such disturbance leads to sickness and death in the minds of the Jawoyn people and cannot be allowed to proceed. This link between the preservation of nature and spiritual belief, however, does not extend to the Jawoyn opposing mining in other less culturally sensitive places. John Ah Kit, the executive officer of the Jawoyn Association in 1991, argued that:

> We are not opposed to mining per se. We have an agreement with two companies who are exploring for diamonds on Jawoyn traditional land. We are not anti-development. We want to contribute to the economy of the Northern Territory and we show that. [Ah Kit, 1999]

A case study: The Mount Todd gold mine

The opportunity to enter a joint venture (JV) with a major mining development arose for the Jawoyn between 1993 and 1996. The Mount Todd gold mine at Katherine was to be developed by Zapopan NL, the Australian arm of the Canada- and Washington-based international mining company, Pegasus Gold Inc. Under an arrangement heralded as the largest ever commercial deal involving Aboriginal people in Australia, the Jawoyn exchanged any possible native title rights to an area of approximately 1200 square kilometres. In addition, they negotiated with the mining company to get entitlements to training, employment, housing and community infrastructure. In return, the Northern Territory government granted the Jawoyn title to over 5000 square kilometres of surrounding land, minus the right to veto any mining proposals. Pegasus claimed that it would be spending $208 million on the development of stage two of the mine. In their own prospectus, Pegasus claimed that:

> In October 1996, Pegasus made a major acquisition of 1200 square kilometres of tenements from Territory Goldfields NL. This area is part of a historic JV agreement with the Barnjarn group of the Aboriginal Jawoyn Association. Under this agreement, the Barnjarn are 10 per cent JV partners. Because of this, the land rights issue is not a concern here. Now Pegasus virtually controls all mineralised land within the region. [Tuchlik & Medway, 1997]

The actual development of the second stage of the mine was to be undertaken in 1996 by the $166 million Mirrkworlk joint venture. This joint venture was between the Henry Walker contract mining company (50 per cent), the Jawoyn Association (25 per cent) and the Aboriginal and Torres Strait Islander Commercial Development

Corporation (ATSICDC) (25 per cent). The Jawoyn invested $10 million in the joint venture through a commercial loan with repayments to be made from the profits of the mine (National Indigenous Working Group on Native Title, 1997). The then chair of ATSICDC, Gatjil Djerrkura, was offered a seat on the Henry Walker company board (Kennedy 1996). Gatjil Djerrkura was later appointed by the Howard government to the chair of ATSIC itself.

In late 1996, the deal between Aboriginal people and Pegasus Gold was held up nationally as 'ground-breaking', a 'win–win' situation for both parties, and importantly, one that was consistent with the Howard government's policy of greater Aboriginal financial autonomy and a reduction in welfare dependence. Unfortunately for the joint venturers, the collapse of the international price for gold during 1997 saw Pegasus Gold enter serious financial trouble. In November 1997, shortly after it was opened, the Mount Todd gold mine was forced to close. A combination of low gold prices and high operating costs were given as reasons for the closure. Moreover, examination of the mining history of Pegasus Gold reveals that the company has a long record of serious violations of its pollution permits in the United States and that its operations have been vigorously opposed by Native American groups, environmental defenders and various government departments (Abel, 1997). The Mount Todd gold mine is now named Yimuyn Manjerr and was purchased by Multiplex Constructions and General Gold Resources for $30 million in February 1999. In July 1999 mining resumed on the site under the control of Macmahon Holdings, which had been awarded a $70 million surface mining contract for the new consortium, which included Pegasus and the new owners.

The Mount Todd case illustrates the difficulties Aboriginal people can find themselves in entering into commercial partnerships with players in the global financial market. As with gold, the uranium market is extremely volatile and can collapse without warning in the face of, for example, another serious accident similar to one that occurred in Japan in 1999. In addition, both industries face major criticism from environmentalists. The gold industry, especially when associated with the cyanide 'heap–leach' method of mining, is often connected with major environmental problems. Leakage of cyanide from leach pads and acid mine drainage — containing nitrates, heavy metals, manganese, arsenic and cyanide — from tailings dams have severely polluted surface and ground water and ecosystems, and have risked human health in many countries, including the US (Pegasus Gold's Zortman–Landusky mine in Montana). In early 2000, at the 50 per cent Australian-owned Baia Mare tailings treatment project (Aurul) in north-western Romania. A tailings dam containing cyanide polluted the Tisza River, poisoning the drinking water of an estimated 2.5 million people in Romania and downstream Hungary (ABC, 2000). Environmental and health impacts of tailings dams are also a potential problem for the uranium mining industry. In the Bihar region in India, the Jadaguda uranium mine is reported to have exposed at least 30 000 people to dangerous levels of radiation from open tailings dams, causing an epidemic of birth deformities, radiation sickness, cancers and other diseases (Rahman, 1999).

Investing hard won Aboriginal capital into ventures that have the potential to be both economically and ecologically risky calls for caution and detailed risk assessment. Leadership within Aboriginal politics is now split on such issues. Positions range from advocating a complete move away from government-based welfare models of development by embracing venture capitalism, to positions that question the ability of venture capitalism to generate ecological and social stability.

CONCLUSION

In this chapter we have argued that support for One Nation derived from a disjuncture between the concerns of people in rural and regional Australia and the major political parties (and smaller parties such as the Greens and the Australian Democrats). In this context, it is possible for a party such as Pauline Hanson's One Nation, or variants which may arise in the future, to tap into the discontent about distant and ineffective governments, rampant economic rationalisation, globalisation, Aboriginal land rights, and environmental barriers to development and wealth creation. All of these sources of discontent are easily connected to tropes of decline and loss in rural and regional Australia and converted into political extremes.

The common element in these forms of discontent is that, with the exception of influencing government through the ballot box, all of the other issues have lives of their own, no longer capable of being controlled by rural and regional interests and their traditional political correlates. Indeed, despite One Nation's rise and fall, the overwhelming direction of federal government policy has been to continue to deregulate and to allow market forces to prevail. These policies have promoted innovative joint ventures and other forms of entrepreneurial activity in all parts of rural and regional Australia, including Aboriginal Australia. As such, policies that remove public subsidies from the welfare sector and replace them with incentives for economic and social self–reliance are consistent with One Nation's views that all forms of public subsidies be removed from Aboriginal people. Under great political pressure from 'the bush', however, the Coalition government has belatedly indicated that it doesn't always want market forces to prevail in rural and regional Australia with respect to the withdrawal of remaining essential services (see Chapters 6 & 9).

New legal precedents, academic contributions and Aboriginal activists have transformed debates about the meanings of conservation, wilderness, country and optimum levels of population. One result of such contradictory and confusing messages about the environment has been a vacuum of effective policy on some of the most pressing of environmental issues, such as dry land salinity and water allocations. In this context, the physical environment is asserting its own changing character into environmentalist, Aboriginal and colonial cultures.

The agenda of greater autonomy and control for indigenous people over their own destiny comes at the price of a new variety of exploitation, one that is potentially just as devastating to Aboriginal people as those of past regimes of domination and assimilation. Greater self-determination to make good or bad commercial decisions is a freedom that has to be exercised by Aboriginal people themselves. While this agenda has emerged partly in response to pressures of neo-conservative politics, Aboriginal people cannot expect that such decisions will not be criticised by pro-environmental and anti-capitalist interests. This is especially the case with Aboriginal involvement in the gold and uranium industries. As demonstrated in the Mount Todd case, when entering partnerships with venture capitalists, Aboriginal people who are seeking independence from the welfare state find themselves in the same risky situation as other classes of investors. They also find themselves immersed in controversial environmental issues of national and international importance.

The tensions between non-Aboriginal members of rural communities, Aboriginal people and environmentalists are likely to continue into the future. Indeed, the tensions are likely to be exacerbated given the increasing diversity of interests within these groups. Recently there have been shifts in the political positions and environmental awareness within all groups. While this has resulted in shifting alliances, it is also leading to divisions in what formerly appeared to be homogeneous blocs. It also clearly shows that the underlying assumptions of One Nation — that 'this nation is being divided into black and white, and the present system encourages this' — are flawed (Australia, House of Representatives, *Debates* 10 September 1996: 3861).

The inherent fragility of One Nation's policies have been exposed and the inherent riskiness of venture capitalism has now been experienced by some Aboriginal communities. At the time of writing, the big environmental issues, such as expanding dry land salinity, diminishing water resources, land degradation and loss of biodiversity, continue to be neglected by State and federal governments. Non-government organisations such as Landcare are working hard to redress some of the damage inflicted on the environment by past mismanagement, but these efforts pale in the face of ongoing vegetation clearing and the expanding demands of intensive agriculture. Critical assessment of recent approaches to rural and regional issues, policies, politics and economics needs to be undertaken by all players in order to develop a more progressive base for social and environmental sustainability for the various Aboriginal and non-Aboriginal interests in rural and regional Australia.

REFERENCES

Abel H (1997) 'The rise and fall of a mining company', *High County News*, Vol. 29, No. 24, 22 December, at: *http://www.hen.org/1997/dec22/dir/Sidebar_The_rise_a.html*.

AFFA (1999) 'Agriculture, Fisheries and Forestry — Australia', at: *www.affa.gov.au/csg/nrmp/landcare.html*.

Ah Kit J (1991) in 'Australia: Jawoyn official on Coronation Hill', at: *www.nativenet.uthscsa.edu/archive/91b/0024.html*.

Australian Broadcasting Corporation (1999) '7.30 Report', 19 November.

Australian Broadcasting Corporation (2000) 'Australian company involved in Hungarian environmental disaster', 'News', at: *http://www.abc.net.au/news/2000/02/item200000209091012_1.htm)*.

Australia, House of Representatives (1996), *Debates*, 10 September, Vol 8, pp 3860–3.

Bailey M (1997) 'Landcare: Myth or Reality?', in Lockie S & Vanclay F (eds) *Critical Landcare*, Centre for Social Research, Charles Sturt University, Wagga Wagga, pp 129–42.

Broome R (1994) *Aboriginal Australians : black responses to white dominance, 1788–1994*, second edition, Allen & Unwin, Sydney.

Butt P & Eagleson R (1993) *Mabo: What the High Court Said*, Federation Press, Sydney.

Country Shires Councils' Association & Country Urban Councils' Association Working Party (1990) *A Future or a Funeral?*, Country Shires Councils' Association & Country Urban Councils' Association, Western Australia.

Davenport D (1997) 'A view from the ground: Farmers, sustainability and change', in Lockie S & Vanclay F (eds) *Critical Landcare*, Centre for Social Research, Charles Sturt University, Wagga Wagga, pp 153–63.

Flannery T (1994) *The Future Eaters*, Reed Books, Sydney.

Harrison C, Burgess J & Clark J (1998) 'Discounted knowledges: farmers' and residents' understandings of nature conservation goals and policies', *Journal of Environmental Management*, 54, pp 305–20.

House of Representatives (Commonwealth) (1996) *Debates*, The Parliament, Canberra, pp 3860–62.

Howitt R (1998) 'Recognition, respect and reconciliation: steps towards decolonisation?', *Australian Aboriginal Studies*, 1998, 1, pp 28–34.

Hutton D & Connors L (1999) *A History of the Australian Environment Movement*, Cambridge University Press, Melbourne.

Kennedy A (1996) 'Miner strikes it rich with staff', *Business Review Weekly*, at: *www.brw.com.au/root_brw/021296/pg_feat14.htm*.

Langton M (1996) 'Art, wilderness and terra nullius', in Sultan R (ed.) *Ecopolitics IX: Perspectives on Indigenous Peoples Management of Environment Resources*, Northern

Territory University, Darwin, pp 11–24.

Langton M (1998) *Burning Questions: Emerging Environmental Issues for Indigenous Peoples in Northern Australia*, Centre for Indigenous Natural and Cultural Resource Management Northern Territory University, Darwin.

Lockie S (1995) 'Beyond a "good thing": political interests and the meaning of Landcare' *Rural Society* 5 (2–3) pp 3–12.

Lockie S & Vanclay F (eds) (1997) *Critical Landcare*, Centre for Social Research, Charles Sturt University, Wagga Wagga.

Macleod N & Taylor J (1994) 'Perceptions of beef cattle producers and scientists relating to sustainable land use issues and their implications for technology transfer', *Rangelands Journal*, 16, pp 238–53.

Martin P (1995) 'The constitution of power in Landcare: A post-structuralist perspective with modernist undertones', *Rural Society*, 5 (2/3) pp 30–7.

Murphy D & Woodford J (1999) 'Salt of the earth turns Australia's rivers to poison', *The Australian*, 23 October, p 1.

National Indigenous Working Group on Native Title (1997), 'NIWG Fact Sheets', at: *www.faira.org.au/niwg/fact_sheets/fs6.html*.

National Institute of Economic and Industry Research (1998) *State of the Regions: A Report to the Australian Local Government Association 1998 Regional Cooperation and Development Forum*, NIEIR, Melbourne.

One Nation (1999a) *Pauline Hanson's One Nation: Policies and Political Goals*, at: *www.onenation.com.au/policy.html*.

One Nation (1999b) *Pauline Hanson's One Nation, 1998 Queensland State Election Primary Industries Policy*, at: *http://www.onenation.com.au/qldstate/polprim.htm*.

Rahman A (1999) 'Nuclear deformity and death in villages of the damned', *Sydney Morning Herald*, 11 December, p 22.

Reynolds H (1989) *Dispossession: Black Australians and White Invaders*, Allen & Unwin, Sydney.

Reynolds H (1996) *Aboriginal Sovereignty: Reflections on Race, State and Nation*, Allen & Unwin, Sydney.

Roberts G (1999) '... Barren the next', *Sydney Morning Herald*, Saturday, 30 October, p 38.

Rose B (1995) *Land Management Issues: Attitudes and Perceptions Amongst Aboriginal People of Central Australia*, Central Land Council, Alice Springs.

Rose D B (1996) *Nourishing Terrains: Australian Aboriginal Views of Landscape and Wilderness*, Australian Heritage Commission, Canberra.

Rural Needs Research Unit, University of Newcastle Research Associates Limited (TUNRA) (1997) *Rural Needs and Climate Variability*, TUNRA, Newcastle.

Scott G (1998) 'Uranium Issues', at: *www.ozemail.com.au/~greentt/westarn.htn*.

Sproull R (1999) 'Rio's miner miracle', *The Australian*, 10 November, p 52.

Toyne P (1994) *The Reluctant Nation: Environment, Law and Politics in Australia*, ABC Books, Sydney.

Tuchlik K & Medway C (1997) 'Diggers and dealers forum', 1997 Pegasus Gold Corporation, at: *www.reyngraph.com.au/dnd/dnd97/peg.html*.

Wand P (1996) 'Untitled', in Northern and Central Land Councils, *Land Rights: Past, Present and Future*, Conference papers from Canberra, 16–17 August 1996, Northern and Central Land Councils, Casuarina, pp 228–29.

Wells D (1996) 'Untitled', in Northern and Central Land Councils, *Land Rights: Past, Present and Future*, Conference papers from Canberra, 16–17 August 1996, Northern and Central Land Council, Casuarina, pp 241–42.

8

THE MANAGEMENT OF GOVERNMENT AND ITS CONSEQUENCES FOR SERVICE DELIVERY IN REGIONAL AUSTRALIA

ROLF GERRITSEN

Globalisation, and the macroeconomic policy response arising from the challenge of globalisation by successive Australian governments, is usually blamed for the spatial and socio-economic effects that are currently popularly labelled the 'rural crisis'. This chapter argues that the phenomena that constitute the rural crisis are caused not just by the dominant (so-called 'economic rationalist') policy responses to exogenous economic pressures. A combination of policy-making atrophy (a complementary problem to economic rationalism and caused by a similar set of assumptions), plus a set of organisational mechanisms that have shaped the way governments conduct their business, are probably as important as globalisation in shaping the contemporary problems of rural Australia.

Together these macro-economic and public management effects have interacted with a tendency towards 'jurisdiction shifting' in our federal system. At the local level this is manifest in local governments increasingly being subject to the burdens of broadening service delivery responsibilities (for example, for the environment, economic development, public safety) without any compensating broadening of the revenue base of the local state (see Chapter 11).

The clear implication of this hypothesis is that successive State and federal governments have organised their management of policy making and implementation in a manner that has exacerbated the socially adverse effects of globalisation and proved deleterious to Australia's rural and regional communities. The result has been increasing poverty in particular regional areas of Australia — small rural towns, manufacturing centres, coastal 'welfare' regions and some outer urban areas of Australia (Fincher, 1999).

THE CONTEXT OF THE PROBLEM

Globalisation is a catch-all descriptor for a set of international technology and information flows — as well as trade and international power relations — that have profound local effects (Giddens, 1994; Harvey, 1989; Wiseman, 1998). It has long been realised that globalisation has had differential national and intra-national impacts (for Australia see Browett & Leaver 1989; Lawrence 1987). The analysis of some of these impacts is certainly one of the major reasons for the concerns that motivate this book.

The contemporary rural and regional crisis in Australia is caused by a combination of three factors. The first is the social and commercial consequences of the restructuring of our agricultural and pastoral industries over the past half century (see Chapter 3). The second factor — to a degree both cause and effect — is inter-regional population movements. These include the drift to the east and south-west coasts and the drift which follows the recentralisation of private sector services away from smaller regional towns and settlements to large regional cities (see Chapter 4). The final factor is the recentralisation of governmental services, with spatial results that have mirrored those caused by the restructuring of the private sector (Gerritsen, 1998: 30–38). Globalisation is the principal causal agent of the first of these factors. To a degree, globalisation has also produced the incentives that have created the second factor, the migration of private sector services to larger regional towns and cities. The policy sets and approaches which are a consequence in part of globalisation have created the policy and managerial frameworks that have further exacerbated the rural crisis and inhibit any holistic approach to regional policy by State and federal governments.

Since the mechanisation that began in the 1950s, Australian agriculture has been in a process of continuous evolution. This has involved increases in scale, diversification into new products, an increase in the capital intensity of production, the advent of new production processes and the wholesale application of new advanced technologies. This evolutionary process accelerated during the 1980s and has generally contributed to a continuing depopulation of agricultural and pastoral areas. The rural labour market has changed profoundly, most obviously in the massive decline of itinerant and seasonal unskilled and semi-skilled labour markets (to the great disadvantage of Aborigines in particular). Paradoxically, while the rural poor are relatively worse off, many regions of Australia feature impressive growth rates and increases productivity and value, at least per employed person (Productivity Commission, 1999a: figures 1.2–1.4).

It is apparent that the successes of Australian agriculture in adapting to declining terms of trade are partly contradicted by the increasing maldistribution of wealth and income in non-coastal rural and regional Australia. This perverse distributional result of globalisation is not confined to inland rural and regional Australia, but is worse there than in most parts of metropolitan Australia. It creates a challenge that by and large Commonwealth and State governments have not met over the past 15 years.

The growing capital intensity of agriculture is a common phenomenon in all advanced economies. What is different in Australia (and New Zealand) is that, unlike, for example, the European Union, the USA and Japan, there has not been a parallel growth in agricultural protectionism. In part, this is because, since the late 1970s, farm groups have agreed with and assisted Australian governments to reduce the effective rate of agricultural protection (Gerritsen, 2000). Australian farm elites (principally, as organised in producer pressure groups) have been intrinsic to the manufacture of the national policy packages of deregulation and reduction, in producer assistance that have devastated regional Australia. The farmer political elite has suffered from the same 'partialisation' of policy frameworks — that is, by having an almost exclusive focus upon economic efficiency — as has bedevilled the State and federal policy-making elites.

The depopulation of rural Australia has interacted with globalisation to encourage private sector services to recentralise their operations in large regional centres. The rural branch closures of the four major retail banks have attracted most of the popular attention, but this phenomenon has occurred across a variety of retail, wholesale and agricultural service industries (see Chapter 9). Boarded up shop windows have been the result in the main streets of the smaller towns and settlements of rural and regional Australia.

Supposedly the depopulation of rural and regional Australia has also driven the sweeping cutbacks in State and federal services, though these cuts have usually been justified in terms of seeking improved economies or organisational efficiencies. In addition, in many instances the new fashion for corporatising and privatising government business enterprises has contributed both directly and indirectly to that depopulation. Australia Post, for example, cut the number of its post offices after corporatisation by 25.6 per cent between 1991 and 1997 (Gerritsen, 1998: 73). In a large number of cases these offices were replaced by community mail agencies, usually operating out of an already established local business such as a general store or newsagency. The replacement of a stand-alone post office with a community mail agency typically meant the removal of at least three jobs from a local community. This phenomenon can also be seen in the massive staff reductions in decentralised State Rail and Telstra depots.

These cutbacks have also been an inevitable consequence of the reductions in expenditure on direct service delivery — as distinct from income transfers — that have characterised governmental fiscal strategies since the 1980s. In part the States are reacting to the 50 per cent drop (in real terms) of the level of Commonwealth general purpose grants between 1985 and 2000. The cuts also have the advantage of being able to 'jurisdiction shift'; the burden of the unemployment created by State service shrinkage falls upon the Commonwealth budget. The States' environmental duties can be devolved to local government. The consequences of the vertical fiscal imbalance in our federation bear disproportionately upon the residents of rural and regional Australia.

Declining State fiscal resources, exacerbated by the narrowing of their own-source revenues and reduced intergovernmental transfers, have interacted with the changing nature of government in Australia. There has been a constant state of transformation, a process that has gathered momentum over the past two decades. Throughout the 20th century there was a tendency to shift from the direct provision of the services — such as agricultural extension, education, police, health, rail and communications services — that characterised government in the years before World War 1, towards regulatory interventions to secure governmental objectives (Butlin, Barnard & Pincus, 1982). So, whilst we supposedly live in an age of small government, the reality is that there has merely been a change in the nature of the burden of government.

Paradoxically, the supposed age of small government has also seen the rapid expansion of regulatory activities, such as those in the area of consumer product standards and behaviour regulation (for example, restrictions on tobacco consumption) and, especially, the field of environmental affairs. This growth of regulation has occurred at the same time as real per capita reductions in direct service provision. In part this shift to regulation has been encouraged by the fiscal stringency characteristic of Australian governments over the past 15 years; the budgetary conservatism reflecting a power shift to central agency control over whole-of-government outlays.

But there are also elements intrinsic to the organisation of government agencies themselves that have affected, mostly adversely, the impacts of globalisation upon regional Australia. Firstly, governmental service delivery agencies have responded to budget cut-backs by shifting to cost free (for them) regulation. In addition, within service delivery agencies a power shift analogous to the larger shift from front-line to central agencies has also occurred. The budgetary stringency has assisted a centralisation of power within front-line agencies.

This centralisation is encouraged by the need for performance monitoring and other features of what Hood (1990) initially characterised as the 'New Public Management'. Emerging to prominence during the 1980s, this new organisational set features a more explicit focus on results (as against a supposedly traditional public administration concern with administrative process); decentralised program management; a priority on efficiency, productivity and competition; as well as flexible approaches to achieving cost-effective policy implementation (OECD, 1995). Behind the advent of the New Public Management is the hidden agenda of rolling back the Keynesian-style welfare state.

The centralisation of power within front-line agencies again encourages the implementation of unpopular change at the organisational periphery. So the structures and practices of bureaucracy, as reshaped by the New Public Management, encourage the recentralisation of administrative activity that is intrinsic to the adverse effects of globalisation in many parts of rural and regional Australia. Regulation is a capital city based activity; regulatory departmental headquarters expand in consequence. Fiscal cutbacks and personnel 'downsizing' impact through reduced employment at the decentralised rims of departmental and State agency operations in rural and regional Australia. The managerial power structures also operate to provide incentives to require the organisational periphery to sustain the most pain when restructuring and 'downsizing' is occurring.

The exact extent of these effects upon services and the population centres is difficult to determine, the waters being considerably muddied by the advent of new information technology driven modes of organisation. Thus the Commonwealth government's social welfare agency, Centrelink, has introduced interactive technology to serve its customers needs. This technology allows the reduction of staff numbers, thereby presumably facilitating the budget objectives of its 'owner', the Department of Social Security. In this instance the new technology may provide an overall customer benefit, but the reduction in staff certainly hampers community development.

So the recentralisation of government services is a result of a complex combination of factors. This recentralisation is not just a reaction to the post-1985 reduction in governmental expenditures. Nor is it explained as simply an organisational reaction to the depopulation of rural Australia (to which it has undoubtedly contributed). The organisational and spatial form that this reduction of public outlays has taken has been shaped by the advent of the New Public Management. This in turn has interacted with the new macro-economic orthodoxy to create a policy system that appears incapable or unwilling to deal with the issues raised by the spatial differentiation and unequal access to public goods that are the consequence of these policy fashions.

In Australia it is an interacting combination of these three factors — the general thrust of macro-economic policy, micro-economic methodology's domination of policy making at each individual policy arena level; and the New Public Management — that have provided the particular framework for the regional casualties of globalisation.

THE NEW PUBLIC MANAGEMENT AND THE REGIONAL CRISIS

Since the mid-1980s the manner in which Western governments conduct their business has altered profoundly. As discussed above, these changes in the process of government administration have been characterised as the New Public Management (NPM) (Hood, 1990; Stewart, 1997). As mentioned, characteristics of NPM include a more explicit focus on results; a priority on efficiency, productivity and competition; decentralised program management and flexible approaches to achieving cost-effective policy implementation.

The NPM contrasts with traditional public administration principally in the establishment of principal–agent relations, which has driven a shift towards contractualism both in relation to out-sourcing services and in purchaser–provider splits within public sector agencies (Hood, 1990). The NPM has encouraged a trend to see private management practices as worthy of public emulation. Indeed, for the current Prime Minister, this has been an explicit driver of continuing changes to the *Australian Public Service Act* (Howard, 1998: 5).

In most cases the philosophy of small government and global competitiveness has also underpinned this policy paradigm shift. This new policy paradigm is the result of the overturning of the previously dominant Keynesian macro-economic paradigm, a process that began in the late 1970s and was completed a decade later. The new orthodoxy, based upon a revival of Marshallian neo-classical micro-economics as the basis for policy, has focused upon small government, almost as an end in itself (Argy, 1998: 80–87). Indeed, in Australia during the 1990s the accelerating emphasis upon the fiscal imperatives of small government virtually displaced the new processes of accountability (freedom of information, administrative appeals, equal opportunity, etc.) instituted during the 1980s (Zifcak, 1997; Curtin, 2000) and supposedly intrinsic to the new public sector managerialism.

The focus upon so-called 'economic rationalism' — in reality a small government restructuring of the state — has produced a degree of civic discontent (Curtin, 2000), most recently reflected in the Victorian election. The initial manifestation of this discontent was in the rise of a powerful political protest movement embodied in the surprise showing of Pauline Hanson's One Nation in the 1998 Queensland election and the 1998 federal election. In the media, the

One Nation phenomenon was generally interpreted as a regionally based protest, though in reality it also had important class components. This latter element was apparent in the relatively strong One Nation vote in the metropolitan margins and predominantly lower socio-economic residential areas.

The NPM occurs within a context in which the dominant microeconomic framework eschews holistic interventions, replacing these with a myriad of supposedly efficient 'markets' that interact together to provide the optimal aggregate outcome. The NPM's acceptance of market-like elements within its management practices follows naturally from the dominant policy paradigm. The NPM has, however, encouraged behaviour that has made the rural and regional crisis worse than it would have otherwise been. This result is through particular features of the approach, such as the concentration upon individual agency or program performance (usually only measured quantitatively) and establishing quasi-market relations between agencies. In essence, my argument is that rational individual agency behaviours have collectively contributed to the rural crisis. This is because each individual agency's actions, while rational and efficient within the context of the NPM, have ignored the cumulative collective effects of their behaviour and its impact upon whole-of-government service delivery.

An illustration will clarify the point. In 1992 Telstra, which was then being corporatised, moved onto an enhanced cost-recovery model for its maintenance and service extension. This increased budgetary pressure on Telstra's middle managers meant that there was an incentive to concentrate efforts in areas which could earn a 'profit' (mostly the major metropolitan centres of each State). In Wilcannia in western New South Wales, the Telstra depot was closed and maintenance organised from Broken Hill. This was a success from management's point of view. As a consequence of this 'success', however, 90 jobs were lost from a small township of 1200 people. Naturally the population declined — to about 850 in 1996. But more seriously, local crime rates immediately rose dramatically. The number of cases before the monthly circuit court in Wilcannia increased from between 20 and 30 to consistently over 120 over the next two years (until the Keating government's *One Nation* and *Working Nation* regional employment programs again reduced the crime rates). So the effect of an individually rational action by Telstra middle management was collectively disastrous for both the NSW government — whose law and public safety costs immediately rose in that locality — and the Commonwealth, which had extra unemployment benefits to pay. An individually rational action by a public agency contributed to increased costs and difficulties for other public agencies.

The cumulative effect of individual agency rationality can be disastrous. In Cooma over the 1996–97 financial year (in which the Howard government's regional program cut backs impacted most severely), 361 jobs were lost either directly or indirectly. This was a $11.8 million loss to the annual product of the town. In Lismore, similar consequences ensued in that same year (COSBOA, 1997: 86–106).

Further examples of this collective action-cum-NPM dilemma in regional service delivery are legion. In the 1998 budget in one State, the Minister for Police discovered that his budget was to be cut (or at least it was subject to an 'efficiency dividend') by about 10 per cent over the next two years. His response was to pass the problem to his police commissioner. The commissioner, very efficiently, told his divisional commanders that each of their budgets would be cut by the requisite amount in order to secure the efficiency dividend. The commissioner's remuneration was performance-based, so he had an incentive to respond rapidly in this simplistic manner. Each divisional commander likewise passed the problem down the organisational food chain. Eventually it ended with regional police commanders, who responded by securing savings through reduced police numbers at small stations (that is, those in small townships and villages). The reduction in numbers of police in rural areas was not supposed to reduce their efficiency. Regional call centres replaced after hours staffing of the local police station. Some brighter regional commanders even announced mobile and tactical squads, which would replace police living in small localities.

In a sense this model is similar to the Centrelink example (discussed above). From the perspective of the police service, its managers have responded as efficiently and effectively to the budgetary imperatives as possible. Their management's response was affected by the incentives created by the performance-based remuneration intrinsic to the NPM. For the smaller localities involved, however, this individual rationality of the police service will probably be collectively disastrous. This is because the local police are not just the guardians of law and order. Similar to the bank branches (discussed in Chapter 9), local police have important indirect economic and community functions. Economically, they contribute to the total pool of employment in the town, thereby assisting the local clubs and retailers to survive. The departure of the police will have multiplier effects. The local economy will become smaller and suffer asset deflation, providing a disincentive to further investment by current businesses. This in turn will shrink the small town's economy, contributing to further asset deflation and under-investment. In addition, because the police staff's children have left the local primary school, it may lose a teacher. Again, this is because of the efficiency driven design of school staffing in the education departments. Staff–student ratios cannot be amended sufficiently to allow the survival of intellectually sustainable education in smaller centres. The rich local farmers may send their kids to metropolitan and regional boarding schools. The decline of one governmental service provides a 'market' reason for others to scale down their efforts in such small towns. Their individually rational response (for example, to deliver their local service part-time from a regional centre) further encourages economic disinvestment. Richer farmers may begin doing most of their shopping in the nearest larger regional centre. The absence of police personnel will mean that sporting and social clubs are likely to suffer shortfalls of volunteers. The poor social, educational and other services will mean that the family amenity of the small town is eroded so that it becomes difficult to secure skilled tradesmen (and impossible to get skilled professionals), so that other services deteriorate. This process has been accurately described as a 'downward spiral' (Sorenson, 1992).

Eventually the 'social capital' (Putnam, 1993) of the community is similarly eroded. Local sporting teams can fold for want of a coach or enthusiastic parents, the local Lions Club can become moribund or completely dependent upon two or three people. Even though the gross regional product of the area is increasing, because of the consolidation of agriculture and the growing scale efficiencies of the surrounding farms, the reality is that the small town can be doomed. This has important equity implications for the populations stranded in the town, without the skills, imagination or inclination to leave for areas where labour markets are growing.

The recentralisation of public services exemplified by the above processes also has longer term organisational implications for regional Australia. The recentralisation of services impelled by budget cut-back strategies also leads to a loss of local knowledge and expertise in policy implementation. This usually results in a lack of appreciation of local factors by the relocated agency, which will create long term efficiency difficulties, particularly in-time costs in communication and organisation. Eventually these extra time costs will swallow the efficiency gains of the original recentralisation. This means that the regional decline created as a collective if unforeseen consequence of each agency's pursuit of rationality will add to the problems of all governments, ultimately negating the gains of each agency's original efficiency improvement.

At the larger level, some of the blame for these phenomena can be sheeted home to the Australian system of intergovernmental relations. The administrative aspects of the rural crisis are not entirely created by the incentive structures of the NPM. Some of the recentralisation and jurisdiction shifting engaged in by State governments is explicable by the vertical fiscal imbalance in our federation. The States are dependent upon the Commonwealth for over 50 per cent of their expenditures. They are caught in a severe fiscal squeeze if Commonwealth–State financial transfers decline, as they have in real terms over the past 15 years (see Chapter 10). Of course, the States have intensified their own plight by engaging in a Dutch auction with each other to reduce their own revenue bases; as in the cases of the abolition of probate and the escalating exemptions from payroll tax. Nevertheless, even if no systematic managerial preconditions existed, the narrowing State fiscal base provides a financial incentive for administrative recentralisation and devolution of State responsibilities via regulation to local government (see Chapter 11). This situation has occurred because successive governments have emphasised productive efficiency — and, to a degree, allocative efficiency — at the expense of equity principles, such as horizontal fiscal equalisation.

CONTEMPORARY POLICY ATROPHY

The combination of the new macro-economic orthodoxy and the NPM has encouraged regional policy atrophy. Policy now is ad hoc and politically opportunist and unable to provide a holistic understanding of the rural–regional situation (see Chapter 10). This is partly because each agency addresses regional issues through its own perspective and objectives. This individual rationality is explicable by the coda of the NPM.

The current federal Coalition came to power with a central agency inspired determination to reduce supposedly wasteful overlap and duplication in Australia's intergovernmental system. It began by scrapping a range of programs, especially regional employment programs, that impacted immediately upon the social situation in Australia's regions. The electoral reaction, especially the One Nation successes, has since 1998 produced an excitable policy activism within the Coalition. But the fundamental organisational problems are no nearer to being tackled. Each department now has its rural–regional program or programs. There is a plethora of individual programs, from flagpiece initiatives such as the Natural Heritage Trust, the Regional Assistance Program, and the Rural Transaction Centres, to smaller initiatives. 'Regional' has become a bureaucratic badge-word, included in the title of new program proposals as an aid in the struggle to obtain funding from the federal cabinet and secure the careers of their bureaucratic drivers.

Yet there continues to be a lack of holistic understanding of the complexity of regional development issues. For example, the Commonwealth Department of Communications' 'Networking the Nation' is potentially a very useful program. Notwithstanding the program is being put into communities where the State departments of education (responding to their own internal imperatives) are cutting resources to the local schools systems. The impact of the federal program will be lessened by the weakening individual educational capacity and deteriorating infrastructure in precisely those areas that most need the program.

One of the problems with the continuing commitment to reducing the size of the public sector has been growing concerns with the capacity of federal (and by implication State) agencies. In June 1999 the Australian National Audit Office report on public service staff reductions concluded that the loss of specialist skills and corporate memory potentially imposed significant risks, especially in the context of escalating contractual relations with private providers (ANOA, 1999).

The current federal government has reacted to perceptions of widespread regional discontent with more political activity than policy analysis. The Liberal Party has paid for fortnightly regional television addresses by the Prime Minister. In January 2000 the Prime Minister conducted a highly publicised tour of regional centres.

But policy making is still driven by central agencies completely ignorant of regional realities. For example, when the Goods and Services Tax (GST) tax package was designed, the government decided to reduce its petroleum excise by seven cents a litre in order to secure a cost-neutral imposition of the GST on petrol prices. Yet for this policy, the Commonwealth Treasury's calculations were based upon assumptions that the Sydney retail petrol price of 77 cents per litre was a national standard. The reality was that in most rural areas of Australia petrol prices are far above this and the excise–GST arrangement will lead to price increases, which the government has explicitly promised will not happen.

A core problem of the Commonwealth's role in regional development and service delivery is that the current government is fundamentally ambivalent about its role in regional development. This equivocation reflects, in part, the scepticism entrenched in the Commonwealth's central agencies. These agencies see this area as intrinsically a State and Local government responsibility (NCA, 1996). The 1998 attempt by the Commonwealth Treasury in the initial GST legislation (before it was amended in the deal with the Democrats) to remove the Commonwealth's general purpose grants to local government is an illustration of central agency attempts to circumvent this type of role by the Commonwealth. Given that over the last 15 years power in inter-agency relations has shifted away from front-line service delivery agencies towards central policy agencies (such as Treasury, Prime Minister and Cabinet, Premier and Cabinet), this central policy preference is significant.

At the State level there are widely varying commitments and policies with regard to regional development. In Victoria (at least until the 1999 State election), the State virtually abdicated from regional development, legislating it into local government's arena of responsibilities.

Arguably only Western Australia pursues a holistic approach to this policy area, incorporating economic, social, cultural and environmental elements on a distinct statutory basis (South Australia, 1999: 17). It is apparent that the strictures and practices of the NPM have also reduced State governments' ability to develop coordinated regional development services.

COMPETITION VERSUS EQUITY

Another core problem is the little recognised conflict between two fundamental policy principles — competitive efficiency and horizontal equalisation or equity. This conflict is dramatised by the tensions between the national competition policy (NCP) and the equalisation objective inherent in Australian federalism. The strict focus upon competitive efficiency intrinsic to the NCP is a relatively recent departure in Australia's public policy history.

The long postwar boom of the 1950s and 1960s led to the expansion of government outlays and revenue as a proportion of Gross Domestic Product (GDP). An important corollary of this evolution was the increasing power, size and influence of front-line agencies (that is, agencies such as education departments, that actually deliver services). Since the mid-1980s, the central agencies of have fought to re-establish control over the line agencies and to restructure the role and operating mode of the State. This battle initially emerged from a desire to establish administrative and political control over public sector deficits. The NPM has been the administrative aspect of that struggle for control. On the politico-economic levels we have seen initiatives such as user-charging, privatisation and asset sales. The political keystone of this fight for control of how government does business, and what business it does, has become the Council of Australian Governments (COAG). Ostensibly designed to overcome the problems of intergovernmental overlap and duplication, COAG is in reality a set of institutions driven by central agencies at State and Commonwealth levels. Each set of central agencies is united by a common desire to achieve whole-of-government control over their respective line agencies (Gerritsen, 1997: 135–38).

The NCP is another element in this package of policy and administrative measures aimed at permanently reshaping the way Australian governments operate and what they do. It is officially an attempt to reduce supposedly unfair advantages enjoyed by the public sector in delivering economic and infrastructure services. The NCP undoubtedly has had an impact upon rural and regional Australia. Massive reductions in regional employment in telecommunications, rail and electricity authorities are admitted (Productivity Commission, 1999b:

xxxvi ff.). Small rural local governments, especially, have blamed the competitive neutrality provisions of the NCP for threatening their councils' role in maintaining local employment. Consequently, the NCP is now being looked at much more critically in decision-making circles (for example, see Senate, 1999, passim).

What is principally relevant here, however, is that the NCP poses a fundamental contradiction to the guiding principle of Australian federalism: horizontal fiscal equalisation (HFE). The NCP seeks 'competitive neutrality', or the creation of perfect markets and an end to cross-subsidisation. HFE seeks equity, or the financial redress of geographic disadvantage, of necessity a contrary principle to competitive neutrality.

Established in 1934, the HFE principle is authoritatively and accurately described as the linchpin of Australia's federation (Mathews, 1994). In essence it posits that citizens in a federation should have the right to roughly equal levels of government services if their sub-national government makes a roughly equal revenue-raising effort to the other sub-national governments. It is specifically a spatially based principle of equity. Since 1974, this principle has also been applied to local government through an annual Commonwealth financial assistance grants transfer to the State governments, which on-pass it to each local government on a needs basis. In reality, local governments receive general purpose grants only providing about 50 per cent of the requirement for horizontal equalisation.

Even this inadequate fiscal equalisation is contested. The nature of the determination—quantification of the fiscal transfers and the level of equalisation are subject to continual political wrangling (for example, Western Australia Treasury, 1999). New South Wales, for example, continually claims that fiscal equalisation allows the smaller States to engage in business attraction auctions, which have perverse effects from a national allocative economic efficiency standpoint (New South Wales, 1996). Successive relativity reviews by the Commonwealth Grants Commission have resulted in the gradual erosion of the degree of fiscal equalisation embodied in intergovernmental financial transfers. It appears that, over the last decade, HFE has not been a principle of the organisation of Australian governments. This directly threatens the rights and welfare of rural and regional Australians.

A simple example may elaborate this last point. Before the NCP reforms and the Australian local airport program, Sydney airport effectively cross-subsidised the entire network of Australian airports. Its landing charges were higher than required, in order to subsidise the operation of less busy airports in other parts of Australia. Once the Commonwealth ceased to own all the airports, each airport was required to set its own charges (subject, presumably, to appeal to the

Australian Competition and Consumer Commission if another rival airport thought it was engaging in anti-competitive pricing). Before the new system was introduced the standard national landing charge was $3 per kilogram. In January 2000, Sydney, the nation's busiest airport, was charging 60 cents per kilogram. Rockhampton airport in central Queensland, which is now owned by that city's council, was forced by the high maintenance costs for the fixed infrastructure to set landing charge at $8 per kilogram.

The overall national welfare — in terms of the allocative efficiency of the economy — may be assisted by such reforms. But for business in regional centres (and Rockhampton with a population in 1996 of approximately 55 000 is a major regional centre, not a rural backwater), it means significant cost penalties erode their competitiveness and profitability. This has important implications for the right of the citizens of Rockhampton to have access to air travel and the convenience of air freight.

The aggregation of rural television networks during the 1990s also provides similar outcomes and dilemmas. Comfortable local TV monopolies were replaced with State-wide or regional television stations. These new aggregated television stations then had to compete in the same markets. The pressures of aggregation, in conjunction with the financial pressures of increased competition for the same pool of advertising dollars, means that local news is created on shoestring budgets. In most localities communities now have access to a greater variety of television programming. But their local news is usually homogenised and dominated by product from one centre. One important means for creating community identity and social capital has virtually disappeared in the interests of competition. The productivity gains are accompanied by social losses; the results do not unequivocally favour one perspective or the other. Clearly, the balance between the NCP and the HFE has in the last five years tilted too far towards a priority upon competitiveness, with a comparative neglect of geographic equity issues.

CONCLUSIONS

As in most Western nations, the nature of the Australian state has changed radically, particularly since the mid-1980s. Mirroring that change has been the redefinition of how the State is to be managed. Public management is now conceptualised as a public–private interaction, involving the operation of bureaucracies plus their connections with a variety of other institutions through the processes of governance (Frederickson, 1997: 84); the whole system operating to dominant private sector values. The prevailing emphasis is the individual performance, usually measured in terms of productive efficiency, of each agency and program within that agency. In reality this has meant constantly inventing means for delivering programs with static if not declining real financial resources. This latter aspect of service delivery is consequent upon the deficit fetishism that has dominated macro-economic policy making since the mid-1970s. This combination of fiscal restriction and new methods of organising government provides a context in which the system's front-line agencies are not concerned with the outputs and impacts of the other line agencies in the inter-governmental system.

Consequently, in the policy arena of local and regional community development, mutually reinforcing trends such as fiscal decentralisation and the localisation of policy responsibility result in collective chaos. As a consequence local governments and regional development agencies are increasingly being required to conduct their activities through col-laborative mechanisms (that have been labelled the 'hollow state' — Milward et al., 1993) with the private sector. In essence these partner-ships are an attempt to mask the reality of the diminution of the fiscal resources available at the local level. This has disproportionately impacted upon precisely the rural and regional areas of Australia that are — in employment and living standards — most adversely affected by globalisation. The resulting regional disequilibrium has been exac-erbated by the introduction of NPM and a new preoccupation on the micro-economic performance of individual government agencies. In such a 'hollow state', units of government are separated from their col-lective outputs and negotiated contracts and influence replace statuto-ry authority (and direct accountability), hierarchical relations and fiscal distribution. Goals are not uniform or authoritatively organised by the state. This further encourages private sector market-like behaviours because these are supposedly more 'efficient'.

This uncertainty over policy and implementation systems means that local and regional community development inevitably becomes a predominantly political arena. In Australia this is best indicated by the contemporary scramble for the burgeoning specific purpose grants provided from a national government , which is increasingly concerned to reconnect with rural and regional people who feel disenfranchised within the current policy-making system. In this political arena the local state apparatus is disadvantaged by its unequal policy sovereignty. State governments are shifting from service delivery and production to regulation. It is this new regulatory mode that is increasingly being made the responsibility of local government. Yet the freeze on the fis-cal capacity of local administrations means that spatially differential consequences occur for service delivery. Most of these consequences systematically disadvantage rural Australians relative to metropolitan

Australians. Equally seriously, ultimately it is the mechanisms by which the governments — principally State and Commonwealth — are organised that prevent any holistic amelioration of the social, environmental and service access aspects of the contemporary rural crisis.

REFERENCES

ANOA (Australian National Audit Office) (1999), *Staff Reductions in the Australian Public Service*, Auditor General's Report No. 49, Australian National Audit Office, Canberra.

Argy F (1998) *Australia at the Crossroads. Radical Free Market or a Progressive Liberalism?*, Allen & Unwin, Sydney.

Browett J & Leaver R (1989) 'Shifts in the global capitalist economy and the national economic domain', *Australian Geographical Studies*, 27 (1), pp 31–46.

Butlin N, Barnard A & Pincus J (1982), *Government and Capitalism: Public and Private Choice in Twentieth Century Australia*, George Allen & Unwin, Sydney.

COSBOA (Council of Small Business Organisation of Australia) (1997) *Creating Employment in Regional Australia*, COSBOA, Canberra.

Curtin J (2000) 'New public management meets civic discontent? The Australian Public Service in 1999', *Australian Journal of Public Administration*, (March 2000).

Fincher R (1999) 'New geographies of disadvantage: Implications for service delivery', *Australian Journal of Public Administration*, 58 (3), pp 55–60.

Frederickson H G (1997) *The Spirit of Public Administration*, Jossey-Bass, San Francisco.

Gerritsen R (1997) 'Some progress was made: Intergovernmental relations in the second Keating Government', in Singleton G (ed) *The Second Keating Government: Australian Commonwealth Administration 1993–1996*, Institute for Public Administration Australia, Canberra, pp 124–42.

Gerritsen R (1998) *Deregulating Australia Post: Another Attack on Regional Australia?* ACRLGS Monographs in Applied Policy No. 1, University of Canberra, Canberra.

Gerritsen R (2000) 'Antipodean exceptionalism? Australian farmers and world trade reform', in Greenwood J & Jacek H (eds), *Organised Business and the New Global Order*, St Martins Press, New York.

Giddens A (1994) *Beyond Left and Right: The Future of Radical Politics*, Polity Press, Cambridge.

Harvey D (1989) *The Condition of Postmodernity*, Basil Blackwell, Oxford.

Hood C (1990) 'De-Sir Humphreyfying the Westminster model of bureaucracy: A new style of governance?', *Governance*, 3 (2), pp 205–14.

Howard J (1998) 'A healthy public service is a vital part of Australia's democratic system of government', *Australian Journal of Public Administration*, 57 (1), pp 3–11.

Lawrence G (1987) *Capitalism and the Countryside: The Rural Crisis in Australia*, Pluto Press, Sydney.

Mathews R (1994) *Fiscal Equalisation — Political, Social and Economic Linchpin of Federation*, Federalism Research Centre, Australian National University, Canberra.

Milward H B, Provan K G & Else B A (1993) 'What does the hollow state look like?', in Bozeman B (ed), *Public Management: The State of the Art*, Jossey-Bass, San Francisco, pp 309–22.

NCA (National Commission of Audit) (1996) *Report to the Commonwealth Government*, AGPS, Canberra.

New South Wales (1996) 'Submission by the Government of New South Wales to the Industry Commission inquiry into state, territory and local government assistance to industry', Department of Premier & Cabinet, NSW Government, Sydney.

Organisation for Economic Cooperation & Development (OECD) (1995) *Governance in Transition: Public Management Reforms in OECD Countries*, OECD, Paris.

Productivity Commission (1999a) *Modelling the Regional Impacts of National Competition Policy Reforms, Supplement to the Inquiry Report*, AusInfo, Canberra.

Productivity Commission (1999b) *Impact of Competition Policy Reforms on Rural and Regional Australia*, Report No. 8, AusInfo, Canberra.

Putnam R (1993) *Making Democracy Work: Civic Traditions in Modern Italy*, Princeton University Press, Princeton.

Senate (1999) *Competition Policy: Friend or Foe, Economic Surplus, Social Deficit?*, An Interim Report of the Senate Select Committee on the Socio-Economic Consequences of the National Competition Policy, Commonwealth Parliament, Canberra.

Sorenson A (1992) 'The Australian country town: present trends and future prospects', Paper delivered at the ANZRSA Conference, Ballarat, December.

South Australia (1999) *South Australian Regional Development Task Force Report*, Government of South Australia, Adelaide.

Stewart J (1997) 'Theorising New Public Management, *Public Sector Papers 1–97*, Centre for Research in Public Sector Management, University of Canberra, Canberra.

Western Australian Treasury (1999) *Fiscal Subsidies Within the Australian Federation: Western Australia's Net Subsidy to Other States*, Intergovernmental Relations Division, WA Treasury, Discussion Paper.

Wiseman J (1998) *Global Nation? Australia and the Politics of Globalisation*, Cambridge University Press, Melbourne.

Zifcak S (1997) 'Managerialism, accountability and democracy: A Victorian case study', *Australian Journal of Public Administration*, 56 (3), pp 106–19.

9

LOPPING THE BRANCHES: BANK BRANCH CLOSURE AND RURAL AUSTRALIAN COMMUNITIES
NEIL ARGENT & FRAN ROLLEY

Stand with your back to the coastline, strain your hearing landwards, and you begin to catch it: a distant, half-forgotten murmur — the voice of the Bush, the sound of rural Australia. It is proud, despairing, angry, frustrated, hopeful against the odds, full of anxious fear. It's the voice of a people, a culture, a way of life confronted, in 100 different ways across the country, with challenge, with transformation, if not with impoverishment and imminent extinction. [Rothwell, 1997: 1]

I'm fed up with people saying the Government is doing nothing — it is. But rural communities must respond with courageous leadership and motivation ... I'm sick of hearing people complaining about losing banks ... [Former Deputy Prime Minister, Tim Fischer, cited in O'Kane, 1997: 19]

The rural crisis, at least in its contemporary guise, is now over ten years old. In many ways it has been one of the few constants for rural communities in an epoch of increasingly rapid economic, technological and social change. Nevertheless, given the complexity of forces restructuring rural society and economy over the last two decades, this discourse of crisis has changed in emphasis and focus from time to time, place to place.

The rural crisis of the early 1980s, for instance, appeared concerned primarily with the plight of the family farm and the farming family, beset by drought, low broadacre commodity prices, unfair and unfavourable international trading conditions and growing farm debt (see Lawrence, 1987). The rural crisis of the late 1980s and early 1990s echoed many of the concerns of the earlier period of exigency, but to these were added a number of other factors. These included growing farmer unrest over high interest rates, perceived bank aggression to indebted farm clients after a phase of 'easy lending' (Cronin, 1993), and concern at the withdrawal of government support for rural industries, including the removal of the wool industry's floor price scheme.

Over the past five years or so, and corresponding approximately with the incipient rise and decline of One Nation as a political force, concerns over the future of rural society in Australia have broadened and come to emphasise increasingly the social welfare of rural people. A number of recent fora have highlighted the growing recognition that the sustainability of social life in small town Australia is under threat from a complex of economic, demographic and social changes, and the particular responses to these changes by rural citizens. These fora include the Human Rights and Economic Opportunities Commissioner's 'Bush Talks' (Sidoti, 1998), ABC Radio National's *Late Night Live* forum on the 'City and the Bush', ABC's *Lateline* program 'Bitter Harvest', a Commonwealth House of Representative Standing Committee on Economics, Finance and Public Administration (HRSCEFPA) Inquiry into Regional Banking Services (1999) and the South Australian Parliament's Social Development Committee Inquiry into Rural Poverty (1994), to mention but a few. This discourse of crisis has become pervasive, in a geographical and temporal sense, through the agency of a media easily satisfied with the simple dichotomous imagery of 'city' and 'bush', 'core' and 'periphery'. This rigid binary was nowhere better expressed than in National Party leader and regional services minister, John Anderson's idea of 'two nations' (Anderson, 1999), and the notion, peculiar to New South Wales, that Sydney rules the rest of the State from behind the 'sandstone curtain'.

However this discourse is expressed, either in the mawkish, melodramatic tones of the opening quote, or in the following official tenor of denial and blame of the former Deputy Prime Minister, one of the obvious challenges to any serious comprehension of the 'rural crisis' is to unpack its rhetoric and material referents. It is important to recognise, for example, that rural Australia encompasses a great diversity of settlement types and sizes, spread across a number of broad biophysical zones and associated bands of population density (Holmes, 1987; Bureau of Rural Sciences, 1999). The rural crisis of the 1980s and 1990s primarily has affected the extensive cereal–livestock farming zones of each State; areas which, notwithstanding the beneficial but short-lived impact of the 'population turnaround' during the late 1970s and early 1980s, have experienced relatively high rates of population loss since the 1950s (Hugo & Smailes, 1992). On the other hand, rural settlements in environmentally amenable areas, particularly those in riverine and coastal environments, have grown dramatically over the past two decades or so, in substantial part due to the inflow of retirees. Many regional centres, termed 'non-capital cities' by Beer, Bolam & Maude (1994: 6–7) have also experienced strong rates of population growth over the past 20 years (Beer et al., 1994; Productivity Commission, 1999: 20–22; and see Chapter 4). These regional centres have been misleadingly dubbed 'sponge cities' for their alleged role in 'soaking up' out-migrants from smaller inland towns (see Salt, 1998; Productivity Commission, 1999: 27–28). However, as Beer et al., (1994: 45–46) observe, '... regional cities gain some of their in-migrants from their hinterlands, similar or larger numbers of migrants are drawn from the State capital, and the remaining migrants come from a wide variety of regions'.

In this chapter, we interrogate one aspect of the putative rural crisis by investigating how private small businesses and rural residents have been affected by the recent spate of bank branch closures. Our concern, then, is less with the relative fortunes of each level of the functional hierarchy of towns, but more with how the changing spatial structure of banking services in rural Australia has affected the functions and viability of rural businesses, and rural residents' access to basic but necessary financial services. Case studies drawn from rural New South Wales and Western Australia are used to illustrate and expand upon these themes. One of the key points to emerge from this analysis is that the range of traditional banking services, once easily accessible by the bulk of rural people from their local bank branch, has been hastily withdrawn from many towns and increasingly concentrated in regional centres. This 'regionalisation' of financial service provision has followed similar processes of spatial rationalisation over recent years in other critical areas, like hospitals and allied health services, railways and governmental agencies (Rolley & Humphreys, 1993; Wahlquist, 1996).

This process of service reallocation has revealed the vital contributions that a financial services shop-front makes to the economic and social development of rural towns and their encompassing regions. Bank branches not only offer the basic financial transaction services (that is, deposit-taking, cash withdrawal, accounts management, lending) that have come to be accepted as necessary for 'financial citizenship' (Leyshon & Thrift, 1995: 336), but also embody considerable symbolic and real economic capital for their towns. Branch closures not only lead to local employment loss and increased local costs in accessing face to face financial services, but also represent to local people the perceived non-viability of their town. The case study of financial service restructuring herein demonstrates that, while it may be customary for the media to focus on local issues as causes for rural decline, it is also important to be aware of the linkages between local events, regulatory changes and their corporate sector responses.

FORCES FOR CHANGE IN RURAL BUSINESSES: AN HISTORICAL OVERVIEW

> More so than in any other country subject to European colonisation, Australia's rural settlement has been severely handicapped by problems of sparse population and associated low demand for local infrastructure, creating difficulties in the provision of services needed to sustain a dispersed population. [Holmes, 1981: 80]

The apparently increasing social and economic distance between the city and the country, so central to the discourse of the rural crisis, is mirrored empirically in an urban system lacking the intermediate-sized centres needed to blur the distinction between 'Sydney and the bush'. Although 'the bush' looms large in the national self-image, Australia is one of the most urbanised nations in the world (Logan, Whitelaw & McKay, 1981; Holmes, 1987). The development of this relatively attenuated urban system in Australia was largely the result of an early dominance of extensive commercial agriculture based on relatively large rural holdings and low population densities (Beer, Bolam & Maude, 1994). The resultant low demand for goods and services by rural consumers produced a distinctive urban system characterised by metropolitan primacy and a settlement hierarchy comprising typically only three or four other layers. The basic component of this hierarchy was the standard country town, usually of more than 600 but less than 5000 people. The basic function of the country town network as it developed was to facilitate the flow of goods and services from the dominant metropolitan centres to the scattered rural populations, and to expedite the flow of primary products to ports. Apart from special-function towns based largely on mineral resource extraction, the great majority of inland country towns developed as service centres to serve trade areas largely organised in an 'incomplete nested hierarchy' (Bowie & Smailes, 1988: 233). Nested within the trade area of the standard country town may be townships which offer only the most basic services, such as a general store, post office and church, whilst the standard country town itself may be overshadowed by a regional centre.

This is not to suggest that this pattern was followed exactly by each of the separate colonies. In New South Wales, for example, the rural settlement pattern effectively followed the spread of the squatters throughout the colony, with sparsely-located towns and hamlets emerging to administer justice and service the needs of the extensive pastoral economy. Much of the better arable and pastoral country of the first colony had been alienated by the late 1830s. The establishment and extension of a railway network and river trade, together with the discovery of gold in 1851, facilitated the extension of farm settlement into the more marginal country in the western half of the colony through the latter half of the 19th century (Jeans, 1972).

In Western Australia, on the other hand, the expansion of agricultural settlement was hampered, and therefore metropolitan primacy was abetted, by a narrow economic base and a concomitant lack of public resources at least until the 1880s. Thereafter, the colonial government began a capital-intensive campaign to expand the local economy and population using, as in New South Wales, the railway as a tool for frontier expansion. This campaign was backed by the capital generated through the gold rushes in Kalgoorlie and Coolgardie of the 1890s (Tonts, 1998). The environmental and economic unsuitability of substantial portions of the State for yeoman settlement, however, has meant that Perth's dominance of the urban hierarchy has remained largely unchallenged.

Bowie and Smailes (1988) provide a detailed description of the history, role and functions of country towns in Australia. Historically, rural settlements existed to provide the social and economic infrastructure needed to support farm businesses and farm families, with a 'tangible interdependency' developing between the farm sector and the rural service centres (Joseph & Smithers, 1999). Primary producers form the basis for the economic structure of country towns, and agriculture has served as the mainstay for the local rural economy (Smailes, 1979). The core central-place functions of these towns comprise the private and public tertiary sectors, with the former including sales and services, consumer goods and services, and transport, finance and property businesses. The public tertiary sector (employment in national, provincial and local government as well as semi-government agencies) has traditionally been important in most country towns.

The Australian rural settlement system generally, and the historically established relationship between the farm sector and the widely spread network of rural centres discussed above, is currently undergoing rapid change in response to a complex of economic, technological and demographic forces. Many of these dynamics have been in operation for a substantial part of this century, while others are more recent in origin.

CONTEMPORARY FORCES FOR CHANGE

Now looked upon as the halcyon era for the farm and rural sector, the years following the Second World War until the late 1960s were nevertheless marked by significant economic and technological changes that transformed Australian agriculture and, importantly, the nature and strength of its links with the rural town network. From the early 1950s, farm mechanisation and amalgamation helped farmers attain the economies of scale necessary to compete on international markets. The number of tractors on farms, for example, increased from 103 800 in 1950 to 212 400 in 1957. Over the same period, the number of fertiliser spreaders increased from 44 100 to 74 400 and hay balers from 1100 to 25 100 (Hefford, 1985). Accordingly, agricultural output increased by 35 per cent in the 1950s and by the same amount again in the 1960s (Gruen, 1990). These trends had the obverse effect on farm employment. In 1950–51, the agricultural workforce totalled 466 000, peaking at 480 000 in 1953–54. The period to 1960–61 saw the loss of 40 000 farm employees, and a further decline to 414 000 employees in the following decade (Freebairn, 1987).

As Bowie and Smailes (1988: 251) state, the increased farm incomes of the long postwar boom 'favoured the regional centres and the larger "standard" country towns'. Smaller country towns were (and still are) affected much more by the number of farm families and employees in their hinterlands, than by farm income per se (Smailes, 1979). The pressure on the smaller centres was exacerbated in the immediate postwar years with rapid improvements in the quality of road networks, along with declining real fuel costs, which cut travel times and reduced the real cost of mobility. This allowed capital cities to cast even greater trade shadows upon the rest of the urban hierarchy (Smailes, 1969; Walmsley & Weinand, 1991).

With the end of the long boom during the late 1960s, the period since has been characterised by extensive restructuring of the Australian economy, including substantial shifts in the structure of employment and major changes in the ways in which goods and services are provided (Fagan & Webber, 1994). Accompanying — indeed facilitating — this economic change has been the demise of the Keynesian welfare state (Martin & Sunley, 1997), and in Australia the associated retraction of previous levels of state assistance for both the farm and rural sectors. Rural Australia has experienced these forces directly in a number of ways.

The changing structure of international demand over the past 40 years is reflected in the declining terms of trade for Australian agriculture. Returns to farming relative to costs of production were approximately four times higher in the mid-1950s than they are today (Productivity Commission, 1999: 50). Naturally, the farm sector has responded to these forces by attempting to achieve ever greater economies of scale — the 'get big or get out' syndrome of the 1980s — with the total number of farms decreasing simultaneously with the growth of average farm size.

The economic restructuring of rural Australia and deterioration in international markets has been accompanied by significant demographic change within the rural sector. Population out-migration from rural areas and small inland towns has long been a significant feature of rural Australia. At the turn of the century, for example, 65 per cent of Australians lived in non-metropolitan regions. By 1947, this had fallen to 49 per cent. It declined further to 36 per cent by 1971. Since then the non-metropolitan share has stabilised, although there have been substantial shifts in the population within regional Australia (ABS, 1997). Large towns (20 000–49 999 people) and small cities (50 000–499 999) have experienced rapid population growth over the last 25 years. In 1996, these towns and cities together accounted for 18.9 per cent of the Australian population compared with 13.3 per cent in 1971. During the same time, the proportion of the population living in centres between 1000 and 19 999 people, and the population living in small villages, hamlets and on surrounding farms, has been relatively stable (Productivity Commission, 1999: 19).

After the Great Depression of the 1930s small town growth slowed and rural populations declined in many areas. Regional populations stopped growing because of technological changes in agriculture, widespread rural recession and the effects of the war. Although this process was temporarily reversed during the postwar expansion of the early 1950s, after this 'the familiar story of mechanisation, rural depopulation and a downward spiral affecting country towns began in earnest' (Bowie & Smailes, 1988: 251). The urban system in rural areas has adapted to lower levels of demand as a result of declining farm populations. In Australia, as elsewhere in the developed world, there have been strong centralising tendencies affecting the lower orders of the hierarchy, arising from postwar improvements in consumer mobility, more specialised demand and the increasing benefits from scale economies of firms (Holmes, 1983; Beer et al., 1994). Many country towns have long looked directly to the State capitals for goods and services that are not locally available, largely as a result of the historical development of transport networks and the dominance of the capitals (Smailes, 1969; 1996). In addition, rural areas have historically been disadvantaged in the sense that political and economic power has been located in the national and State capitals and statutory power has been located in State rather than local governments (Walmsley, 1980).

Decisions about the location of services in rural Australia, for example, have traditionally not been ones where there has been a great deal of self-determination (Lawrence & Williams, 1990). Thus a crucial element in the dynamics of decline facing many inland communities lies in the fact that, as economic activity and service provision is shifted into regional centres, whatever influence the community may have had is further weakened. This results in even greater concentration of services in regional centres and a further withdrawal of economic infrastructure from local areas. Increasingly, many of the decisions that affect business in regional and rural areas are taken in the State capitals (or beyond).

Collectively, the economic, demographic and technological changes already outlined have brought marked changes to rural communities. The following case study of the restructuring of rural financial service provision since 1983 illustrates these changes, and their interconnectedness to regulatory change and the responses of major corporations. A focus on the restructuring of banking services in rural Australia is useful because, as the large quantity of media and political attention devoted to this issue over the past two years demonstrates, rural communities' relative degree of access to face to face financial service delivery is an increasingly important measure of a town's viability, both in a symbolic and a strictly economic sense. The Human Rights and Equal Opportunity Commissioner, Chris Sidoti, during his recent 'Bush Talks' consultations and meetings, paid special attention to the role of bank branch closures in triggering or exacerbating a vicious cycle of decline for targeted towns, remarking that the 'support of and investment in small business and industry in rural Australia are necessary to address the downward spiral of rural life' (Sidoti, 1998: 7).

THE GEOGRAPHY OF FINANCIAL SERVICE PROVISION IN RURAL NEW SOUTH WALES AND WESTERN AUSTRALIA

The geographical distributions of the 'non-metropolitan' bank branch networks of New South Wales and Western Australia have been compiled from the Telecom and Telstra telephone directories.[1] To establish how well the geographical distribution of the bank branch networks of both States fits the distribution of the population, location quotients (LQs) were calculated for the period 1981 to 1998 respectively (Tables 9.1 and 9.2). Location quotients of greater than one indicate a concentration of branches in a particular area, whereas LQ values less than one indicate an under representation of branches relative to population. A LQ value of one indicates that there is a parity between the distribution of branches and population. These tables utilise the classification schema for settlement and remoteness developed by the Department of Primary Industries and Energy and Department of Health and Human Services (1994). Figures 9.1 and 9.2 illustrate bank branch networks and regional classifications for New South Wales, and Figures 9.3 and 9.4 do so for Western Australia.

FIGURE 9.1
NON-METROPOLITAN BANK BRANCH NETWORK, NSW, 1981

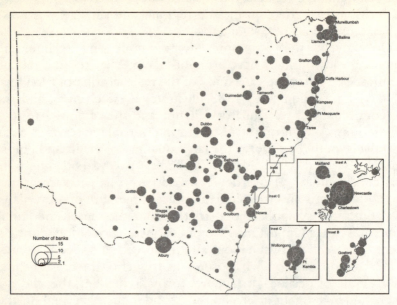

SOURCE Telecom telephone directories, 1981.

FIGURE 9.2
CLASSIFICATION SCHEME, NSW

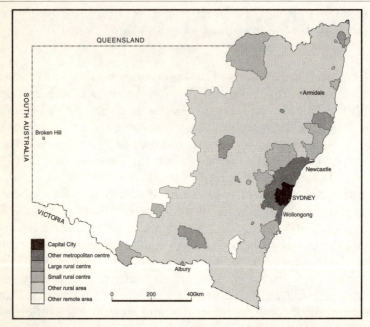

SOURCE Department of Primary Industries and Energy and Department of Human Services and
Health, 1994.

FIGURE 9.3
NON-METROPOLITAN BANK BRANCH NETWORK, WA, 1981

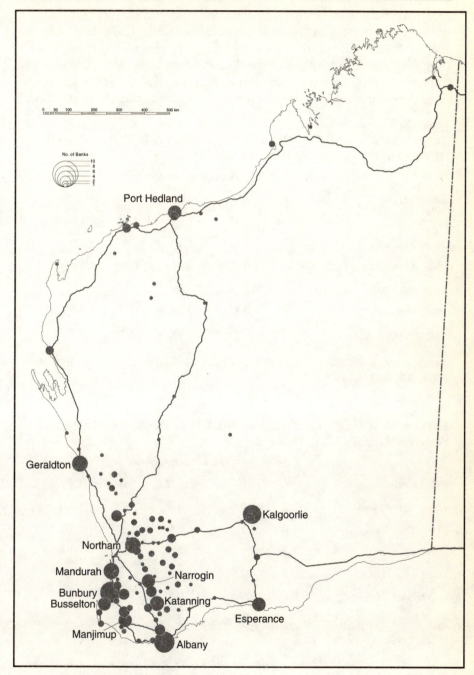

SOURCE Telecom telephone directories, 1981.

Tables 9.1 and 9.2 illustrate the difficulties of interpreting bank branch representation vis a vis population. The results of NSW and WA for 1981 demonstrate that the 'remote' and 'other rural area' categories were better furnished with bank branches than their relative shares of the State populations would suggest, whereas all 'rural centre' categories were under-represented. Between 1981 and 1998 WA's 'remote centres' were an exception in that for all study years their LQs demonstrated branch representation closely proportional to population.

TABLE 9.1
BANK BRANCH DISTRIBUTION IN RELATION TO POPULATION,
NEW SOUTH WALES, 1981–98

RRMA zones	Location quotients				
	1981	1986	1991	1996	1998
Remote	1.58	1.45	1.64	1.45	1.83
Other rural area	1.71	1.55	1.49	1.57	1.65
Small rural centre	0.87	0.97	0.88	0.99	1.08
Large rural centre	0.82	0.76	0.70	0.83	0.90
Other metro centre	0.78	0.81	0.76	0.79	0.82
Capital city	0.93	0.95	0.99	0.95	0.91

SOURCE Telecom and Telstra White and Yellow Pages, 1981, 1986, 1991, 1996, 1998; ABS, 1988a, 1993a, 1998a.

TABLE 9.2
BANK BRANCH DISTRIBUTION IN RELATION TO POPULATION,
WESTERN AUSTRALIA, 1981–98

RRMA zones	Location quotients				
	1981	1986	1991	1996	1998
Other remote area	2.1	2.1	2.2	1.6	1.4
Remote centre	1.1	1.1	1.0	1.0	1.1
Other rural area	2.0	1.9	1.9	1.8	1.6
Small rural centre	0.9	0.9	0.9	0.7	0.7
Capital city	0.8	0.8	0.8	0.9	0.9

SOURCE Telecom and Telstra White and Yellow Pages, 1981, 1986, 1991, 1996, 1998; ABS, 1988b, 1993b, 1998b.

NOTE The Department of Primary Industries and Energy and Department of Health and Human Services classification uses seven settlement–remoteness categories: capital city, other metropolitan centre, large rural centre, small rural centre, other rural area, remote centre, and other remote area (DPIE & DH&HS, 1994).

FIGURE 9.4
CLASSIFICATION SCHEME, WESTERN AUSTRALIA

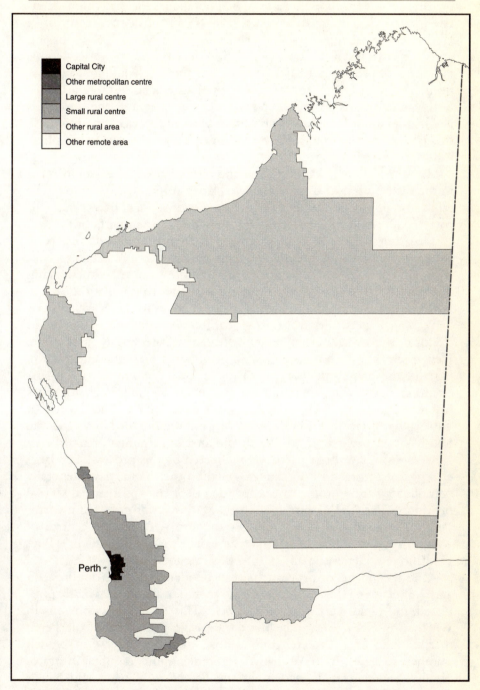

■ Capital City
Other metropolitan centre
Large rural centre
Small rural centre
Other rural area
Other remote area

Perth

SOURCE Department of Primary Industries and Energy and Department of Health and Human Services, 1994.

It is important to note that LQs do not necessarily provide any basis for judgements about the comparative degree of *equity* in service provision. Under representation of bank branches for the regional centres ('small' and 'large rural centres' in NSW; 'small rural centres' in WA), the 'capital cities' and 'other metropolitan centres' (Wollongong and Newcastle) reflect higher population densities and lower concomitant costs of providing banking services to these concentrated populations. The high LQ scores for 'other rural areas' and 'remote areas' of both States results from low population densities and the perceived need, at least until recently, to be able to provide services and tap these disparate markets through the provision of banking services with physical shop-fronts.

Paradoxically, the LQs for rural and remote NSW reveal an increase in the distribution of bank branches relative to population despite the rapid loss of a large number of branches over the last five years. This pattern is a result of the fast rate of branch closure in parts of Sydney, emphasising that bank branch closure is an urban *as well* as a rural issue. For WA, the LQs (Table 9.2) illustrate a more predictable trend, with all rural zones, excepting the remote centres, experiencing decreases in the relative distribution of branches to population.

Figures 9.5 and 9.6 display the major changes to the NSW and WA bank branch networks from 1981 to 1998 respectively. Two broad trends in the spatial rearrangement of branches are readily discernible. First, there has been a considerable pruning of the rural and remote parts of the branch network, with many small country towns experiencing a net decline in branches, and many single-branch localities losing their facilities by 1998. The Central West, the Northern Tablelands, the South-Eastern and Murray regions of NSW, and the South-West, the Central Wheatbelt and an area running north of Perth to Geraldton have been particularly affected by this process. The larger regional centres in both States, on the other hand, have generally consolidated and in some cases expanded their roles as financial service providers. The NSW centres of Coffs Harbour, Lismore, Tamworth, Dubbo, Orange and Wagga Wagga and the WA regional centres of Kununurra, Broome, Karratha, Newman, Margaret River, Port Hedland and Geraldton all fall into this category.

The second major process that can be identified from Figures 9.5 and 9.6 relates to the reallocation of branches to the more densely populated and rapidly growing coastal belt. This trend is less obvious in WA than in NSW, with only Mandurah, lying just south of the Perth metropolitan area, experiencing a substantial net increase in branch numbers to 1998. In NSW, growth in branch numbers, albeit in strategically sited centres, is evident in the Far North Coast, Mid-North Coast and South Coast regions. More complex trends are in play in the

FIGURE 9.5
CHANGE IN THE NON-METROPOLITAN BANK BRANCH NETWORK,
NEW SOUTH WALES, 1981–98

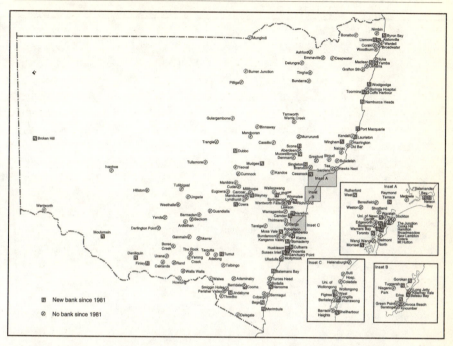

SOURCE Telecom and Telstra telephone directories, 1981, 1986, 1991, 1996, 1998.

Central Coast, Newcastle and Wollongong regions. Here, a significant 'shuffling' of bank branches appears to have occurred, whereby the major industrial centres have shed many branches (and, perhaps, their position as the financial hub to their hinterlands) to neighbouring residential centres. Central Newcastle, for example, experienced a net loss of ten branches from 1981 to 1998; however, centres such as Nelson Bay, Warners Bay, Kotara and Morriset (which are on or near the periphery of Newcastle), and Shellharbour, Warrawong and Figtree (surrounding Wollongong) experienced net growth in bank branches over the study period. In the Central Coast region to the immediate north of Sydney, the same pattern is evident. While some relatively minor net losses have occurred in this region, quite spectacular growth has focused on the following Central Coast localities: Bateau Bay (growing from zero to four branches from 1981 to 1998), Erina (zero to nine), Gorokan (one to six), Tuggerah (zero to six) and Kincumber (zero to two). This expansion is almost solely attributable to the establishment of 'kiosk' style branches in large supermarket centres. For example, all banks have recently opened branches in the Westfield shopping centre at Tuggerah.

FIGURE 9.6
CHANGE IN THE NON-METROPOLITAN BANK BRANCH NETWORK, WESTERN AUSTRALIA, 1981–98

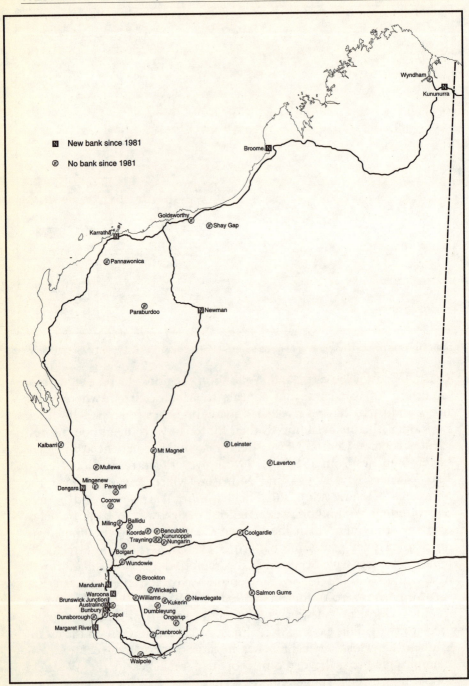

SOURCE Telecom and Telstra telephone directories, 1981, 1986, 1991, 1996, 1998.

In summary, then, two opposing trends appear to have developed in 'non-metropolitan' NSW and WA in the post-financial deregulation period. In the agricultural heartlands and remote areas of both States, a twin process of rationalisation and consolidation is apparent, with regional centres buttressing their position at the expense of the smaller rural towns. Along the coasts, in what might be termed a population growth corridor, there has been relatively large numbers of branch closures in the major industrial centres, while smaller neighbouring localities, including some previously 'unbranched' centres, have experienced a growth in branch provision.

Also of significance is the timing of these closures. Table 9.3 shows the sequence of branch rationalisation for the NSW and WA rural centres that have lost all bank branches from 1981 to 1998. The period immediately preceding and following financial deregulation (1981–86) saw only ten NSW and four WA country towns lose their banking functions; however the decoupling of rural centres from the traditional bank branch network proceeded apace during the mid to late 1990s. Eighty-four per cent of all rural NSW towns that have had all branches removed over the study period did so after 1991. Nearly half of this retrenchment has occurred since 1996. In WA, the process of rationalisation has been slightly less dramatic, although the most recent period (1996–98) has witnessed an escalation of branch closures. Little wonder, then, that the issue of rural bank branch closure has evoked so much recent media and community interest. It is also important to note that this analysis of the growth of branchless towns provides a conservative picture of the impact of recent closures. Many towns have lost one or more branches over the study period without becoming 'branchless', yet portions of their populations have nevertheless been inconvenienced by the loss of their local branch.

TABLE 9.3
RURAL NEW SOUTH WALES AND WESTERN AUSTRALIA BANK
CLOSURES: 'BRANCHLESS' LOCALITIES, 1981–98

	1981–86	1986–91	1991–96	1996–98	Total
NSW					
No. of localities	10	4	38	35	87
% of total branchless	11.5	4.6	43.7	40.2	100
WA					
No. of localities	4	8	11	17	40
% of total branchless	10.0	20.0	27.5	42.5	100

SOURCE Telecom and Telstra White and Yellow Pages, 1981, 1986, 1991, 1996, 1998.

The critical question, of course, is how these selective patterns of financial service retraction and expansion have affected rural people's, including business operators', access to necessary financial services. According to Leyshon and Thrift (1995: 313), access to the financial system, and, by implication, to basic financial services in the contemporary era, is 'a social necessity'. Furthermore, an individual's access to and knowledge of a range of financial services is an increasingly important measure of citizenship (Leyshon, Thrift & Pratt, 1998). The swathe cut through the rural bank branch networks of NSW and WA, depicted in Figures 9.1, 9.3, 9.5, and 9.6, often with little notice given to the communities affected or without satisfactory alternative banking arrangements established, has rendered the residents of the now 'branchless' communities as the 'financially excluded'. This process is akin to that documented in the UK by Leyshon and Thrift (1995: 1) where the 'flight to quality' in bank lending towards more secure and therefore wealthier borrowers was shown to have a mirror image in the physical withdrawal of financial services from poorer areas. While it is important to recognise that financial service retraction is an urban as well as a rural phenomenon, bank branch closures in rural and remote areas have particularly serious consequences for rural residents and their communities.

Rural people are accustomed to the need for lengthy travel to access essential goods and services. However, a town's loss of all face to face banking services usually impacts severely upon its residents. For instance, with the closure of the last bank branch in Trundle, Central Western NSW, local residents were forced to drive up to 70 kilometres to access once locally provided financial services. In the case of Mungindi, on the NSW–Queensland border, locals faced a 120 kilometres drive one way to either Moree (NSW) or St. George (Qld) following the closure of the town's last bank in 1996 (Beal & Ralston, 1997). In these circumstances, branchless town inhabitants tend to withdraw larger amounts than normal to partially compensate for the loss of convenient access to the full gamut of financial services (HRSCEFPA, 1999: 27). This poses security concerns, particularly for the rural elderly. Many older people and the physically handicapped in branchless towns also face the obvious difficulty of accessing private transport to regional centres, with public transport in many rural areas provided on an infrequent basis (Department of Fair Trading, 1997: 4–5).

Not surprisingly, small businesses in recently branchless localities bear the brunt of the banks' 'flight to quality' (Leyshon & Thrift, 1995: 312). First, the change in local consumer behaviour impacts directly and negatively upon the turnover of local enterprises, with local spending leaving the town. Second, businesses themselves confront an additional set of problems to local townspeople when trying to access necessary banking services. Business operators in branchless towns are forced to travel further to deposit business takings, enduring increased operating costs and decreased productivity, not to mention inconvenience. Of course, the temptation is for business owners to hold onto cash takings for longer to avoid making daily trips to the nearest branch, but this too poses increased security risks for the business. Due to local residents', and particularly the elderly's, decreased access to cash, many rural business enterprises are forced to extend short-term credit to some purchasers, which can also lead to bad debts. Perhaps the most significant impact upon rural businesses of the loss of face to face bank services is the decline in local trade that results from residents being forced to travel up the functional and urban hierarchy to access financial services. Beal and Ralston (1997) estimate that, on average, $320 per month per person in general shopping expenditure is lost to branchless town businesses due to residents combining shopping with banking in the nearest regional centre.

Of course, as the previous section has made clear, rural people have made good use of the improved road infrastructure and the development of safer and faster cars over the past three decades to gain access to a wider and, in many cases, cheaper range of shopping goods (and experiences). It would therefore be easy to overstate the role of bank branch closures in expanding the apertures through which trade leaks out of rural town economies. Nevertheless, the NSW Local Government and Shires Association supports the notion that the regionalisation of banking is harming small town businesses, finding that supermarkets in branchless towns had experienced a 20 per cent decline in turnover with the loss of the last bank branch in town (HRSCEFPA, 1999: 28).

Additionally, branch closures usually lead to the direct loss of relatively highly paid and trained staff from the affected community. The multiplier effects of these direct losses can be significant, with the loss of even a few bank staff and their families causing 'knock-on' effects upon schools and similar services which often cannot afford to lose many students for fear that staffing levels will be reduced. A less easily quantifiable aspect of bank branch closure is its impact upon the overall level of financial acumen and expertise of the community. Prior to the early 1990s, bank managers at the local level could generally be regarded as repositories of local knowledge, having intimate knowledge of the relative credit worthiness of a range of local operators. The shift in recent years towards more centralised and instrumentalist modes of assessing the credit rating of loan applicants has eroded the value of this 'embodied' knowledge (Leyshon & Thrift, 1995: 319; Leyshon et al., 1998). Key bank staff, with their embodied knowledge and training, also often filled high profile and important positions within local sporting and social organisations. The loss of this pool of personnel therefore drains a community of one of its key resources of social capital and morale. Taken as a whole, these impacts suggest that the loss of a bank branch tends to represent to local residents, in a highly graphical way, the perceived non-viability of their town by large metropolitan-oriented corporations (Department of Fair Trading, 1997: 8–9).

TO CLOSE OR NOT TO CLOSE? A CRITICAL EVALUATION OF THE RATIONALE FOR FINANCIAL SERVICE WITHDRAWAL

From the major trading banks' perspective, the traditional bank branch model of providing financial services is being rendered less effective by a complex of factors, including long-term demographic change, rapid technological advances in electronic financial products and their delivery, increasing levels of personal mobility and intensified competition from new entrants into the financial system. There is also the widely held yet simplistic view within industry circles that rural Australia is over branched (McIntosh Baring, 1996). The banking sector has certainly sought to propagate this perspective as the enlightened common-sense rationale behind the rapid and widespread retraction of bank branches described above (see KPMG, 1998). To make sense of the ways in which the delivery of financial services is changing and, importantly, to understand why it is changing, it is necessary to tease out these separate factors.

RURAL BANKING AND DEMOGRAPHIC CHANGE

First, there is little if any evidence to support the contention that population decline is driving the pruning of rural and remote bank branches. Argent and Rolley (1998) found that, of the 72 rural and remote NSW towns left 'branchless' between 1981 and 1996 for which population data was readily obtainable, 44 (61.1 per cent) experienced population growth from 1981 to 1996. Just over one-third of these 72 centres declined over the study period, while one centre experienced no net population change. Furthermore, the 44 towns that increased their population grew by a healthy average of 61.2 per cent over the 15 years from 1981 to 1996.

THE RISE OF ELECTRONIC DELIVERY CHANNELS

There is no doubt that technological advances have revolutionised some facets of financial service delivery. As Figures 9.7 and 9.8 show, the number of automatic teller machines (ATMs) and 'electronic funds transfer at point of sale' (EFTPOS) terminals have grown rapidly and achieved wide public acceptance as convenient modes of accessing cash and, in the case of EFTPOS, of cashless purchasing. The number of

FIGURE 9.7
GROWTH IN ATMs AND ATM TRANSACTIONS, AUSTRALIA, 1994–98

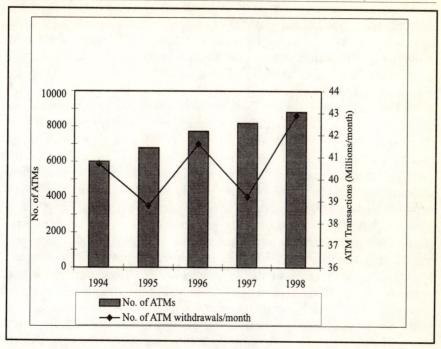

SOURCE Australian Payments Clearing Association, 1988.

FIGURE 9.8
GROWTH IN EFTPOS TERMINALS AND EFTPOS TRANSACTIONS, AUSTRALIA, 1994–98

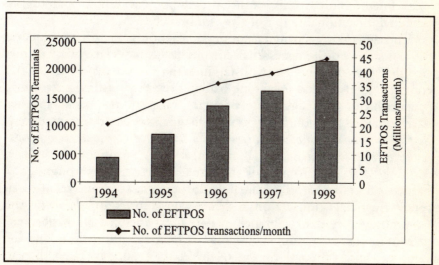

SOURCE Australian Payments Clearing Association, 1988.

ATMs and EFTPOS terminals increased by 47 per cent and 500 per cent respectively from 1994 to 1998, while the number and value of EFTPOS transactions has grown two-fold over the same period. Interestingly, though, the number of cash withdrawals from ATMs has increased by only 7 per cent over the same period. In short, the banks can claim, with some justification, that electronic delivery channels have made financial consumers' access to cash (or non-cash) speedier and more convenient.

Additionally, the banks have placed considerable emphasis on Internet and telephone banking to meet their customers' needs and thereby further undermine the economic viability of their bricks-and-mortar branches. Some banks have publicly gloated over the take-up rates of Internet banking, with the National Australia Bank recently announcing that, in a two month period, its pilot customer base had expanded from 8000 to 27 000 online users. Similarly, Westpac has claimed that its Internet banking services are used by 77 500 customers, with the take-up rate growing by 10 000–15 000 users per month (Cuthbertson, 1999: 6). As if to further emphasise how rapidly and radically retail banking is changing, and how outmoded the extensive bank branch network is becoming in the wake of these changes, two of the four major trading banks have formed alliances with two national retailers (the Commonwealth Bank with Woolworths; Westpac with Coles). While the joint Commonwealth Bank–Woolworths initiative, 'Ezy-Banking', has been developed 'to provide more flexible opening hours and convenient locations to suit the pressures of modern living' (Scott, 1999: 3), this alliance underscores the ongoing regionalisation of commercial services in rural areas. Furthermore, if this venture proves popular, it may open up the potential for rationalisation of *regional* branches.

This apparent growing customer satisfaction with 'virtual' banking has not sounded the death knell for physical face to face financial service delivery, though. Notwithstanding the banks' hyperbole to the contrary, Internet and telephone banking represent a tiny, if growing, proportion of their aggregate financial transactions. 'Bank branches have remained an enduringly popular channel to carry out transactions, *despite the imposition of retail fees aimed at shifting customers to cheaper forms of electronic delivery*' (Boreham, 1998a: 26, emphasis added). Although varying from bank to bank, transactions through bank branches account for approximately 25 per cent to 35 per cent of all retail financial transactions. While apparently in decline, the Commonwealth Bank's branch network experienced a 26 per cent growth in over-the-counter business between 1992 and 1996, and the value of those transactions was 64 per cent greater in 1996 than in 1992 (Boreham, 1998b: 37). These growth figures have been achieved despite the banks' surreptitious attempts to drive away customers from bank branches. A recent Reserve Bank of Australia report on bank fees (Reserve Bank of Australia, 1999: 3) disclosed that while transaction fees for customers' use of their own ATM have increased on average by 100 per cent between 1991 and 1999, fees for over-the-counter trans-actions have grown by 330 per cent.

The figures for online banking usage do, of course, disguise con-siderable geographical, demographic and socio-economic differences in the use of and access to these flexible modes of financial service pro-vision. For many rural people, depersonalised modes of service delivery such as Internet and telephone banking form a powerful barrier to access (Joseph & Chalmers, 1997: 401). The provision of adequate communications infrastructure is another barrier exacerbating unequal access to these facilities. Whereas approximately one-quarter of Australian farmers have Internet access, inadequate communications infrastructure is limiting the roll-out of the information highway into rural Australia. 'Half the farmers do not have the phone lines capable of accessing some of the Web sites' (Lamba, 1999: 18). Concerns over the security of conducting financial transactions across the Internet are an additional major barrier to farmers and other rural residents in embracing virtual banking. Not surprisingly, the banks have down-played these inconvenient realities in the wake of a sustained and intense adverse public reaction to the flurry of branch closures described in part above.

The banking industry's assertions regarding the non-viability of the rural bank branch network have not gone unchallenged by rural peo-ple and public commentators. During the conduct of 1999's HRSCEFPA Regional Banking Inquiry, rural spokespersons presented evidence to suggest that branches have closed despite being profitable. In the words of the Inquiry Committee, '... it is neither fair nor con-structive to perpetrate th[e] impression which in some way could be seen to put the responsibility for a bank closing on the community rather than the banks' (HRSCEFPA, 1999: 21). The supposed causal link between local borrowing and saving patterns, branch viability and closure is further blurred by the recent trend for lending functions to be regionalised by the banks. Both the NSW Department of Fair Trading's Regional Banking Forums (Department of Fair Trading, 1997: 10) and the HRSCEFPA Regional Banking Inquiry (1999: 21) observed that the viability of some branches has been unfairly judged due to the fact that, in some cases, large accounts have been transferred to regional branches, at times without the prior consent of the cus-tomers themselves.

Moreover, there are other reasons to suspect why corporate deci-sion making relating to administration and competitive strategy is central in influencing the way bank branch viability is measured in rural Australia. Even before financial deregulation in 1983, the intensification of competition within the Australian banking sector was identified as a determinant for the future rationalisation of the bank branch network (Taylor & Hirst, 1983). To compete with the arrival of merchant banks into the wholesale commercial loan market, local banks were forced to search for greater economies of scale while simultaneously paring their costs. Mergers offered one such avenue for the banks. The ANZ Bank, for instance, shed 249 branches upon its acquisition of the English, Scottish and Australian Bank in 1969 (Taylor & Hirst, 1983: 268). Following the 1981 mergers between the National Bank of Australia and the Commercial Banking Company of Sydney to create the National Australia Bank, and between the Bank of New South Wales and the Commercial Bank of Australia to create Westpac Bank, Taylor and Hirst (1983: 270) forecast a rash of duplicated branch closures, particularly in rural areas. A total of 601 branches nationally were deemed to be at risk. Ford (1991) details the impact of post-deregulation mergers on the bank branch network as banks attempted to achieve national rather than a regional distribution of branches.

Although the threat of foreign bank expansion into retail banking following deregulation in 1983 is yet unfulfilled, competitive pressure within the Australian banking sector greatly intensified through the 1990s. The so-called 'big four' trading banks have occasionally preyed upon smaller regional banks, and there have also been mergers between the regional banks themselves. This continual search for increased scale economies and lower operating costs — amidst the emergence of new non-bank financial institutions and 'footloose' mortgage originators, declining interest rate margins and advances in banking technology — has forced banks to appraise the cost efficiency of their branch structures. Branch closures have almost inevitably followed this appraisal process.

Interestingly, similar competitive pressures caused a proliferation of bank branches during the 1950s and 1960s. The official banking sector responded to the growth of the non-bank financial institution sector during the 1950s and 1960s by embarking on a major spatial expansion of services. The trading bank branch network grew from 3942 in 1950 to 5779 in 1963, while the savings bank branch network expanded still faster, from 5011 to 18 532 branches over the same period (Committee of Economic Enquiry, 1965).

NEW MODES OF FACE TO FACE FINANCIAL SERVICE DELIVERY

In the hiatus between the final locking of the branch's front doors and the anticipated boom of modem-based money management by rural customers, other institutions have developed innovative and potentially locally empowering approaches to providing physical banking services to recently branchless or threatened rural communities. Running against the recent trend for rural financial services to be regionalised are the Bendigo Bank, via its 'community bank' concept, and the joint Commonwealth and State government-funded CreditCare scheme, which establishes credit unions in communities which have recently joined the ranks of the 'financially excluded'. These initiatives have given the lie to the major banks' arguments that rural bank branch closures are a response primarily to the affected town's lack of economic viability.

Partially in response to the public antipathy focused on rural branch closures and the generally positive media attention given to alternative service providers, the major banks have been forced to rethink their cost recovery and service reduction strategies. One response has been to develop their own non-branch modes of servicing rural communities' banking needs. Westpac, for instance, is experimenting with an agency-type arrangement located in the local newsagent in the town of Canowindra, Central West NSW, as a replacement for its branch facility (Boreham, 1997: 19). The Colonial State Bank is introducing a similar initiative on a trial basis, offering branch franchises to existing small town retailers such as pharmacists, newsagents and grocers (Boreham, 1998c: 50). These models of service provision have drawn criticism from local residents, however, because of the potential for customer confidentiality and security to be compromised. There is no guarantee that local communities will accept these 'second-best' modes of service provision. To rural residents, they may appear to be a case of the banks privatising the gains and socialising the costs of deregulation, increased competition and technological advances in financial service delivery.

It would not be unfair to suggest that the recent geographically extensive campaign of rural bank branch closures has diminished access to financial services for large sections of rural and remote, as well as metropolitan, Australia. For many in these areas, the closures have produced financial exclusion. In stark contrast to this process of financial exclusion, however, some of the major trading banks have begun to court high wealth financial consumers using, of all things, bank branches. Both the ANZ Bank and National Australia Bank are in the process of establishing 'premium banking facilities' across Australia, with ANZ Bank's showpiece St. Kilda branch costing $500 000 in renovations. As a rather unsubtle exercise in 'financial inclusion', the 'premium banking' concept aims to give physical support to the apparently typical situation faced by retail banks whereby 20 per cent of customers generate 80 per cent or more of profit. This 'flight to quality' is unambiguously and unabashedly pitched at the high-wealth strata of urban society. Revamped branches seek to create an ambience in which affluent customers feel more disposed to purchasing more of the bank's products. In these new branches:

[t]here are no queues. Customers are assigned a number and can recline on couches. Premium customers are ushered to a separate sanctum — accessible by an issued card — and offered tea and coffee while — if — they wait. 'It is really rewarding those customers who have shown loyalty and have a major part of their financial services business with us,' says ANZ head of global banking, Peter Hawkins. [Boreham, 1999a: 21]

Premium bank customers are those that 'have a business relationship of more than $100 000 in loans and investments, as well as annual household income of at least $70 000' (Boreham, 1999b: 32). The contrasts with the recent restructuring of the rural bank branch network could not be stronger.

CONCLUSION

An increasingly stark geography of financial exclusion and inclusion is being created. The major banks are prepared to expend heavily to lure high wealth, predominantly metropolitan customers into a tighter relationship with them; while seeking to off-load basic retail financial services to the rest of their customers via well-known retailers like Coles and Woolworths, and simultaneously stripping back the traditional branch network. As we have seen, these changes can offer greater flexibility for the individual financial consumer (not to mention the bank), depending upon their location, class and ability. For small rural towns, and particularly small businesses in the towns, the loss of local financial services produces large costs. In this respect, the centrifugal forces placing face to face banking services back in towns deserted by the major trading banks is an important counter to the dominant centripetal forces pulling a range of vital public and private services from small town rural Australia.

There is no denying that the established rural settlement system and functional hierarchy has, and will continue to, undergo transformation in response to demographic, economic and technological change. The case study of financial service provision in rural NSW and WA here, however, demonstrates that this process is interwoven with organisational and institutional change. New players are emerging to supply supposedly high cost face to face financial services to rural communities (for example, Bendigo Bank) at the same time that there is growing pressure for mergers between the 'four pillars' (ANZ Bank, Westpac, National Australia Bank, Commonwealth Bank) — a move that, if successful, would almost guarantee further branch closures. In order to comprehend the implications of these changes, what is required are fewer bromides of the 'only certainty for rural Australia is ongoing change' type (Walker et al., 1997), and more critical discussion of what services rural people are entitled to, or what they can legitimately expect to negotiate via the political system. That debate has barely begun.

NOTE

1 Official statistics on bank branch numbers in Australia are available from the Australian Prudential Regulatory Authority. Prior to 1999 this data was reported in the September edition of the *Reserve Bank of Australia Bulletin*. Before June 1990 the Australian Bureau of Statistics published quarterly data on trading and savings bank branch and agency numbers for each State. Geographically, this data is broken down into the categories of 'metropolitan' and 'non-metropolitan'. The metropolitan category basically consists of capital city and suburban branches only. Therefore it is inaccurate to infer that the 'non-metropolitan' category refers exclusively to rural areas (see Argent and Rolley, 1998).

REFERENCES

Anderson J (1999) 'One nation or two? Securing a future for rural and regional Australia', Address to the National Press Club, Canberra, 17 February, at: *http://www.dot.gov.au/media/anders/speeches/as1_99.htm*

Argent N & Rolley F (1998) 'Submission to The Federal House of Representatives Standing Committee on Economics, Finance and Public Administration Inquiry into alternative means of providing banking and like services in regional Australia', Submission No. 120, Vol. 5, S971–997.

Australian Bureau of Statistics (ABS) (1988a) *Census '86 — Persons and Dwellings in Legal Local Government Areas, Statistical Local Areas and Urban Centres/(Rural) Localities: New South Wales*, (Cat. No. 2462.0), ABS, Canberra.

Australian Bureau of Statistics (1988b) *Census of Population and Housing, 30 June 1986: Census 86 — Persons and Dwellings in Local Government Areas and Urban Centres — Western Australia*, (Cat. No. 2465.0), ABS, Canberra.

Australian Bureau of Statistics (1993a) *Census '91 — Census Counts for Small Areas: New South Wales*, (Cat No. 2730.1), ABS, Canberra.

Australian Bureau of Statistics (1993b) *1991 Census of Population and Housing — Census Counts for Small Areas: Western Australia*, (Cat. No. 2730.5), ABS, Canberra.

Australian Bureau of Statistics (1997) *Australian Demographic Trends 1997*, (Cat. No. 3102.0), AGPS, Canberra.

Australian Bureau of Statistics (1998a) *Census '96 — Selected Characteristics for Urban Centres and Localities: New South Wales and Australian Capital Territory*, (Cat. No. 2016.1), ABS, Canberra.

Australian Bureau of Statistics (1998b) *1996 Census of Population and Housing — Selected Social and Housing Characteristics for Statistical Local Areas: Western Australia*, (Cat. No. 2015.5), ABS, Canberra.

Australian Payments Clearing Association (1998) *Payment System Statistics*, at: *http://www.apca.com.au/Paymentstatistics.htm*

Beal D & Ralston D (1997) *Economic and Social Impacts of the Closure of the Only Bank Branch in Rural Communities*, Centre for Australian Financial Institutions, University of Southern Queensland, Toowoomba.

Beer A, Bolam A & Maude A (1994) *Beyond the Capitals: Urban Growth in Regional Australia*, AGPS, Canberra.

Boreham T (1997) 'Westpac banks on newsagents in the bush', *The Australian*, 15 December, p 19.

Boreham T (1998a) 'Branch loyalty leaves banks on a limb', *The Australian*, 11 June, p 26.

Boreham T (1998b) 'Value of branch transactions rises', *The Australian*, 30 November, p 37.

Boreham T (1998c) 'Bushwhacked banks redraw rural battle lines', *Weekend Australian*, 21–22 March, p 50.

Boreham T (1999a) 'Just the ticket for the new world of banking', *The Australian*, 26 February, p 21.

Boreham T (1999b) 'Premium seats', *The Australian*, 2 March, p 32.

Bowie I & Smailes P (1988) 'The country town', in Heathcote R (ed) *The Australian Experience: Essays in Australian Land Settlement and Resource Management*, Longman Cheshire, Melbourne, pp 233–56.

Bureau of Rural Sciences (1999) *Country Matters: Social Atlas of Rural and Regional Australia*, Bureau of Rural Sciences, Canberra.

Committee of Economic Enquiry (1965) *Report of the Economic Enquiry*, Vol. 1, AGPS, Canberra.

Cronin J (1993) *Operation Bankwatch*, Unpublished booklet.

Cuthbertson I (1999) 'Banks branch out', *The Australian* (Computers — The Cutting Edge), 20 July, p 1, 6.

Department of Fair Trading (1997) *Banks: Are You Being Served?*, Report of the NSW Regional Banking Forums, Department of Fair Trading, Sydney.

Department of Primary Industries and Energy and Department of Human Services and Health (1994) *Rural, Remote and Metropolitan Areas Classification: 1991 Census Edition*, AGPS, Canberra.

Fagan R & Webber M (1994) *Global Restructuring: The Australian Experience*, OUP, Melbourne.

Ford M (1991) 'Restructuring Australia's banking industry during the 1980s: Global forces and local effects', unpublished BA (Hons) thesis, Department of Geography, University of Melbourne.

Freebairn J (1987) 'Natural resource industries', in Maddock R & McLean I (eds), *The Australian Economy in the Long Run*, Cambridge University Press, Melbourne, pp 133–64.

Gruen F (1990) 'Economic development and agriculture since 1945', in Williams D (ed) *Agriculture in the Australian Economy*, Third Edition, Sydney University Press in association with OUP, South Melbourne, pp 19–26.

Hefford R (1985) *Farm Policy in Australia*, University of Queensland Press, St. Lucia.

Holmes J (1981) 'Sparsely populated regions of Australia', in Lonsdale R & Holmes J (eds) *Settlement Systems in Sparsely Populated Regions: The United States and Australia*, Pergamon Press, New York, pp 70–104.

Holmes J (1983) 'Telephone traffic dispersion and nodal regionalisation in the Australian States', *Australian Geographical Studies*, 21, pp 231–50.

Holmes J (1987) 'The urban system', in Jeans D (ed), *Space and Society*, Sydney University Press, Sydney, pp 49–74.

House of Representatives Standing Committee on Economics, Finance and Public Administration (1999) *Regional Banking Services: Money Too Far Away*, CanPrint Communications, Canberra.

Hugo G & Smailes P (1992) 'Population dynamics in rural South Australia', *Journal of Rural Studies*, 8(1), pp 29–51.

Jeans D (1972) *An Historical Geography of New South Wales to 1901*, Reed Education, Sydney.

Joseph A & Chalmers A (1997) 'Growing old in rural New Zealand: towards an appreciation of the sustainability of lives and communities', in Epps R (ed), *Sustaining Rural Systems in the Context of Global Change: Proceedings of the Joint Conference of the IGU Commission for the Sustainability of Rural Systems and Land Use–Cover Change Study Group*, University of New England, Armidale, pp 399–408.

Joseph A & Smithers J (1999) *Towards an Understanding of the Interrelated Dynamics of Change in Agriculture and Rural Communities*, Paper presented at the International Geographical Union Commission for the Sustainability of Rural Systems Conference, Vancouver, Canada.

KPMG Management Consulting Pty. Ltd. (1998) *Australian Bankers' Association: Demographic Trends and Services Provision in Rural Australia*, Submission to the House of Representatives Standing Committee on Financial Institutions and Public Administration Inquiry into Alternative Means of Providing Banking and Like Services In Regional Australia.

Lamba R (1999) 'Bush telegraph switches on to e-mail', *Weekend Australian*, 17–18 July, p 18.

Lawrence G (1987) *Capitalism and the Countryside: The Rural Crisis in Australia*, Pluto Press, Sydney.

Lawrence G & Williams C (1990) 'The dynamics of decline: implications for social welfare delivery in rural Australia', in Cullen T, Dunn P & Lawrence G (eds), *Rural Health and Welfare in Australia*, Centre for Rural Welfare Research, Charles Sturt University, Wagga Wagga, pp 38–59.

Leyshon A & Thrift N (1995) 'Geographies of financial exclusion: financial abandonment in Britain and the United States', *Transactions of the Institute of British Geographers*, 20, pp 312–41.

Leyshon A, Thrift N & Pratt J (1998) 'Reading financial services: texts, consumers and financial literacy', *Environment and Planning D: Society and Space*, 16, pp 29–55.

Logan M, Whitelaw J & McKay T (1981) *Urbanisation: The Australian Experience*, Shillington House, Melbourne.

Martin R & Sunley P (1997) 'The post-Keynesian state and the space economy', in Lee R & Wills J (eds), *Geographies of Economies*, Arnold, London, pp 278–89.

McIntosh Baring (1996) *Bank Branches: To Close or Not to Close?* McIntosh and Company, Melbourne.

O'Kane T (1997) '"What rural crisis?" asks Fischer', *The Land*, 10 July, p 19.

Productivity Commission (1999*) Impact of Competition Policy Reforms on Rural and Regional Australia*, Draft Report, Canberra.

Reserve Bank of Australia (1999) 'Bank fees in Australia', *Reserve Bank of Australia Bulletin*, June, pp 1–10.

Rolley F & Humphreys J (1993) 'Rural welfare — The human face of Australia's countryside', in Sorensen A & Epps R (eds), *Prospects and Policies for Rural Australia*, Longman Cheshire, Melbourne, pp 241–57.

Rothwell N (1997) 'Cry from the bush: A tale of three towns', *Weekend Australian*, 15–16 February, pp 1–6.

Salt B (1998) *Population Growth Ranking in Australia and New Zealand*, KPMG, Melbourne.

Scott J (1999) 'The supermarket you can bank on', *The Australian*, 13 July, p 3.

Sidoti C (1998) 'Bush Talks', at: *http://www.hreoc.gov.au/news_info/bushtalks/index.html.*

Smailes P (1969) 'A metropolitan trade shadow: the case of Adelaide, South Australia', *Tijdschrift voor Economische en Sociale Geografie*, 60, pp 329–345.

Smailes P (1979) 'The effects of changes in agriculture upon the service sector in South Australian country towns, 1945–1974', *Norsk Geografisk Tidsskrift*, 33, pp 125–42.

Smailes P (1996) 'Accessibility changes in South Australia and the country town network', in Lawrence G, Lyons K & Momtaz S (eds), *Social Change in Rural Australia*, Rural Social and Economic Research Centre, Central Queensland University, Rockhampton, pp 119–38.

Social Development Committee (1994) *Rural Poverty in South Australia: Interim Report of the Social Development Committee*, Fourth Report, Parliament of South Australia, Adelaide.

Taylor M & Hirst J (1983) 'Australian banking: the current round of rationalisation and restructuring', *Australian Geographical Studies*, 21, pp 266–71.

Telecom and Telstra Corporation (1981, 1986, 1991, 1996, 1998) *White Pages* & *Yellow Pages*, Telstra Ltd., Melbourne.

Tonts M (1998) 'Rural restructuring, policy change and uneven development in the Central Wheatbelt of Western Australia', unpublished PhD thesis, Curtin University of Technology, Perth.

Wahlquist A (1996) 'The gutting of rural NSW: bush bleeds as 30,000 regional jobs disappear', *The Land*, 8 August, p 6.

Walker G, Corby D & Murphy T (1997) 'Finance industry restructuring: Implications for regional Australia', Paper presented at the 15th Pacific Regional Science Conference Organisation, 8–12 December.

Walmsley D (1980) *Social Justice and Australian Federalism*, Department of Geography, University of New England, Armidale.

Walmsley D & Weinand H (1991) 'Changing retail structure in Southern Sydney', *Australian Geographer*, 22 (1), pp 57–66.

10
REGIONAL POLICY AND DEVELOPMENT IN AUSTRALIA: RUNNING OUT OF SOLUTIONS?

ANDREW BEER

O ver the last decade local and regional development has attracted renewed academic and policy interest in Australia and internationally. In that period this country has witnessed a raft of inquiries into regional policy and regional development. Even if we limit our purview to federal interest in this area, there is an extensive list of work. Some of the most significant works include the report of the Taskforce on Regional Development (1993), the Industry Commission's reports into *Impediments to Regional Industry Adjustment* (IC, 1993) *and State, Territory and Local Government Assistance to Industry* (IC, 1996), McKinsey & Co's (1994) report *Lead Local, Compete Global,* and documents relating to the release of *Working Nation* (Keating, 1994). Moreover, regional development has come to represent something new and quite different when compared with policy debates and programs two decades ago (Teitz, 1994).

This flurry of activity in regional development policy and these new approaches to promoting the growth of regions have not necessarily resulted in a better quality of life for people living in depressed areas. In many instances the residents of non-metropolitan regions — often referred to as 'regional Australia' — face even greater pressures than in the past, through the withdrawal and restructuring of public services, the decline in the terms of trade for many agricultural commodities, employment loss from manufacturing industries and persistently high levels of unemployment. As several researchers have shown, it was precisely this 'regional Australia' that provided the backbone of support for the One Nation party, and its brand of populist politics in the 1998 federal election and the New South Wales and Queensland elections of the same period (Davis & Stimson, 1998).

This chapter seeks to examine the changing face of regional development in Australia at the Commonwealth, State and local government levels. It maps out the nature of local and regional development policies and programs in Australia and investigates the processes driving policy and political change within this sphere. The chapter draws upon the applied literature on regional development and regulation theory to consider why there has been so much turbulence within economic development over the last two decades, and whether regional development in Australia has come to an impasse. It further speculates on whether the major impediment to creating greater prosperity in Australia's regions is the failure of theories on the growth of regions, or whether it is a consequence of poor application due to inappropriate and inflexible political and administrative structures.

UNDERSTANDING ECONOMIC DEVELOPMENT POLICIES AND PROGRAMS

Australia is currently at the crossroads in respect to regional policy. The highly centralised 'top down' sponsor-oriented approach to regional development, which dominated in the 1960s, has proved to be not a very effective one, in spite of all its promises and expectations. The disillusionment with this approach, coinciding with the economic recession, has resulted in a relative neglect of regional thinking in socio-economic policy formulation until very recently. The importance of the regional dimension has again come to the fore during recent attempts to overcome current economic difficulties. It seems, however, that the approach to regional development has to be different today to the approach dominating in the past. [Zagorski, 1989: xi]

Zagorski's (1989) pronouncement on the state of regional economic development in Australia appears timeless: regional economic development was at a crossroads in 1989, as it was in 1975, as it was in 1944 (Logan, 1978) and as it is again now. Moreover, policy makers and politicians remain committed to finding new approaches from those 'dominating' in the past.

Local or regional development remains problematic in Australia.[1] In part this reflects both the problems of vertical fiscal inequality and the peculiar policy and program ambiguities generated by Australia's model of federalism. The federal government is perhaps the only tier of government with sufficient resources to address the problems of uneven development between regions, but on occasion federal governments have found it convenient to argue that they lack a clear political or constitutional mandate for involvement in this arena (National

Commission of Audit, 1996). State and local governments have fewer resources but more clearly defined responsibilities. This imbalance between the political power to act and the resources to do so has generated complex and far reaching tensions within regional development: with the federal government periodically engaging and then withdrawing from regional programs; State governments shifting their priorities over time; and local governments filling the gaps, when and how they can (see Chapter 11).

There have been identifiable cycles within regional policy in Australia but it would be incorrect to imply that there has not been fundamental progress. As Zagorski (1989) suggested, there has been substantial and far-reaching change over time and developments in Australia have been consistent with international trends. In broad terms, there has been a shift from Fordist approaches — such as growth pole theory — to post-Fordist approaches that place a greater emphasis on the culture of entrepreneurialism (Cooke, Uranga & Etxebarria, 1998) and engagement with global markets (Hall & Hubbard, 1996; Harvey, 1989). In Australia this trend has contributed to a proliferation of regional and local economic development programs and policies over recent years (Beer & Maude, 1997). A number of these policy initiatives have come and gone in a relatively short period (Beer, 1998), without making any real impact on the state of Australia's regions. Importantly, the programs and policies followed in the early and mid-1990s were very different from those operating a decade earlier. They also differ from those policies and programs now emerging at the forefront of regional policy and practice as we enter the 21st century.

REGULATION THEORY

The work of researchers informed by regulation theory sheds considerable light on the processes of change and development within regional policy in Australia. Regulation theory has built upon the work and insights of Aglietta (1979) in examining the role of governments and government institutions in creating and supporting the conditions for accumulation under capitalism (see also Jessop, 1995). Some authors within what McLeod (1997) has dubbed the 'Leeds School' of economic geography have argued that new modes of social regulation have arisen in advanced economies since the mid-1970s to support new systems of accumulation (see Peck & Tickell, 1992; 1995; Tickell & Peck, 1995). Importantly, regulation theory suggests governments will proceed — often in a chaotic manner — through a series of broad policy frameworks as they attempt to create the conditions that best support economic growth. This includes the shift to neo-liberal — or 'economic rationalist' — approaches to government (Peck & Tickell,

1995), changes to how cities and regions are governed (Harvey, 1989; Haughton, Peck & Strange, 1997) and, more recently, 'Third Way' philosophies of government that emphasise community empowerment and mutual obligation in social welfare.

There is not the scope to adequately address the regulation theory literature here, but reference will be made to three key ideas. In the first instance it is essential to recognise the importance of crises, or perceived crises, within governments in triggering change in government structures and actions (Hay, 1995). In common with other developed nations, Australian governments in the 1980s and 1990s faced a number of economic challenges as a consequence of restructuring and global economic shifts and these acted as a catalyst for change in local development policy and programs. Second, the notion of crisis is also central to the argument put forward by Peck and Tickell (1992) that change in the structures of government is indicative of severe difficulties within the economy and the search for an 'institutional fix' to the problems of accumulation. Finally, Goodwin and Painter (1996) discussed the process of 'institutional searching' common to many post-Fordist societies. Economic restructuring not only leads to the search for new forms of government intervention, it also leads governments to change existing administrative structures.

Regulation theory has been criticised for reading too much into the processes of economic and political change within advanced economies. Lovering (1995), for example, argued many of the processes and phenomena that regulation theorists see as evidence of the emergence of new institutional structures are in fact better understood as an outcome of the application of economic rationalist philosophies. While acknowledging this criticism, regulation theory offers valuable insights into the policy environment shaping regional development in Australia: it recognises that the proliferation of local and regional development initiatives is a consequence of a new set of imperatives affecting post-Fordist economies (Amin, 1994). It also makes an explicit link between crises within economies (economic and social) and renewed efforts to develop or redevelop the landscape of local and regional development.

THE NATURE OF REGIONAL DEVELOPMENT IN AUSTRALIA

In all Australian States and Territories there is a myriad of institutions and agencies working for the development of localities and regions (Beer, 1997). They are variously supported by, or attached to, local government, a community group, a federal government department or operate as an agency of the State government. In a number of instances an agency will draw support from more than one tier of government.[2] These agencies may be a business enterprise centre, a regional development board, an economic development unit within a local government, an Area Consultative Committee or represent some other institutional configuration. Some agencies — such as those set up under the federal government's Rural Partnership Program — were only established in a limited number of localities and there are a number of agencies that were established as 'one-off' experiments, or are historical curiosities.[3] Any given locality may be covered by three or four different agencies, all of which are working at a variety of scales and in response to the priorities of different stakeholders. Most States have set up regional development structures that deliberately exclude their capital city (Beer & Maude, 1997).

This section briefly reviews the structure of federal, State and local government involvement in regional development in Australia. It then goes on to consider the overall structure of regional development in Australia, and the important questions of efficiency and effectiveness in the current sets of institutional arrangements. This will lead to the next section on recent trends in local and regional development.

FEDERAL GOVERNMENT PARTICIPATION IN REGIONAL DEVELOPMENT

Federal government involvement in regional development in Australia has a very chequered history and has been the focus of sustained academic interest (Stilwell, 1974; 1993; Vipond, 1989; Harris, 1989; Self 1990; Forth, 1996). Given the volume of published material, this section will only briefly touch upon federal programs prior to the 1990s and then focus on the most recent policy approaches. Logan (1978) provides a very useful summary of earlier policy frameworks.

POSTWAR INITIATIVES

The first serious attempts at national regional policies and programs came in the 1940s and they were pursued as part of the broader postwar redevelopment effort. In 1944 the State and Commonwealth governments agreed upon a process of planning and action for what was essentially a decentralisation program. A number of regions were established across Australia and committees were formed in each region to advise both the State and national governments on regional development. As Logan (1978: 26) has pointed out, 'little was achieved in this period because of the absence of a clear statement of objectives, the lack of statutory power by regional development committees and their inability to fire the collective imagination of the people'.

POLICIES UNDER THE WHITLAM GOVERNMENTS

Regional development — as decentralisation — re-emerged on the national political agenda in the late 1960s and early 1970s. During the 1960s regional policy became one part of the federal Labor Party's policy platform, which in turn prompted the Coalition government to introduce legislation in 1972 that established the National Urban and Regional Development Authority (NURDA) (Stilwell, 1974: 171). The election of the first Whitlam Labor government in 1972 brought further direct federal involvement in urban and regional policy with the establishment of the Department of Urban and Regional Development (DURD) and the renaming of NURDA as the Cities Commission. The Whitlam government(s) pursued decentralisation by promoting a number of growth centres (with Albury–Wodonga nominated the first such centre in 1973) and attempted to develop a national strategy for urban and regional development. There were other programs with a regional or urban dimension, including the Area Improvement Program — which provided funding to local governments in a select number of areas designated as disadvantaged — and the Regional Employment Development Scheme. The true focus of the Whitlam government, however, was on the problems of the rapidly growing cities. As Vipond (1989) has noted, interest in regional development and the resolve to establish 'new cities' as growth centres was in large part an offshoot of the more prominent urban policy agenda. She observed that 'These essentially urban interests coincided with the need to resolve the acute rural problems that had also arisen. New cities might invigorate some of the declining rural areas' (Vipond, 1989: 67).

THE FRASER GOVERNMENT

The Fraser Coalition government (1976–83) wound up DURD and most federal urban and regional development initiatives. Between 1977–78 and 1980–81 a modest Regional Development Program was implemented. This program provided general assistance for projects in non-metropolitan areas, but its funding of $36.5 million ensured that it had a limited impact.

THE HAWKE AND KEATING LABOR GOVERNMENTS

The election of the Hawke Labor government in 1983 did not result in the federal government immediately re-engaging with urban and regional policy. Instead, the government focused on restructuring the economy, dealing with unemployment and managing the budget deficit (Taylor & Garlick, 1989). Over the life of the Hawke Labor governments (1983–91), and more notably the Keating governments (1991–96), federal involvement in regional development was often presented under a different guise — labour market assistance, the sustainability of rural communities etc. — and administered by the relevant program area.

The Country Centre's Project (CCP) was one small but later very influential initiative of this period. The project was a trial of local economic development practice by the federal government. An emphasis was placed on community self-help, local management of economic development initiatives and private sector participation (Taylor & Garlick, 1989). While total funding for the project was relatively insignificant, and only 11 centres were included, the CCP was perceived by some within the federal government to be a success and was recognised as a fundamental shift in regional policy (Taylor & Garlick, 1989; Epps, 1999). It represented a move away from a framework in which central government policies were implemented on a 'problem' region, to one where governments worked in consultation with the community to facilitate 'longer run social and economic growth' (Taylor & Garlick, 1989).

More substantial involvement in regional affairs came via other programs. Through the Office of Labour Market Adjustment (OLMA) the Hawke government sought to address unemployment in areas adversely affected by economic restructuring and cyclical change. Funding under this program was targeted to areas with above average unemployment or other structural difficulties. Both metropolitan and non-metropolitan regions were assisted through support for local economic development organisations, labour market training and education. Funding was also available to support the establishment of business incubators, local enterprise ventures and micro-businesses, and to assist existing enterprises in expanding their capacity (DEET, 1995a). OLMA programs had modest budgets. Total program expenditure in 1994–95 was just $27 million, spread across 150 OLMA regions (Deloitte Touche Tohmatsu, 1995). Funds were divided into three sub-programs of $10 million for business incubators, $13 million for regional employment initiatives and $4 million for regional employment assistance.

Program and policy development at the local level was informed by 130 OLMA committees. These committees typically comprised local business people, local government representatives and other community leaders. To use one area as an example, in Fairfield–Liverpool in western Sydney, the OLMA committee oversaw the establishment of a Regional Skills Development Council and the establishment of a number of worker co-operatives. It investigated the impact of public transport on access to employment and established a food industry development group (DEET, 1995b). From the mid-1980s through to 1995, when OLMA programs and committees were merged with the Area Consultative Committees (discussed below), OLMA was an important part of local economic development in Australia. It made a substantial contribution to the survival and success of many local development bodies, through the funding of positions and projects.

The mid-1990s saw a major shift in the direction of federal regional policy and programs. As Australia's economy struggled out of the recession of the early 1990s, it became apparent that some parts of the nation were not growing and confronted both high unemployment and record levels of long-term unemployment. The Keating government responded by releasing its *White Paper on Employment and Growth* (Keating, 1994) and introducing a number of programs, including some that explicitly addressed regional issues.

Area Consultative Committees (ACCs) were created to work with communities to make employment and training programs more relevant to local needs. ACCs were established with the central goals of advising on, and generating support for, the Keating Labor government's major employment initiatives, namely the Job Compact, the Youth Training Initiative, entry level training opportunities and New Work Opportunities. They were also expected to assist in the development of an employment strategy linked to plans for regional economic growth, including the identification of skills needed for regional growth, and to facilitate growth in job opportunities for regional communities (DEET, 1995a: 1).

Some 61 ACCs were established throughout Australia, spread across urban and rural areas. They were set up as advisory bodies with a membership drawn from business, trade unions and related organisations. Committee responsibilities included establishing priorities within existing programs, raising community concerns and commissioning studies. It is important to recognise that ACCs were established to operate within strictly defined limits. They were set up to advise the Department of Employment, Education and Training, rather than run their own programs and projects. Their operations were also restricted to labour market issues.

The Regional Development Program (RDP) was announced as a second part of the *White Paper on Employment and Growth*. Under the RDP the Keating government committed itself to providing $150 million over four years to facilitate regional development. The program was intended to bring about the development of regions that were visible on world markets, as suppliers of commodities, as tourist destinations, or as major centres for business (Brown, 1996; Department of Housing and Regional Development, 1994; McKinsey and Co., 1994; 1996). The RDP's philosophy and structure emphasised the importance of regional Australia gaining access to world markets and thereby overcoming the limitations set by Australia's small population. It emphasised the processes driving local economies, and wherever possible it attempted to define regions on the basis of common industries and market opportunities, rather than inherited administrative boundaries. It also placed great emphasis on the development of local leadership and strategic planning. Conceptually, it drew heavily on the Country Centre's Project and sought to introduce many of the ideas that emerged from that earlier experiment.

The RDP had a number of component parts. There was, firstly, a $70 million regional infrastructure fund for regional projects which removed obstacles to development and enhanced competitiveness. The second element was labelled 'Structures, Strategies and Projects' and it supported the establishment of Regional Development Organisations (RDOs) and provided financial assistance for strategic planning. RDOs were to be independent, incorporated bodies that represented their communities and worked for economic growth. RDOs were encouraged to seek additional funding for both operating costs and projects. Funds were sought from the private sector, other federal government programs, State government programs and local government. Management and skill enhancement was the third component of the RDP and it was intended to encourage 'best practice' approaches to economic development as well as improve the skills of those involved in regional development. Activities included the establishment of Best Practice Centres, the distribution of management and economic development education modules and the development of improved skills through formal training, and the provision of cadetships.

RDOs were managed by boards whose members were drawn from the community. Unlike ACCs, the boards employed their own staff to serve as a secretariat and oversee projects. They were less well funded than ACCs, but had a broader brief to address any issues considered important by the local community, including infrastructure, questions, labour market training, the environment, the perception of the region and business information needs. The Regional Development Program was abolished in August 1996 as part of the budget cuts imposed by the new Howard Coalition government. Its abolition was consistent with the recommendations of the National Commission of Audit (1996), which argued that regional economic development was the preserve of State and local governments and that there was no need for Commonwealth involvement.

HOWARD COALITION GOVERNMENT INITIATIVES

In its 1999 budget the Howard government introduced a statement on regional development entitled *Regional Australia: Meeting the Challenges* (Anderson & McDonald, 1999). In this statement the Coalition spelt out its philosophies and approaches to the development of 'regional' Australia. This statement had two central underpinnings:

in the first instance, the statement reasserted the federal government's view that it could best contribute to regional development through a prosperous national economy. It argued that:

> In the past three years, the Federal Government's primary focus in assisting Australia's regions to realise their enormous potential has been to deliver sound macro- and micro-economic management of the Australian economy ... These strong economic foundations have provided the launching pad for strong and sustainable economic employment growth, bringing benefits to regional Australia such as substantial reductions in interest rates. [Anderson & McDonald, 1999: 1]

The Regional Australia Strategy was the second foundation of the Coalition's policies. This strategy embraced a 'whole-of-government approach' with the federal government 'working with communities to plan viable futures and deliver results' (Anderson & McDonald, 1999: 1).

The Howard government's policies and programs for regional development are very different from those introduced by the Keating Labor government in 1994. The Keating governments addressed the problems of regional development by creating new institutions (such as ACCs and RDOs) and introducing major new programs, such as the Regional Development Program. The policies pursued by the Coalition are of more modest scale and place a greater emphasis on using existing frameworks to achieve the government's regional development goals. The budget statement announced a one-off Regional Australia Summit for October 1999 that would 'draw together business and community representatives from across the nation to address the challenges facing rural and regional Australia' (Anderson & McDonald, 1999: 2). There would also be a program of regional forums at which members of the federal government — ministers and officials — would consult within the regions as to how best assist each area to develop its potential.

Within the processes of government, the Coalition introduced major changes. These included formal regional impact statements requiring departments to address the potential regional impacts of all cabinet submissions, and the establishment of a memorandum of understanding on regional development between key departments such as Transport and Regional Services, Agriculture, Forestry and Fisheries, and Education Training and Youth Affairs. The Howard government also placed great emphasis on the services it provides to the regions. It announced that part proceeds of the sale of the second tranche of Telstra were to be used to provide some 500 Rural Transaction Centres around Australia and expand a number of other services, especially regional health services. The transaction centres would provide access to electronic banking and account payment in communities bereft of banks or other financial institutions.

Regional Australia: Meeting the Challenge (Anderson & McDonald, 1999) is as important for the issues on which it is silent as it is for those it discusses. What is absent is a commitment by the federal government to funding general regional development programs: there is no regional infrastructure funding program, there is no financial support for existing regional development bodies and there is no funding for programs or projects submitted as priorities by the regions. The Regional Assistance Program comes closest to a general regional development focus, but it is explicitly tied to labour market outcomes and could be seen as a legacy of the previous government, particularly as it is administered through the Area Consultative Committees. On the other hand, the Howard government has brought regional development and services into the centre of federal government business. For example, the Regional Forums Program received high-level support from virtually all departments. It is worth restating, however, that no new funds were made available to address issues raised in the forums and no policy initiatives will be spawned out of this process.

STATE GOVERNMENT PARTICIPATION IN REGIONAL DEVELOPMENT

Any discussion of State government participation in regional development is bedevilled by two factors. In the first instance, Australia is a federation and each of the six State and two Territory governments pursue regional development policies in their own unique fashion. There is no single approach to regional development amongst the States, though there are many common elements. Second, regional development policies and programs are always changing, such that any review of State programs is inevitably out of date within a year.

It is possible, however, to draw together some features that summarise the various State government approaches to the promotion of local and regional growth (for more detail, see Beer & Maude, 1997). All State governments have a commitment to local and regional development and in most instances this is expressed through the funding of regional development agencies and other organisations. Victoria does not separately fund agencies, but since the restructuring of local government in 1995 has required regional development to be one of the priorities of individual local governments. The New South Wales and the Western Australian governments fully fund their own agencies (called Regional Development Boards and Regional Development Commissions respectively). These agencies are amongst the most well funded in Australia, with the Development Commissions in Western Australia having budgets in excess of $1 million. Their staffs are State government employees and there is a strong articulation between the activities of these agencies and the broader State government administration. In South Australia, Regional Development Boards are the primary vehicle for promoting the growth of regions and are jointly funded and controlled by the State government and local governments. Until recently, the Queensland government made no direct financial contribution to regional development agencies in its jurisdiction, but it introduced ongoing funding for some regional development organisations in 1999.

It is one of the cruel ironies of regional development in Australia that the poorer and less developed States and Territories struggle to support regional development initiatives. In Tasmania, regional development agencies have been weakly developed, with the Tasmanian government providing grants to a number of community and regional development bodies. Most of the State's efforts in business advice and other assistance for firms are undertaken through its department, Tasmania Development and Resources (TDR) (Beer & Maude, 1997). The situation is even more parlous in the Northern Territory. While the Territory government established Regional Economic Development Committees in the 1990s, it was left to the local communities to support them and they subsequently failed to develop as operational units outside Darwin.

Most State government-sponsored regional development agencies are administered by a board drawn from the community, local businesses and other stakeholders. In New South Wales, the relevant minister appoints all board members, while in Western Australia some members are appointed by the minister, some are drawn from the community and others come from the constituent local governments. South Australia's Regional Development Boards have members drawn from the community and local government. The functions performed by these agencies vary between and within States. A survey of agencies undertaken in 1996, however, found that most considered that business development — that is, assisting the businesses within their region to grow — was their 'core business' (Beer, 1997). Other important roles included lobbying the State and Commonwealth governments, work on infrastructure projects, marketing and promoting their regions and tourism. In some jurisdictions the responsible agency is able to provide infrastructure subsidies to attract companies into its region.

Clearly, most State and Territory governments consider it necessary or desirable to establish independent or quasi-independent agencies to encourage the growth of regions. There are other common features. These agencies are generally limited to the non-metropolitan parts of each State, and in some ways can be seen to be the last vestiges of decentralisation policies. Most agencies work in a separate but parallel fashion to State government departments whose task it is to attract businesses. These departments of State Development, Commerce and Trade, or Industry and Trade are the first and often only point of contact between large firms and the government, with the local development agency not involved in an initiative that could significantly affect the future economy of their region. State government subsidies to industry were valued at $5.7 billion in 1994–95 (Industry Commission, 1996: xxiii). The fact that regional development agencies do not participate, or have limited influence, in attracting very large projects into their regions is one of the apparent gaps in the functioning of these bodies.

LOCAL GOVERNMENT PARTICIPATION IN REGIONAL DEVELOPMENT

Local governments have an important but often unrecognised role in regional development. They were the second most numerous respondents to a survey of regional development bodies undertaken in 1996 (Beer, 1997), and they also contribute to regional development through their sponsorship of other agencies such as business enterprise centres, regional development boards (especially in South Australia), main street programs and other community initiatives.

Municipalities have primary responsibility for local and regional development in Victoria and they are required by legislation to give this function considerable priority. In many other States and Territories, local governments have established their own economic development units to ensure that their city or shire can grow. In some parts of New South Wales local governments have established their own development corporations to push the growth of their area. Local governments will also undertake direct action, providing subsidies through land grants, infrastructure subsidies and other benefits. The Industry Commission (1996: xxiii) found these subsidies were worth $220 million in 1994–95.

EFFICIENCY AND EFFECTIVENESS OF REGIONAL DEVELOPMENT ACTIVITIES IN AUSTRALIA

The structure of regional development in Australia raises questions of efficiency and effectiveness. The framework for regional development in this country can be criticised on a number of grounds. In the extreme, some people have argued that regional development policies and programs are little more than window dressing, a politically inspired sop to rural or union interests (see Isserman, 1994; Eisinger, 1995). It is very difficult to measure the impact of regional development initiatives as macro-economic trends are often more influential in determining a region's growth or decline. A development agency's work will have an impact over the long term, often beyond the time frame of any evaluation cycle, and it is often difficult to make an explicit tie between development outcomes and the actions of the relevant agency (for a fuller discussion, see Maude & Beer, forthcoming; Turok, 1989).

It is important to look more deeply into concerns over the effectiveness of regional development in Australia as there are essentially not one but two fundamental questions. In the first instance, we must determine whether Australian governments have pursued appropriate regional policies. The question is, have we as a nation followed the strategies and policies most likely to result in economic growth for our regions? Second, we must question the implementation of regional development. Have policies and programs been implemented in the most effective fashion possible?

APPROPRIATE REGIONAL POLICY?

What represents 'best practice' in regional development is a very complex question. Fortunately, bodies such as the Organisation for Economic Co-operation and Development (OECD) and the European Union have devoted considerable attention to this issue, drawing upon the experience of their member nations. The OECD's Territorial Development Unit argues that it is possible to identify both successful and unsuccessful regional development strategies (OECD, 1997b; Huggonnier, 1999). Huggonnier (1999: 6–7) argues that strategies that do not work include:

- those that provide massive financial assistance through bureaucratic channels to lagging regions;

- artificial interventions that try to stimulate substantial growth in a limited number of sites. These 'growth-poles' either fail or result in enclave development where footloose industries locate for the period of their subsidy, without any links to the wider economy;

- infrastructure projects that bear no relationship to the demand for that service or facility;

- the maintenance of direct assistance to declining industries in order to protect one or more local economies; and

- infrastructure decision making based on short-term demands rather than long-term needs. Weaker regions tend to have the longer-term needs while wealthier regions often suffer from immediate bottlenecks. Decisions made in the absence of a strategic plan operate to the advantage of wealthier regions.

On the other hand, Huggonnier (1999: 7–8) was able to identify three positive actions in regional development:

- the creation of an environment more suitable for small and medium-sized enterprises;

- encouraging entrepreneurialism or the formation of new businesses (through networking, institutional frameworks etc.); and

- consolidating and improving local infrastructure.

In the OECD's view, the creation of networks and industry clusters is an important path for stimulating and maintaining growth (OECD, 1997b; Huggonier, 1999). Building connections to the global economy through industry clusters and business networking is seen to raise regional incomes and create more resilient economies. The OECD (1997b) has suggested that attracting foreign direct investment is also important as it places the region into the global market place. Foreign direct investment policies then need to be complemented by networking and cluster programs that generate substantial linkages between foreign investments and the surrounding small businesses.

How does Australia's regional development framework measure up against these criteria? On the positive side, regional policy and practice in Australia since the late 1980s have been very much focused on two of the successful strategies, encouraging firm formation and creating a supportive environment for small and medium-sized enterprises. Australian governments have not pursued many of the ineffective policies. Under normal circumstances, governments do not provide substantial assistance to lagging regions, they do not generally pursue growth-pole strategies, and they are more likely to be guilty of providing infrastructure after demand has become apparent than before it. Australian federal governments have also vigorously dismantled tariff barriers and, while some remain, few local economies would be effectively protected by the remaining low tariffs. However, Australia does not have an unblemished record in regional policy. Australian governments have tended to make infrastructure decisions on the basis of short-term needs rather than longer-term priorities, and this has operated to the advantage of the capital cities and the considerable disadvantage of non-metropolitan areas. This has been reflected both in the broad-scale funding decisions of government and in the absence of an infrastructure element within most regional development policies — the Keating Labor government's Regional Development Program being the notable exception.

IMPLEMENTATION

Having appropriate policies in place is a fundamental step for facilitating regional development but implementation is equally important. The scale and funding of operations of regional development agencies in Australia is one area open to critical assessment. The 1996 survey of regional development bodies found that on average agencies had a budget of just $220 000 and employed 2.2 staff (Beer, 1997). How can such small organisations influence the economic future of regions covering thousands of square kilometres with populations in excess of 100 000? In addition, many practitioners reported that they were active in a large number of policy and program areas — effectively stretching their resources and limiting their impact in any one field. There was, of course, considerable variation, with Western Australia's Development Commissions comparatively well funded, while community-based organisations in Queensland and Tasmania operated on shoestring budgets. Moreover, many agencies suffered from insecurity of funding; that is, they were dependent on Commonwealth or State government funds that were on occasion tied to a one- or two-year funding cycle, with no certainty of renewal. This insecurity in funding sources and outcomes has contributed to the very high 'death' rates amongst regional development agencies in Australia (Beer, 1997).

The complexity of regional development in Australia also raises questions of effectiveness. All three tiers of government are involved in local or regional development in some shape or form, and in a number of instances there is the appearance of duplication of effort. Many regions have two, three, four or even more agencies claiming to represent the region and to be working for its future. Garlick (1996: 8) judged this situation harshly and drew attention to the questionable legitimacy of some of these bodies, arguing that

> there has been a plethora of agencies and groups, both inside and outside the region, trying in a variety of ways to come to grips with an array of potentially complex economic management issues. Apart from being generally unco-ordinated and undisciplined in their efforts, these groups have not always been true creatures of the regional community, being, more likely, creatures of some remotely determined institution.

The problems of overlap and duplication appear less acute in nations with different systems of government and political institutions. Europeans, for example, have developed the principle of subsidiarity — a philosophy that holds that the roles and responsibilities of government should be vested with the lowest tier of government able to perform that function (Roberts, 1997). In Australia, the converse appears to apply, with all parts of the federal system claiming, at various stages, pre-eminence in regional development. These claims, of course, carry their own contradictions: on occasion each tier of government finds it politically expedient to expect the other tiers to fund local initiatives or shoulder the burden of financing development agencies. It is notable also that Australian governments have not adopted the philosophy of 'partnership' in local development that seems common in parts of the world such as the USA (OECD, 1997a).

The complexity of regional development in Australia is not limited to the number of agencies claiming to represent a region. There is even more complexity in the programs and funding opportunities available to the agencies. Typically, an agency will perform its core functions and then seek to extend its impact by securing funds from federal or State government departments to undertake projects or deliver programs. The types of functions agencies will tender to perform include the delivery of education and training services, environmental programs, urban beautification, and the development of business incubators. One consequence is that regional development bodies end up undertaking the projects and programs they can be funded for, rather than the tasks that would best promote the growth of their region. Looked at another way, there are very high information costs within regional development, as the managers of agencies need to be familiar with the full gamut of government portfolios and programs that affect them, and be skilled in securing grant income. In addition, many agencies complain that funding guidelines are too strict and that no latitude is given to match the real needs of a region to funding opportunities (Beer, 1997). This issue was highlighted in the 1996 survey of regional development agencies and was a prominent concern at the Spencer Gulf Area Regional Forum (Beer, 1997; Spencer Gulf Area Regional Forum Steering Group, 1999).

Doubts over the effectiveness of regional development agencies in Australia have important consequences: they contribute to a climate in which governments at all levels continually question the merits or demerits of regional development activities. This in turn cuts short the life of some regional development agencies and contributes to a set of perceptions in which regional development measures are expected to fail. Unfortunately, these expectations can be self-fulfilling.

TRENDS IN REGIONAL DEVELOPMENT POLICY AND PRACTICE

All tiers of government in Australia are involved in local or regional development in some way. Policies and programs have evolved over time and continue to change in the face of new opportunities and constraints. In the mid-1980s local employment initiatives were seen to be at the forefront of regional development practice (Fagan, 1987). In the early 1990s a number of State governments (such as Western Australia and South Australia) established their regional development programs (Beer & Maude, 1997).

Many of the shifts in regional development policy are linked to broader crises within the political or economic system. This relationship between wider societal change and change within regional development is entirely consistent with regulation theory (Beer, 1998). Local employment initiatives were introduced as a program of the federal government when unemployment was at a level unprecedented within the postwar period. Similarly, the *Working Nation* employment programs and the Regional Development Program were regional policy responses to new challenges facing the federal government — in this instance, high levels of unemployment and an economy made moribund by the 'recession we had to have'. In 1996 the Howard government reinterpreted the crisis facing the economy, changing it from one of under-performance in global markets and economic growth to one of fiscal crisis and the need for responsible economic management. This view remains fundamental within federal policies, though tempered somewhat by the political crisis generated by voter backlash against the Coalition in the 1998 federal election and the strong showing of Pauline Hanson's One Nation.

An increased prominence for local or regional development is one of the practical outcomes we can 'read off' from the regulation perspective. In a globalised economy, small nations such as Australia will inevitably be confronted by greater social, economic and political challenges as new opportunities arise and as some parts of the economy — and some regions — suffer from increased competition. In turn, this will inevitably force governments to seek solutions to the problems of uneven spatial development.

Regional development in this country is currently in a state of flux and the insights offered by regulation theory would suggest it is likely to remain in this state for a considerable period. As discussed above, the federal government announced major initiatives in the 1999 budget, the South Australian government received the report of its Regional Development Taskforce in March 1999 and the Queensland government has reviewed its involvement in regional development. The Western Australian government is coming to the end of a major review of regional development in that State. The Carr Labor government in New South Wales has also substantially modified its approach to regional development. Importantly, many of the approaches and views being put forward at the end of the 1990s and the beginning of the 2000s are very different from those promoted just five years previously, but are not too dissimilar from those promoted 20 or 30 years ago. These changes clearly reflect the processes of 'institutional searching' that Goodwin and Painter (1996) discussed. There are a number of facets to the shifting face of regional development practice in Australia and three of the most prominent will be considered here. These are: the community dimension — a greater focus on the provision of services to rural or regional communities; the fiscal dimension — a greater recognition of the need for all the resources of government to address the needs of regions and, the program management dimension — the need to knock down the barriers between existing programs.

THE COMMUNITY DIMENSION: THE PROVISION OF SERVICES

Government statements and programs on regional development in the late 1990s placed a much more explicit emphasis on the provision of services to regional communities than they did five years previously. This new perspective was expressed in a number of ways. The Howard government renamed its Department of Transport and Regional Development as the Department of Transport and Regional Services after the 1998 election. At least three States — South Australia, Queensland and New South Wales — have an Office of Regional Communities, or its equivalent, within their administrative structure (South Australian Regional Development Taskforce, 1999: 161–63). These offices have a policy function and work to co-ordinate the better provision of services outside the capitals. One could suggest, perhaps somewhat cynically, that it is cheaper for governments to 'co-ordinate' services than to meet the real needs of these communities.

The provision of services does not feature prominently within the international literature on strategies to promote the development of regions, though the provision of appropriate infrastructure is considered crucial (OECD, 1997b). Its prominence within the policies of this nation reflects both Australia's geography — especially the remoteness and sparse population of some areas — and the impact of 15 years or more of economic rationalism that has stripped bare the services provided in many non-metropolitan localities. Governments that are loath to spend money at all are keen to draw attention to the sums they spend already in regional areas, albeit on basic social and physical infrastructure such as roads, primary schools, telecommunications and health facilities. The federal government has pursued this policy approach. Its formal statement to the Regional Forum conducted in Whyalla (SA) in July 1999 listed its service expenditures in the region (Verova, 1999). In addition, the Coalition government has consistently emphasised its contribution to rural and remote Australia through the supply of access to mobile phones, electronic banking services and health services. Services are important, but these programs lack a clearly articulated philosophy of how their provision or better co-ordination will generate sustainable growth within communities.

THE FISCAL DIMENSION: USING ALL THE RESOURCES OF GOVERNMENT

Governments are increasingly inclined to examine the impact of their own expenditures on the growth of the regions. There is a strong element of déjà vu in this trend, as it marks a return to the ideas of the 1970s when decentralisation and the growth of new cities was to be led by the public sector. South Australia's Regional Development Taskforce (1999) commented on the desirability of decentralising public sector employment, while the NSW Labor government announced in 1999 that 1400 public sector positions would be transferred out of Sydney to regional centres. In Western Australia, one goal for the review of regional development has been to provide the National Party leader, Hendy Cowan, who is also the Deputy Premier and Minister for Regional Development, with a sound basis for challenging the existing pattern of State government expenditures, which he considers too focused on metropolitan Perth.

THE PROGRAM MANAGEMENT DIMENSION: ACCOUNTABILITY AND REGIONAL NEEDS

The necessity of program management and accountability in government presents one of the greatest challenges to the development of regions. As discussed in an earlier section, the Commonwealth and State governments make substantial funding available for regional programs, but the resources are tied to the priorities they have identified and are often administered through tightly targeted guidelines. This is recognised as a major problem both by commentators and practitioners within regional development. The point was clearly articulated by the Spencer Gulf Regional Forum Steering Group (1999: 8), which argued that:

> The regions recognise that government resources are in short supply and that not all initiatives or needs can get public funding. They are therefore particularly concerned when they see the actions of governments resulting in overlap and duplication. In some instances they see services are being provided that they don't need, or don't need as much as some other priority. The regions are also concerned that central government funding — State also, but Commonwealth Government funding to a greater degree — is limited by a 'stove pipe' mentality that does not allow for any flexibility in funding projects across portfolios or in interpreting funding guidelines with a measure of flexibility, or what the region's would see as sense. The regions want funding to be made available for their needs and they don't want to be confronted by a myriad of small funding programs, each with complex and relatively expensive-to-administer guidelines. As importantly, they don't want funding to be limited to the priorities of Canberra or Adelaide-based decision makers.

Garlick (1996: 8) also noted the undesirability of 'maintaining the "stove pipes" of vertically designed and delivered services and programs'. This complaint was often heard by the South Australian Regional Development Taskforce, which suggested that existing Commonwealth and State programs be reviewed to make them more flexible while reducing the level of duplication.

Greater flexibility in funding guidelines and enhanced local control of how and where funds are spent, are features earnestly desired by local development practitioners, but they will be difficult to achieve under the Australian system of government. It is a desideratum that for many reasons is unlikely to be met. Perhaps the simplest solution would be to provide greater untied funds to local governments, especially in non-metropolitan areas. Communities would then have the opportunity to determine their own priorities and execute their expenditures against them. The more senior levels of government, however, are unlikely to increase the flow of untied funds. If the distribution of resources between the tiers of government remains unchanged, departments will find it difficult to give local communities control of resources while maintaining accountability. How could a department report to parliament on the expenditure of program funds earmarked for the development of information technology businesses if part of the program funding was used to develop a piggery or fund a road? How would departments present their accounts to the Auditor-General if a region decided that it wanted one fewer nurse for its local hospital but an additional teacher for its school? The challenges would be immense.

The history of urban and regional development in this country would also suggest that success in co-ordination across portfolios — let alone across levels of government — is unlikely. A similar co-ordination task was attempted by the Department of Urban and Regional Development under the Whitlam government. As Painter (1984) showed, this venture was beset by many intractable problems that arose out of the very heart of the processes of public sector administration. On the other hand, the 'whole of government approach' adopted by the Howard government suggests a degree of sympathy with the views of the region. It is questionable, however, whether the co-ordination being attempted by the Coalition can move beyond committees to directly affect how and where resources are directed.

CONCLUSION

This chapter has shown that regional development policy and practice in Australia is a complex and at times confusing field of endeavour. There is no one pattern of local or regional development policy in this country, as there are substantial variations between the States and Territories as well as considerable variation within each jurisdiction. Mal Logan (1978: 23) once commented that 'regionalism in Australia has suffered from the strength of State governments on one hand and the weakness of local government on the other'. Logan (1978) was referring specifically to the tendency of State governments to centralise functions, but both State and federal governments have struggled to deal with the character of something as disparate and diffuse as regional development. They recognise that local communities are best placed to identify their own opportunities for growth, but they strive to maintain control of the development process. Inevitably this stifles the very initiative they seek to foster.

Local and regional development in Australia has progressed through several phases of development. The policy instruments now being applied have a decidedly post-Fordist flavour, with a greater emphasis on assisting small businesses, creating industry clusters and generating an entrepreneurial culture. Intriguingly, the contemporary regional development landscape also contains the shadows of policies from 20 or 30 years ago in moves to decentralise public sector employment and 'co-ordinate' across portfolios. There have been cycles of engagement, withdrawal and re-engagement with regional development. For most of the last 20 years economic rationalist philosophies have dominated in government, especially at the federal level. Governments have been inclined to believe that the most appropriate 'institutional fix' to the problems of the economy has been the drawing back of government interventions and the promotion of market solutions. They have only reviewed this position when confronted by a new crisis — political or economic. The federal government in particular has only re-entered the regional development arena when forced to do so by economic circumstances that threaten its defeat. Similarly, the establishment of reviews of regional development in Queensland, South Australia and Western Australia is an indicator of structural crises within their political and economic systems. Regulation theory would lead us to expect that regional development will remain prominent politically well into the 21st century.

Local and regional development in Australia seems destined for more change and more turmoil as governments continually re-evaluate their policies and commitment to this field of endeavour. The history of regional development in Australia suggests that the federal government, and to a lesser extent the State governments, are incapable of developing a set of long-term solutions to the problems of our regions. New policies and new solutions are being promulgated continually and policies that were effective are cast aside, along with those that were ineffective. Already there is evidence that governments are returning to some of the policies that were tried 20 or 30 years ago. Stilwell (1993: 148) has suggested there are four main policy instruments available for conventional regional policy: regional expenditure policy, regionally differentiated price policies, controls on regional development, and mobility. The second of these is not available in Australia because of Constitutional constraints, and while 'local' approaches to regional development would add somewhat to Stilwell's list, it is clear that there are limited options available to policy makers.

What approach then should Australian governments adopt? The reality is that there are no 'silver bullets' or fool-proof solutions in regional development, but much of the answer lies in building upon the strengths already evident in the existing structure for regional development. First, central governments must recognise the importance of existing regional development agencies and seek to work in partnership with them. Second, there is a need to increase the level of resources available to regional development agencies. Well-funded agencies are more stable and can achieve far more than organisations forced to operate on limited budgets. Third, the State and federal governments need to make modest infrastructure funding available to regional development agencies to allow them to address some of the shortages. Fourth, both levels of government need to develop and implement infrastructure plans that ensure funding goes to long-term priorities, rather than short-term bottlenecks. Public or private funding would then need to be found to implement these plans. Fifth, additional resources need to be devoted to supporting small and medium-sized enterprises. A strong case could be made for devolving much of the federal government's role in this area to local governments and regional development agencies. Sixth, regional development could be advanced and national productivity boosted through greater resources for the development of industry clusters and networking between businesses. Seventh, business formation needs to be encouraged by expanding the number of business incubators and increasing public awareness of their role. Few business incubators operate in Australia when compared with economies such as the USA and the United Kingdom. Eighth, some decentralisation of government functions is appropriate. Too often, government services are only based in the capital cities when they could just as easily be provided in one or more non-metropolitan centres. Ninth, there is a need to further develop strategies that link Australia's regions to global markets. Strategies can include both assisting local firms to export (Instate, 1994) and encouraging foreign direct investment (OECD, 1997b). The Howard government supports some locally delivered measures (for example Trade Start–Export Access), but a far greater effort is needed. Tenth, adequate resources need to be devoted to education and labour market training. This step is fundamental to ensuring that Australia's workforce, in all regions, has the skills and competencies to be globally competitive. Overall, the challenge is for governments to make a long-term commitment to these strategies and provide adequate resources to implement them in full.

NOTES

1 Local economic development and regional economic development are used interchangeably throughout this paper. While public sector policies explicitly distinguish between the two, often there is very little difference in the sorts of activities pursued under the two banners.

2 In Australia private sector support for regional development organisations is generally very limited.

3 See, for example, the set of arrangements set up to cover Albury–Wodonga.

REFERENCES

Aglietta M (1979) *A Theory of Capitalist Regulation*, New Left Books, London.

Amin A (1994) *Post Fordism, A Reader*, Blackwell, Oxford.

Anderson J & McDonald I (1999) *Regional Australia: Meeting the Challenges*, AGPS, Canberra.

Beer A (1997) 'The Australian model of regional development', in the *Proceedings of the Regional Co-operation and Development Forum*, Convened by the ALGA and Greening Australia, ALGA, Canberra, pp 24–38.

Beer A (1998) 'Economic rationalism and the decline of local economic development in Australia', *Local Economy*, 13(2), pp 52–64.

Beer A. & Maude A (1997) *Effectiveness of State Frameworks for Local Economic Development*, Local Government Association of South Australia, Adelaide.

Brown R (1996) 'Industry clusters in the Australian context', Paper presented to the Regional Science Association Conference, 22–26 September, Canberra.

Cooke P, Uranga MG & Etxebarria G (1998) 'Regional systems of innovation: An evolutionary perspective', *Environment and Planning, A*, 39(9), pp 1563–84.

Davis R & Stimson R (1998) 'Disillusionment and disenchantment at the fringe: Explaining the geography of the One Nation Party vote at the Queensland election', Paper presented to the Australian and New Zealand Regional Science Association International, Conference, Tanunda, 21–23 September.

Deloitte Touche Tohmatsu (1995) *Review of the Office of Labour Market Adjustment, Regional and Enterprise Case Studies*, DEET, Canberra.

Department of Employment Education and Training (1995a) *Annual Report 1994–95*, AGPS, Canberra.

Department of Employment, Education and Training (1995b) *Regional Employment 1995–96, Strategies for Jobs Growth Developed by Area Consultative Committees*, DEET, Canberra.

Department of Housing and Regional Development (1994) *Guidelines for the Regional Development Programme*, DHRD, Canberra.

Eisinger P (1995) 'State economic development in the 1990s: Politics and policy learning', *Economic Development Quarterly*, 9(2), pp 146–58.

Epps R (1999) 'Survival of the fitter? New firms and the competitive advantage imperative: The scenario in two inland NSW regional centres', unpublished PhD thesis, University of New England, Armidale.

Fagan B (1987) 'Local employment initiatives: Long term strategy for localities or flavour of the month?', *Australian Geographer*, 8(1), pp 51–6.

Forth G (1996) 'Redrawing the map of regional Australia: The Commonwealth's Regional Development Program', *Australasian Journal of Regional Studies*, 2(1), pp 75–86.

Garlick S (1996) 'The incongruity of place and institution in spatial economic development, some early thoughts', Paper presented to the Australian and New Zealand Regional Science Association International Conference, 23–25 September, Canberra.

Goodwin M & Painter J (1996) 'Local governance, the crisis of Fordism and the changing geographies of regulation', *Transactions of the Institute of British Geographers*, NS 21, pp 635–48.

Hall T & Hubbard P (1996) 'The entrepreneurial city: New urban politics, new urban geographies?', *Progress in Human Geography*, 20(2), pp 153–74.

Harris CP (1989) 'Local government and regional planning', in Higgins B & Zagorski K (eds) *Australian Regional Developments*, AGPS, Canberra, pp 104–22.

Harvey D (1989) 'From managerialism to entrepreneurialism: The transformation of urban governance in late capitalism', *Geografiska Annaler*, 71 B, pp 3–17.

Haughton G, Peck JA & Strange I (1997) 'Turf wars: the battle for control of English local economic development', *Local Government Studies*, 23(1), pp 88–106.

Hay C (1995) Re-stating the problem of regulation and re-regulating the local state, *Economy and Society*, 24(3), pp 387–407.

Huggonier B (1999) 'Regional development tendencies in OECD countries', Keynote Presentation to the Regional Summit, Canberra, October, *www.dot.gov.au/regional/summit/keynote/hugonnier_paper.htm*.

Industry Commission (1993) *Impediments to Regional Industry Adjustment*, Report No. 35, Volume 1, AGPS, Canberra.

Industry Commission (1996) *State, Territory and Local Government Assistance to Industry*, AGPS, Canberra.

Instate Pty Ltd (1994) 'A study of a regional export extension service for the cities of Enfield, Hindmarsh–Woodville and Port Adelaide', unpublished.

Isserman A (1994) 'State economic development policy and practice in the United States: A survey article', *International Regional Science Review*, 1 & 2, pp 49–100.

Jessop B (1995) 'The regulation approach, governance and post-Fordism: alternative perspectives on economic and political change?', *Economy and Society*, 24(3), pp 307–33.

Keating P (1994) *Working Nation: The White Paper on Employment Growth*, AGPS, Canberra.

Logan M (1978) 'Regional Policy', in Scott, P. (ed) *Australian Cities and Public Policy*, Georgian House, Melbourne, pp 23–39.

Lovering J (1995) 'Creating discourses rather than jobs: the crisis in the cities and the transition fantasies of intellectuals and policy makers', in Healey P, Cameron S, Davoudi S, Graham S & Mandani-Pour A (eds), *Managing Cities: the New Urban Context*, John Wiley & Sons, London, pp 109–26.

Maude A & Beer A (forthcoming) 'Apples and oranges: A comparison of the strengths and weaknesses of regional development agencies in two Australian states', *Town Planning Review*.

McKinsey & Company (1994) *Lead Local Compete Global, Unlocking the Growth Potential of Australia's Regions*, McKinsey & Co., Sydney.

McKinsey & Company (1996) 'Supporting regional leadership: Unfinished business', unpublished report to the Department of Transport and Regional Development, August.

McLeod G (1997) 'Globalizing Parisian thought-waves, recent advances in the study of social regulation politics, discourse and space', *Progress in Human Geography*, 21(4), pp 530–54.

National Committee of Audit (1996) *Report to the Commonwealth Government*, AGPS, Canberra.

Organisation for Economic Cooperation and Development (OECD) (1997a) *Partnership in the United States*, OECD Reviews of Rural Policy, OECD, Paris.

Organisation for Economic Cooperation and Development (1997b) *Trends in Regional Policies in OECD Countries*, June 1993–June 1996, OECD, Paris.

Painter M (1984) 'Urban government, urban politics and the fabrication of urban issues', in Halligan J & Paris C (eds) *Australian Urban Politics*, Longman Cheshire, Melbourne, pp 31–44.

Peck J & Tickell A (1992) 'Local social modes of regulation? Regulation theory, Thatcherism and uneven development', *Geoforum*, 23:3, pp 347–63.

Peck J & Tickell A (1995) 'Jungle law breaks out: neo-liberalism and global–local disorder', *Area*, 26(4), pp 317–26.

Roberts P (1997) 'Strategies for the stateless nation: Sustainable policies for the regions of Europe', *Regional Studies*, 31(9), pp 875–83.

Self P (1990) 'The challenge of regional development', *Australian Planner*, 28, pp 18–22.

South Australian Regional Development Taskforce (1999) *Report*, State Government of South Australia, Adelaide.

Spencer Gulf Area Regional Forum Steering Group (1999) 'Regional future brief', Paper prepared for the Spencer Gulf Area Regional Forum, 22–23 July, Whyalla.

Stilwell FJB (1974) *Australian Urban and Regional Development*, Australian and New Zealand Book Company, Sydney.

Stilwell FJB (1993) *Reshaping Australia*, Pluto Press, Sydney.

Taskforce on Regional Development (1993) *Developing Australia: A Regional Perspective* (Kelty Report), Vols 1–3, AGPS, Canberra.

Taylor M & Garlick S (1989) 'Commonwealth government involvement in regional development in the 1980s: a local approach', in Higgins B and Zagorski K (eds) *Australian Regional Developments*, AGPS, Canberra, pp 79–103.

Teitz M (1994) 'Changes in economic development theory and practice', *International Regional Science Review*, 16(1), pp 101–6.

Tickell A & Peck J (1995) 'Social regulation after Fordism: regulation theory, neo-liberalism and the global–local nexus', *Economy and Society*, 24(3), pp 357–86.

Turok I (1989) 'Evaluation and understanding in local economic policy', *Urban Studies*, 26, 587–606.

Verova S (1999) 'The Commonwealth government's response to the regional future's brief', Paper presented to the Spencer Gulf Area Regional Forum, 22–23 July, Whyalla.

Vipond J (1989) 'Australian experiments with regional policies', in Higgins B & Zagorski K (eds) *Australian Regional Developments*, AGPS, Canberra, pp 65–78.

Zagorski K (1989) 'Introduction: Australian regional problems, policy and research', in Higgins B & Zagorski K (eds) *Australian Regional Developments*, AGPS, Canberra, pp ix–xi.

11
THE CHALLENGES FOR LOCAL GOVERNMENT IN THE 21ST CENTURY

MAURICE DALY

Ensuring that local government is participatory, efficient and viable remains one of the great challenges in rural and regional Australia. It is the most pervasive form of government in Australia, and its functions and responsibilities mean it is close to peoples' day-to-day lives — particularly when State, Territory and national houses of parliament are geographically distant. Yet despite this crucial role, local government in Australia — and especially in rural and regional Australia — is deeply troubled. Through the 20th century, the number of local governments across the nation shrank. In 1910 there were 1067 local governments nationwide; by 1991 this had been reduced to 826, and in mid-1999 there were 627. But as the number of councils declined, their responsibilities grew. State and Territory governments passed on to local governments an ever widening array of duties, often without commensurate financial assistance.

These issues are central to wider debates on the economic and social future of rural and regional Australia. Failures and perceived failures by local governments to deliver services and amenities efficiently and equitably can fuel alienation and disquiet about government generally. On the other hand, local government is uniquely placed to act as a catalyst for networking communities with broader regional, national and international organisations and structures. This chapter considers the financial and structural issues that either facilitate or constrain these alternatives.

THE CONTEXT

Although frequently cited as the third tier of government, local government is not recognised in the Australian Constitution. In every State, the role of local government is somewhat uncomfortable. Its powers are derived from the State, and the execution of those powers is monitored by the State. The various State laws that determine local government powers are structured so that councils can only undertake new activities if they are given specific powers to do so. Unless an activity is expressly given to local government under the provisions of the State law, councils are precluded from undertaking that activity (Duncan, 1995).

This high level of dependency hobbles the ability of local government to deal with the challenges arising from rapid change in the industrial base of society (Binning, Young & Cripps, 1999). Only in Queensland does legislation give local government powers as broad as those of the State; but even there the State retains the power to override local government laws and actions. These limitations are important because local government represents the institutional face of government that is closest to the grass roots of society. It is perceived by many to have the potential to reflect and affect the true state of the wellbeing and amenity of local communities in a way that other institutional layers cannot.

Moreover, local government is the only organisation at the local level that potentially represents the whole community. In every community there are a range of organisations: service groups (such as Lions or Rotary), church groups, sporting organisations, youth or aged groups, and special interest groups (concerned with a range of issues from local industries through to heritage and conservation). The council is the natural link between these disparate forces. It is also usually the only organisation with a statutory base, and so has the capacity to present and argue community concerns with the outside world, especially with the State or Commonwealth government. Where issues need a regional, rather than a local voice, councils are usually the natural agents to work together to develop a coherent view on regional issues.

Councils might then be seen as the natural representatives of local communities. They can link communities to the higher levels of government in developing responses to social and economic problems. Yet in practice this does not always happen. There are many reasons why councils have not been as effective a force for local communities as might be expected. One concerns the resource base in which they have to work. Caught between an ever increasing set of demands by their State government masters and their limited abilities to increase revenue, local government is often too straitened by demands and expectations. It becomes an inadequate vehicle for addressing issues that arise from declining industrial bases, high unemployment and falling incomes, infrastructure inadequacies, and the challenges arising from new technologies. It is clear that the expectations that local communities have of their councils is greater in the poorer, smaller and more remote places, and in districts that have suffered from the negative consequences of globalisation.

Another problem results from the distribution of councils across the States. The 41 per cent decline in the number of councils between 1910 and 1999 is not representative of rational and continual reform over time, but of episodic and often highly political forced changes to the organisation of local government. There is also the problem that some council areas have never been restructured, and the rationale for their boundaries lies buried in the 19th or early 20th century. There is a huge level of inertia and incoherence in the local government system. Local government boundaries are often only poorly related to physical environmental systems (such as catchments) and regional economic systems. They are also often too small in area and population to manage and deliver services effectively. Problems of geographical incoherence are exacerbated by problems of functional incoherence.

Local government has a governance role, an advocacy role, a service delivery role, a planning and community development role, and a regulatory role. In many ways local government responsibilities are based on a rag-bag of functions that State and Territory governments generally find too local, or too detailed to bother with. This diversity of functions, however, does not amount to a critical mass. Compared to other Western countries, Australia's local governments' range of functions is narrow and disjointed. Because the focus is so local, and the functions so restricted, councils are prey to the uneven pressures that result from this fundamental basis: the episodic concerns that citizens raise when change affects my home, my street, my environment. Such concerns can be so self-consuming that it breeds an incapacity to respond to changes and challenges that beset provincial and rural centres arising from the broader economic or political domains. Hence, the geographical and functional incoherence of local government breeds a preoccupation with localism as the scale of intervention for issues that may derive, or are best responded to, at larger scales.

Although councils perform very well in some places in directing or assisting improvements in opportunities for business and workers, and in boosting quality of life features, many suffer from inadequate policy formulations. Policy inadequacies sometimes relate to the dominance of long-standing councillors in a remarkably large number of non-metropolitan councils. These elders of the local government scene often struggle to come to grips with the shifting demands placed on their councils in view of social, cultural and economic change. At the other extreme, policy development is often contorted where there is a high turnover of councillors and high level staff (as witnessed in many councils in the 1990s). The combination of inexperience alongside a raft of often single issue concerns has led to quirky and unstable policy environments in some areas.

Local government in Australia is, therefore, caught between the supervisory pressures of the State and the highly variable pressures that surface in individual localities. As a result local government has often become reactive, rather than pro-active. Many councils face a deterioration of their economic bases, with many rural industries experiencing low prices and difficult market conditions (see Chapter 3). Many small and medium towns suffer from this malaise of once mighty rural industries, on the one hand, and the improved accessibility of large centres, on the other. Although there are notable exceptions, a key response by local government has been to emphasise and protect its power. Local government could play a much more constructive role, and could act through a series of vehicles to promote regional development in the face of the many challenges explored in this book. To do this there is a need to rethink the fundamental role and purpose of local government, and what is needed for it to become a more effective force in the next decade. Before considering the potential of local government, it is necessary to understand the functions performed by this level of government in Australia.

WHAT LOCAL GOVERNMENT DOES

Before addressing the needs and potential of local government in the early years of the 21st century it is useful to consider the tasks that it now handles. Listing the primary functions handled by most councils and shires demonstrates their general emphasis on maintenance and control, and the persistent pressure of higher authorities:

- local road construction and maintenance (within State, Territory and federal road strategies);

- building controls (under State guidelines);

- general health surveillance (but not health provision, except for baby health services);

- fire control and emergency services (usually subject to a higher State or regional organising authority);

- aerodromes (subject to Civil Aviation Safety Authority and other regulations);

- heritage and environmental management;

- dog and animal control;

- water and sewerage provision (subject to State specifications);

- town planning (usually subject to State planning provisions); and

- noxious weed control (in line with State programs).

In terms of expenditure, the construction and maintenance of roads and bridges dominate the spending patterns of local governments nationwide (Table 11.1). Total local government outlays in 1997–98 were $9.717 billion, with $2.4 billion, or 24.7 per cent spent on transport and communications. Local government road responsibilities, however, are hemmed in between competing road funding activities of State/Territory and Commonwealth governments. Major regional and State roads fall under the control of senior tiers of government. These governments also control the rail systems, meaning that the main arteries of land transport — principal factors in the economic fabric — are outside the control of the local government system. This separation of responsibilities can militate against streamlined transport planning, including the social and environmental impacts of transport infrastructure. For example, rationalisation of rail systems, the growth of road-trains, and other factors increasing the size and extent of long-distance transport have impacted on councils. The desire of hauliers to take short-cuts and avoid regulatory controls have pushed up the levels of heavy traffic on local roads and bridges, adding to the financial burden of councils.

TABLE 11.1
LOCAL GOVERNMENT OUTLAYS BY PURPOSE, 1997–98 ($ MILLION)

Expenditure categories	NSW	Vic	Qld	SA	WA	Tas	NT	Total
General public services	305	217	347	157	165	52	142	1386
Public order & safety	154	31	18	19	33	1	2	259
Education, health & welfare	281	424	69	30	75	19	10	907
Housing & community amenities	886	357	581	129	60	20	29	2063
Recreation & culture	654	437	353	119	245	47	21	1877
Transport & communications	654	477	704	161	317	76	14	2403
Other	60	163	330	75	53	24	118	824
TOTAL	2994	2107	2404	690	948	239	335	9717

SOURCE ABS, 1999: Table 22. (Numbers may not add up due to rounding.)

The categories in Table 11.1 provide broad indicative measures only. The second largest functional area of local government expenditure nationwide is 'housing and community services' (21.2 per cent) but this includes an enormous range of activities, including aged and youth services, libraries, cemeteries, cultural activities, recreational facilities, dog and animal control, street lighting, street and gutter cleaning, stormwater drainage and flood mitigation.

In per capita terms there is considerable variation between the States and the Northern Territory in the distribution of expenditure across the broad categories of Table 11.1. The highest levels of expenditure on transport and communications occur in Queensland, WA and Tasmania ($206, $175 and $161, respectively). Queensland's expenditure in this area is almost triple that of the Northern Territory (Table 11.2). This reflects not so much a greater willingness by Queensland local governments to spend monies for road construction and maintenance, but a different balance of responsibilities between these jurisdictions in that there tends to be relatively few defined 'local roads' in the Northern Territory (Pritchard, 1993). A similar degree of variation exists with respect to housing and community services spending, with Queensland and the Northern Territory having per capita expenditure levels at least five times greater than the lowest State expenditure on these items, Western Australia. Recreation and culture consume most money per capita in Western Australia and the Northern Territory, and the smallest outlays in Victoria and South Australia. Levels of per capita spending on education, health and welfare are under 6 per cent of total outlays in most States, but reach 14 per cent of total spending in Victoria. Per capita debt levels are highest in Queensland and Western Australia, but the variance between States is not very high.

TABLE 11.2
LOCAL GOVERNMENT OUTLAYS PER CAPITA BY PURPOSE, 1997–98 ($)

Expenditure category	NSW	Vic	Qld	SA	WA	Tas	NT	National average
General public services	48	47	101	106	91	110	754	76
Public order	24	7	5	13	18	2	11	14
Education, health & welfare	45	92	20	20	41	40	53	50
Housing & community	141	77	170	87	33	42	154	113
Recreation & culture	104	94	103	80	135	99	112	103
Transport & communications	104	103	206	108	175	161	74	131
Other	10	35	96	51	29	51	26	45
TOTAL	475	455	702	457	523	506	1779	531

SOURCE National Office of Local Government, 1999. (Numbers may not add up due to rounding.)

The expenditure categories in Table 11.2 mask the wide variety of activities that most councils undertake. It is this very variety that often becomes an obstacle to sound, coherent, progressive regional development. Non-metropolitan councils are frequently so busy with 'housekeeping' matters that they have little time or inclination to notice when the 'house' itself is in need of drastic overhaul. This does not mean that councils themselves are unaware or dismissive of the real problems that face their domains. They often utter loud cries of dismay at the cruel ignorance of policy makers in the cities to the plight of local communities. They also draw attention to the localised implications of the immensely powerful forces of globalisation, against which there seem to be few local defences available. Many councils rail at the enemies without, but are able to provide few solutions to the problems those forces create.

THE CAPACITY OF LOCAL GOVERNMENT TO HELP LOCAL COMMUNITIES

There is a broad range of options available to local governments faced with the challenge of co-operating with, and leading, local communities in the struggle to improve conditions during difficult times. Size and resources affect the capacity of local governments to act, ranging from councils with limited capabilities to those with a strong capability to respond to needs. Generally, non-metropolitan councils with limited capabilities are those with small urban bases, low income generating industries, severe environmental challenges, and low population densities. Councils with high capacity levels are frequently centred around large towns and have populations above 25 000 people. These areas often have stronger economic bases, relatively dense population clusters, less challenging natural environments, accessibility to major provincial cities or State capitals, and well developed infrastructure.

There are a number of essential activities in the promotion of local community development, which even councils with a low capacity and resource base need to consider. Councils can establish reliable information systems about their communities, and then accurately argue for community needs. They can work on their community understanding and interactions to co-ordinate development and create plans for the area. They can identify the basic resources that the community needs, and try to make them available. They can work to enhance both the physical and human resource base. Local governments with better capacity can take all of these things further. They can create development strategies that harmonise with State and federal systems, and can influence the direction of change in those systems. Progress can be monitored through the introduction of benchmarks and best practices. Community standards can be identified, and actions positioned to achieve them. The many operating fronts of local government can be co-ordinated into a powerful force for creating a dynamic of development.

The reality is, however, that local government often finds itself in conflict with the directions of State and federal policies. Macro-economic policies of the federal government have uneven effects across and within States and Territories. Councils are locally grounded agents that are well positioned to review these effects and attempt to get redress for negative outcomes. Redeployment of State agencies, or the failure to build vital infrastructure, are common problems that councils have to face. In these, and in many other situations, councils stand on the front-line of debates on the implications of State, Territory and Commonwealth government policies, and are often the torch-bearers in attempts to redress negativities. No matter how great or small the capacity of council, there is always scope to inform and educate State and Commonwealth authorities on local impacts and needs. Councils become, both formally and informally, the chief paths for local advocacy. The council making appropriate structural adjustments can strengthen the fabric of local communities. Community action by groups beyond the council can be stimulated by council incentives.

Councils with higher capacity levels can do more. They can establish information flows that map the changing place of their communities within broader regional economic and social systems, positioning them to reap benefits from growth and investment impulses in the general economy. Most councils hold potentially rich stocks of information, although they struggle to turn such stocks into strategic weapons. Councils with secure resource bases, and therefore better potential institutional capacity, can be well placed to improve amenity through development. Such councils can establish systems of conflict resolution, which strengthen community actions at the local level, and smooth the points of intersection with external agencies.

Despite the State constrictions on local governments' freedom to act, there are many ways in which councils can help local groups seeking to achieve local goals. Discretionary spending allows councils to determine priorities in infrastructure creation. The expertise of council staff is often a valuable resource, especially in areas like the enhancement of social support systems, the development of environmental management programs, or the facilitation and marketing of local business. Council equipment, expertise and networks may provide the hardware for some development efforts. Council offices, halls, and recreational areas may assist local groups with limited resources. There is also scope for councils to spice their standard operations (such as planning and development controls) with the use of incentives and market instruments to assist the achievement of community objectives. By using their links to other levels of government, councils have the potential to mobilise the intentions of community groups on a range of issues (Binning & Young, 1997).

Councils are required to be accountable, they have a clear statutory base, and have professional financial administrations. As local government operations are audited, they have to follow standard processes in managing assets. Through possessing these attributes, councils can provide professional assistance and legitimacy to local groups. There are various difficulties facing organisations such as catchment management committees, landcare groups, local tourist promotion bodies, historic and heritage societies, and planning and preservation groups. There are issues of public and private liability to face. There are questions surrounding the capabilities of these groups to apply for State or Commonwealth grants. They have to develop the capacity to report in particular ways, and demonstrate their accountability. They may wish to raise and manage funds to support their work, and then face the problems of their jurisdiction in such matters. Councils may well provide the umbrella under which local groups can pursue legitimate local needs.

Where local action is spread across several groups chasing their own goals, councils have the scope to link those goals into a clear vision and assist in creating an operating strategy. In these, and other ways, councils can create consensus across communities. Councils can also be the source of new ideas and concepts. Councils can raise public awareness through education and promotion programs. When properly targeted, councils can induce communities to provide innovative responses to challenges. They can raise awareness of how private actions and operations can be managed to produce collective goods. They can illustrate the ways in which unco-ordinated individual elements within communities can interact with each other to produce negative outcomes for the whole community. They can lead the way in putting in place management practices that ameliorate such negative externalities.

The range of data that councils collect in their normal operations may be an invaluable resort for community groups. Some council data have commercial value, and may become a source of funds for community development. In many areas (from major infrastructure developments through to social policy shifts and on to environmental requirements) councils are the sole recipients of State or Commonwealth government information. They thus become the conduit for informing their communities of, and for developing responses to, the local impacts of major policy initiatives. Councils also have the opportunity to improve the data resources of State and Commonwealth agencies by creating two way flows of information, thus linking local communities into broader institutional settings more effectively.

The opaqueness of, and the lack of connectivity with, State and Commonwealth agencies often frustrate local community development. The procedures of State and Commonwealth bodies are often bureaucratic and complex. The co-ordination of local activities with regional energies is often poorly managed. The centrality of, and at times arcane approval practices associated with, State and Commonwealth granting systems is a further obstacle for local groups. When support is won from a funding agency, it is frequently short term and conditional. Objectives of programs designated at central levels can be poorly targeted in relation to local needs. Local community groups often lack the time or expertise to jump through State or Commonwealth government hoops. Local community groups can be discouraged easily, and because there is never any certainty about being successful in obtaining funds, many community groups give up the struggle. In the face of such difficulties, local government often has the capacity to assist community groups through the maze of obstacles they sense are in the way of achieving resource help.

Another challenge for community groups is the almost standard practice of State and Commonwealth governments to resort to legislative means of defining standards, processes and frameworks that are meant to solve community problems. The result is an increasing set of statutory agencies that prescribe how communities can or should act. Frequently the tasks of implementing or policing the legislation is passed on to local government, often with no enabling resources. Councils challenged with these tasks usually have to work through and with local community groups.

Institutional complexity is thus increased. Because the emphasis of State and Commonwealth agencies is often related to input management and process, there can be a poor focus on local outcomes. By their very nature, the legislative–agency approaches of State and Commonwealth governments may not be appropriate for all regions. In some cases they might not be appropriate for any! This can create alienation and resentment at the local level, produce counter-productive outcomes, or outcomes that do not effectively mesh local concerns with regional strategy goals. In such an environment local government stands as the most effective force in confronting and managing the interface between the local and the external.

Amidst the greatly increased complexity of institutional arrangements in the 1990s, State and Commonwealth governments resorted to managerial buzz-words to explain their purposes. Performance indicators, best practice and benchmarking invaded the territory of local government. They influenced the ways in which objectives were defined, and inevitably fed back into how the activities of non-government, community groups were considered and appraised. In fact local governments have been slow to adapt to the new management environment. Nonetheless, all of this has influenced and constricted the way that community groups have been forced to operate, and the way councils and community groups can cooperate.

LIMITING FACTORS TO LOCAL GOVERNMENT'S ROLE IN RESPONDING TO COMMUNITY CHALLENGES

There are as many instances of councils not fulfilling the kinds of roles described in the previous section as there are success stories. There are many reasons for this. One concerns the relationship between the size of councils, their locations in relation to resource distributions, their human resource bases, and their capacity to change to meet the new realities of the 21st century.

Non-metropolitan councils frequently have populations and resource bases that are too small for them to respond adequately and to initiate change in the highly integrated and broadly competitive environment of contemporary Australia. Globalisation is notably disparate in how it spreads its benefits across space (see Lee & Wills, 1997). Unevenness of opportunities and outcomes is the rule, and change is so rapid and strong in its impacts that great uncertainty is created. In this context the relationships of size and functionality are complex, and broad generalisations on what determines economic and social success are difficult to reach (see the discussion of 'institutional searching' in Chapter 10). Nevertheless, if local government were to be an effective agent for managing the challenges that face non-metropolitan communities across Australia, it might be expected that there would be some rational and discernible relationship between their territorial size and their population bases. The nature of this relationship is a major determinant of what the challenges are, and the resources that would be needed to address them.

Australia is such a large and thinly populated country that a large number of sparsely populated local government areas must be expected. In the interior and parts of the north and west, councils have small populations and cover large territories: low population densities and accessibility constraints imply and suggest extended local government areas. The average population of all local governments across the nation is 25 931. New South Wales and Victoria have average sizes substantially above that, whilst local governments in the other four States and the Northern Territory range between 12 000 and 20 000. The Northern Territory averages only 2828 (Table 11.3). Excluding metropolitan councils from the group reduces the average size substantially across all States, but most significantly in New South Wales, Western Australia, and South Australia (Table 11.4).

States with large areas would be expected to have a high proportion of extensive local government areas with small populations. In this context small is a relative term. In the more densely populated States of NSW and Victoria, council populations below 10 000 might be considered small. In the States with fewer people, councils with populations below 5000 might be regarded as small. In Western Australia, the largest State by area, the biggest local government covers 378 533 square kilometres, and the smallest is just two square kilometres. The population densities in Western Australia range from a peak of 1808 people per square kilometre to 0.03 per square kilometre. The average population of non-metropolitan local governments in Western Australia is only 5604. Underscoring the State variations in local government, the second largest State by area, Queensland, has a considerably higher average population of non-metropolitan councils (17 866). This derives from the lower level of urban primacy in that State. In the smaller, but more populous New South Wales, the average is 11 365. Thus, the relationship between population and territory is not simple.

TABLE 11.3
AVERAGE POPULATION SIZE OF LOCAL GOVERNMENTS BY STATE AND TERRITORY, 1999

State/Territory	No. of councils	Average population size
NSW	177	34 117
Victoria	77	56 799
Queensland *	124	23 894
Western Australia	141	12 242
South Australia *	74	19 296
Tasmania	28	16 416
Northern Territory *	69	2 828
Australia	690	25 931

* These jurisdictions have each separately identified Aboriginal community local governments: 25 in Queensland and 38 in Northern Territory are included in these totals; 42 in South Australia are not.
SOURCE Information Australia, 1999.

TABLE 11.4
AVERAGE POPULATION SIZE OF NON-METROPOLITAN COUNCILS BY STATE AND TERRITORY, 1999

State/Territory	No. of non-metro. councils	Average population size
NSW	132	11 365
Victoria	51	26 492
Queensland *	114	17 866
Western Australia	104	5 604
South Australia *	61	6 629
Tasmania	23	11 918
Northern Territory *	68	1 434

* As for Table 11.3.
SOURCE Information Australia, 1999.

Non-metropolitan councils that are small in population terms generally struggle to generate sufficient income to sustain and protect the livelihoods and amenity of their communities. This relates to a number of factors. One factor curtailing the effective workings of small local government areas is the emphasis on territoriality as against functionality. As noted earlier, there is a lack of functional coherence of local government areas in many places. Boundaries often date back to the 19th century. Although there were numerous amalgamations in the 20th century, they were simple agglomerations of existing councils, often with little regard to questions of resources and efficiencies. Generally the shape of the new units has reflected their historical origins. The large-scale amalgamations in Victoria in the 1990s are the major exception to these observations, where in one fell swoop the number of councils was reduced from 210 to 78 (Evatt Foundation, 1996: 189–90).

The problem with historical boundaries is that they often do not accord with the opportunities and challenges presented by contemporary economic change and current environmental management concerns. They are based on transport and commercial systems related to an earlier era, and have little connection with the drivers of economic, environmental and social change at the beginning of the 21st century. Over a long period, wealth in rural areas was based on extensive agriculture and mining. Local government areas reflected such bases. Commodity price falls and the growth of alternative products in rural areas have generated challenges to the geographical logic of these units. Intensive agriculture, such as vineyard development, has grown. New crops (often designed specifically to suit particular markets) have called for new marketing associations and techniques. Delivery systems, and speed of delivery imperatives, have changed. The significance of using, or developing, technologies has changed. The ability to harness, or relate to, the opportunities provided by communication technology and the Internet has become important. The need to seize the advantages that new communications technologies offer for the delivery of vital services (tele-medicine, distance education etc.) is now more pressing.

One particular situation where the shape and size of local government areas provide major impediments relates to the so-called 'doughnut councils'. These are generally rural councils that surround large provincial cities, although in Western Australia doughnut councils can be found at very small scales: the towns of Northam (population 6500) and Narrogin (population 4800) are examples of small towns with surrounding independent councils. Many doughnut councils fight desperately for their continued existence, arguing that town interests are inimical to those of the agricultural areas. Services, plant, buildings and employees are often duplicated as a result, and costs accumulate. Various attempts have been made by councils to share equipment and machinery, sometimes to share staff, and in other cases to jointly establish planning and other regulatory and development mechanisms. The results of this have been patchy. In the case of small councils operating across large territories it is simply impractical.

The doughnut problem frequently weakens the competitive position of the two (or more) councils involved, and aggravates the kind of problems with which so many parts of rural Australia are struggling. Instead of searching for the complementarities between urbanised centres and rural settings, relationships abound with suspicion. Many of the urban centres were the poor relations of the rural areas when Australia was highly dependent on rural earnings. For many, their prime role was to provide the business–service needs of the rural areas where the wealth was accumulated. Typically, the towns held an elite of professional and business people, but average incomes and employment opportunities were much lower than in metropolitan areas. In the 1980s and 1990s severe periods of hardship in many rural industries began a process wherein rural interests started to perceive the larger urban centres as advantaged competitors for the increasingly dwindling growth resources of provincial Australia (Beer et al., 1994; also see Chapter 4).

Where larger urban centres (perhaps those with populations above 20 000) began to generate their own growth impulses, such growth was seen to be the cause of decline for the small towns and villages scattered throughout rural areas; the so-called 'sponge city' phenomenon (Productivity Commission, 1999). Large retail centres concentrated in the bigger towns, government services retracted into them, professional services grew in line with population, and light industries added to the diversity of their economic bases (Beer, 1999). The larger urban centres 'captured' the trade and activities of their rural hinterlands. Rural attitudes became even more ingrained, and the maintenance of independent local governments swelled in importance. The urge to hold on to power affects people across all levels of society, but it intensifies in small communities facing significant problems of change: much more is expected and assumed of local leaders, who defend their power bases by stressing the virtues of their own accessibility. Such leaders often claim that in representing small, local communities they can articulate and defend their particular priorities in a way that would be impossible in larger units. Maintenance of the geographical base then becomes an imperative if these priorities are to be protected.

The structure of many local government areas is sometimes inadequate to meet the realities and challenges of the driving forces of the new century. In a number of places the reorganisation of existing local government units into groups that were functionally coherent and competitively strengthened would boost their prospects considerably. A great deal of the literature, and the operation of regional development programs in the Western world, is now based on the efficacy of identifying and operationalising clusters of economic activities, which grow through cooperative linkage building, and which become competitive through mutual marketing, transport, and sourcing operations (see Chapter 10). Strong local leadership has generated the most successful of these clusters. Small, discrete, and sometimes dysfunctional, local government units block the opportunity to respond more positively and aggressively to the challenges rural areas face.

Another argument for reshaping local government stems from the importance of environmental management. Most local government areas were created without any reference to biophysical systems. Local government boundaries artificially segment ecosystems and greatly compound the problems of their management. River systems provide a simple, but significant, example. Actions upstream inevitably affect characteristics of the whole set of fluvial processes along the course. Yet, even in quite short river systems (such as those on the North Coast of New South Wales), as many as five different local government bodies might be found administering parts of the river.

There is a natural desire on the part of many people to retain small administrative units because they seem to offer the potential for inclusionary and participatory management, and to protect aspects of amenity. But these same goals may be achieved by a more imaginative approach to local government. Larger local government units could operate via devolved systems of responsibility. Local communities could determine a range of things: from the instalment of roundabouts and traffic-calmers to establishing and maintaining parks, playing fields and bushland areas, through to such things as the protection of heritage items and density levels of housing. Local community units could then be meshed into larger councils with responsibility for a wide range of economic management issues, economic development and job creation, and key social systems including aged care, youth support systems, and educational and cultural advancement.

Even if there was a wholesale reorganisation of the shape and responsibilities of local government in Australia, many councils would still rely extensively on some system of support from the senior tiers of government. The regular drip-feed of external support systems and grants grew in importance throughout the last quarter of the 20th century, although at a pace that was insufficient to allow many councils to meet enlarged responsibilities. Against this background, it is useful to consider more closely how size distributions of councils vary across

Australia. In the very large States, such as Western Australia and Queensland, the intuitive expectation is that sparsely populated shires would be found in greater numbers, simply because of the large land areas. Yet this is not so. The number of very small councils is greatest in Western Australia. In 1999, 65 per cent of councils in that State had populations with less than 5000 people. One in five councils had a population under 1000 people. What is surprising is that a high proportion of the small councils, by population, are found in a broad spine running from Kent, just north of Albany in the south-west, reaching northwards to near Exmouth. This spine borders the most populous districts of the State, and at its extreme is no more than 200 kilometres from the coast. The bulk of the very small councils, therefore, is not spread over the vast, sparsely populated eastern and northern areas of Western Australia. Some of the councils in the spine had populations of less than 500 people, but the area of many of these were only just over 1000 square kilometres. The majority of councils with populations of under 1000 people had areas of between 1000 and 2000 square kilometres: this in a State where the average area per council was 12 242 square kilometres.

In Queensland in 1999, 51 per cent of councils had populations under 5000, including 8 per cent under 1000. Yet the average size of non-metropolitan councils is relatively large because of the State's low level of urbanisation (discussed above) and the tendency for large regional centres to be administered as single local government areas. In South Australia 22 per cent of councils had less than 5000 inhabitants. New South Wales had 25 per cent of its councils under 5000, including one which was under 500 population. Victoria had but one council under the 5000 population mark.

Councils with small populations have, typically, very high per capita expenditure levels, large numbers of employees relative to the council's population, and small revenue bases. In Western Australian local government areas with populations under 1000, average expenditure levels per head are above $2000. In Westonia (population 285) expenditure per capita in 1999 was $6815 and in Menzies (population 350) it was $6857. In Queensland per capita expenditure levels in the small shires are even higher. Isisford (population 310) had per capita expenditure levels of $11 129. In Barcoo (population 490) expenditure levels were $10 204 per capita, and in Boulia (population 600) they were $11 013. These expenditure levels contrast with those of Queensland's large urban councils. In Bundaberg (population 46 000) per capita expenditure was $544, and in Mackay (population 72 000) it was $868 (Australian Local Government Guide, 1999).

Revenue bases do not support such high levels of expenditure in small places. The average income the small Western Australian councils generated from rates was only 24 per cent of their total revenues (in the case of Upper Gascoyne rate revenue was only 6 per cent of the total). The average was 23 per cent in the Queensland local government areas with small populations, and it fell to only 12 per cent in both Tambo and in Aramac. The extra revenue needed to keep these councils afloat is derived from grants and various subsidies. Small councils, in the main, are extraordinarily dependent on high per capita grant funding levels for their viability.

A large component of the explanation for high levels of expenditure in small local government areas lies with their relatively high number of employees. In Western Australian local governments with 1000 population or less, there is one employee per 40 residents; Murchison with one employee per 18 people has the State's highest employment ratio. In Queensland the average for the very small councils is even lower (under one local government employee for every 20 residents), with Isisford having the highest proportion of council workers: with one employee per nine residents. Employment, expenditure, and revenue matters raise questions about the resource bases of local government, and the degree they affect councils' capacities to meet the challenges that Australia now faces.

RESOURCE BASE ISSUES

Most councils in Australia rely on a fairly narrow base of taxes for the bulk of their revenue (Table 11.5). These make up 57.9 per cent of the total income. Taxes are dominant in New South Wales (64 per cent of total revenue), South Australia (71 per cent) and Tasmania (62 per cent). In the Northern Territory they make up only 17 per cent of revenue. Grants represent the second main source of revenue (Table 11.6). Across all States these make up 22.5 per cent of the total. In the Northern Territory the system is highly dependent on grants, where they constitute 62 per cent of revenue. Above average levels of grants are recorded in Victoria (27 per cent), Western Australia (28 per cent) and Tasmania (27 per cent).

TABLE 11. 5
LOCAL GOVERNMENT REVENUE, AUSTRALIA 1997–98

Revenue source	% of income
Taxes	57.9
Public trading surpluses	4.4
Interest	3.7
Grants	22.5
Other	11.5

SOURCE National Office of Local Government, 1999: 7.

TABLE 11.6
GRANTS AS A PERCENTAGE OF TOTAL REVENUE, LOCAL GOVERNMENTS BY STATE AND TERRITORY, 1997–98

State/Territory	%
NSW	18
Victoria	27
Queensland	19
South Australia	19
Western Australia	28
Tasmania	27
Northern Territory	62
Australia	23

SOURCE National Office of Local Government, 1999: 4–5.

Public trading enterprises are not significant except in Queensland, where on average they provide over 15 per cent of council income. Although rates make up the largest stream of income, some States (such as New South Wales) place restrictions on the level of rates and the increase allowed from year to year. There is a complex relationship between population, the economic base, and a council's ability to generate additional income sources beyond rates and grants. When councils generate additional income, they have the capacity to undertake a broader and more imaginative set of programs and to provide services at a much higher level. Councils that can generate enhanced income flow, are likely to become more competitive and less dependent on the State. Wealthy areas produce wealthy councils. These can generate substantial rate income because property values are high, and they can also expand their income through a variety of charges and other mechanisms. Poor councils cannot generate large income from rates because property values are low, and they have little opportunity for making up the deficit through other means. Such councils become highly dependent on government grants.

In South Australia some of the major non-metropolitan centres have a fairly low dependence on rate income: Whyalla (population 24 000) gains 26 per cent of its income from rates, and Port Augusta (population 14 240) gets 36 per cent of its income from this source. Mount Gambier (population 23 075) relies on rates for 51 per cent of its funds and Port Lincoln (population 12 530) receives 58 per cent of its funds from rates. There are similar variations amongst the small centres: Tumby Bay (population 2700) gets 59 per cent of its income from rates but Streaky Bay (population 1900) gets only 30 per cent.

There is less variation in Victoria, where each rural centre (except Delatite) receives between 25 per cent and 35 per cent of income from rates. In Queensland the generality is that rate income declines substantially in local government areas with lower populations. Aramac (population 900) and Tambo (population 700) get only 12 per cent of their income from rates. In Western Australia the situation is similar. The very small councils obtain less than 25 per cent of their income from rates; Menzies (population 350) gets 18 per cent from rates, Perenjori (population 950) 15 per cent, Wandering (population 480) 13 per cent, and Upper Gascoyne (population 252) 6 per cent. In the Central Darling in New South Wales the council is one of its own largest rate payers as farmers in this marginal area are forced to cede their properties to the council when they can no longer pay rates, and by default the council has become a substantial land owner.

Besides grants from governments, councils with a low rate base can generate revenue in two ways. First, they can impose charges and licences for services and broadly they can introduce user-pay systems (on items such as aged care services, children's services and sanitation). The charging regime for local government services nationally has been restructured recently with the advent of the national competition policy, requiring councils to undertake commercial functions in a transparent manner consistent with principles of competitive neutrality (Productivity Commission, 1999). The poorer and often smaller councils, however, are disadvantaged in providing and charging for services. Second, local governments can involve themselves in business undertakings such as water, sewerage, abattoirs, saleyards, landfill, gas and electricity, and property development. The opportunity to do these things successfully is generally confined to the larger towns and rural cities. There are regulatory differences between the States in terms of which functions councils can consider when looking for additional income.

Water and sewerage services are an exception. In most rural areas the council is the only agency capable of supplying such services. In New South Wales, for example, 122 (out of 177) councils supply sewerage services, and 113 supply water. State-wide, the revenue from providing sewerage services is around $230 million and the cost is $130 million. For water, revenue is around $225 million and the cost is $140 million. The revenue derived by councils supplying these services is $465 million out of a total revenue stream of $2.2 billion. Net revenue from the two services is $195 million. The level of net revenue, however, does not necessarily relate to the levels of profit accruing to councils: the cost of maintaining and replacing infrastructure for utilities is high and depreciation rates are steep.

Grants constitute a significant part of local government revenue across Australia. In 1997–98, local governments received around $2.2 billion in total grants, with financial assistance grants representing $1.2 billion of this. Other Commonwealth grants equalled $0.2 billion. State grants totalled $0.7 billion. Of the 66 per cent of all grant funds that come from the Commonwealth, the majority take the form of financial assistance grants. The Whitlam Government started the Commonwealth's involvement in the direct funding of local government. This was largely in response to the debt problems of local government of that time. Between 1940 and 1970 local government's share of public debt rose from 17 per cent to 37 per cent, with Queensland and South Australia having the most indebted local government (then, as now). The sector was unable to increase its taxing powers, nor therefore its revenue. Commonwealth financial assistance grants were designed to return a greater share of tax income to local government. Financial assistance grants are distributed between the States on a per capita basis. The principles on which allocations are established is stated in the *Local Government (Financial Assistance) Act 1995*. The allocation mechanisms within each State vary, but there is a general bias towards rural areas and the per capita levels of grants are much larger for smaller and more remote councils. The minimum per capita grant in New South Wales for 1999–2000 was $14.08. Two-thirds of metropolitan councils receive this. The average State per capita grant was $46.92 and the non-metropolitan average was $84.02. Financial assistance grants generally cover only recurrent expenditure items; capital expenditure is not taken into account in estimating the size of the grant needed. Yet, even with the restriction to recurrent items, it has been calculated that the grants cover only a portion of the estimated needs: in New South Wales this is about 60 per cent. As Table 11.7 shows, the grants climb in value from urban to rural, and from large to small. The other main area of Commonwealth funding for local government relates to local roads. In 1990 it was decided to direct Commonwealth funding for local roads away from the roads authorities of the States to the Local Government Grants Commissions of each State (the bodies responsible for allocating general purpose grants). In 1999–2000, financial equalisation grants reached $880 million and local road grants $390 million: a total of $1.27 billion.

TABLE 11. 7
PER CAPITA FINANCIAL ASSISTANCE GRANTS TO LOCAL GOVERNMENTS, NEW SOUTH WALES, 1999–2000

Urban regional medium size	$ 55.52
Urban regional small	$ 69.38
Rural agricultural very large	$114.72
Rural agricultural large	$165.89
Rural agricultural medium	$218.30
Rural agricultural small	$343.42
Remote	$389.54

SOURCE NSW Local Government Grants Commission, 1999.

CONCLUSION

The grants system is clearly needed to keep local government afloat, but it presents a real problem for local government reform. The States are totally responsible for the structure of local government, but they contribute almost nothing to their budgets. The 34 per cent of grant money that comes from the States is tied to special purposes, and represents under 5 per cent of normal revenue for councils. Moreover, in areas like environmental management and planning, councils have had to progressively absorb additional functions, frequently because State governments directly or indirectly devolve these responsibilities to them. At the same time the rationalisation of State government through corporatisation, centralisation and staff cuts has weakened even further the capacity of many rural and regional centres to function adequately. The much publicised effects of bank closures (partly psychological because of the immense symbolic importance of banks in small towns: see Chapter 9) have had a much smaller impact than the retreat of State authorities in rural Australia.

The fact that States do not have to absorb most of the costs that councils cannot meet distorts the process of reform. The problems identified about council functioning in the previous section (small councils, doughnut councils and economically or environmentally dysfunctional councils) are encouraged to remain because they are propped up by federal money. Local government reform is a politically sensitive subject, largely because of the power bases occupied by councillors, and while someone else pays the bills, true reform will not be forthcoming. This reduces enormously the capacity of local government to act as an agent to improve the economic and social well-being of rural Australia.

Reform within States has largely concentrated on improving accounting and efficiency factors within existing systems. Several States in the 1990s revised their local government laws to provide for such things as transparency of operations, strategic planning, co-ordinated organisational structures, and asset accounting and management. Each of these reforms has been laudable individually, but they have not addressed many fundamental issues regarding the negative aspects of size–functionality relationships, nor did they attempt to review the most apposite responsibilities of local government. Essentially, the reforms said: keep doing what you have always been doing, but do it better.

One of the perhaps unintended consequences of the reforms has been a jump in the salaries of council officers. The requirements of the new laws seemed so onerous to councillors that their ends could only be met by reverting to fixed-term contracts for their managers, and pumping up the salary levels in the hope of attracting people with the requisite skills. To illustrate the point, in 1999 the Prime Minister's salary cost 0.13 cents per Australian resident. In the larger councils in New South Wales the salary of the general manager was often greater in total than that of the Prime Minister. The salary of the general manager of a large rural town (population around 50 000) costs the community $2.75 per resident, and the same position in a very small rural council area costs $220.80 per resident. In the latter case it was not the local residents who footed the bill. That same council got $693.50 per capita in general purpose grants from the Commonwealth government.

The salary impositions rippled through the system. The senior layers of council administrations received increased salaries in recognition of the greater complexity of local government administration. Salaries dominate council expenditure after road spending. In New South Wales, per capita expenditure on general administrative services (a useful proxy for the costs of central administration) was 45 times that of aged–disabled services; 45 times that of children's services; 18 times that of cultural amenities spending; ten times that of general health services; and six times that of library services.

Reform is needed to make local government more relevant to the challenges of the new century. Local governments should get more rather than less functions, but these functions should be funded more adequately and directly than at present. Local government should be empowered to raise its own resources and to act creatively and independently to safeguard and improve the lot of their people. To do this requires an overhaul of both the regional structure of local government and the responsibilities accorded to it. Until this happens local government will remain the lame duck of Australian politics, limping along in a battle for survival and, in many cases, not being able to do much for those injured by the shifting foci of economic activity and wealth creation.

REFERENCES

Australian Bureau of Statistics (ABS) (1999) *Government Financial Statistics*, (Cat. 5512), ABS, Canberra.

Australian Classification of Local Governments Steering Committee (1994), *The Australian Classification of Local Government*, AGPS, Canberra.

Australian Local Government Association (1997) *Regional Environmental Strategies*, Discussion Paper, ALGA, Canberra.

Bates G (1995) *Environmental Law in Australia*, Butterworths, Sydney.

Beer A (1999) 'Regional Cities within Australia's Changing Urban System, 1991–96', *Australasian Journal of Regional Studies*, 6(1), pp 329–48.

Beer A, Bolam A & Maude A (1994) *Beyond the Capitals: Urban Growth in Regional Australia*, AGPS, Canberra.

Binning CE & Young MD (1997) 'Biodiversity, incentives and local government', Paper presented at 'Pathways to Sustainability International Conference', Newcastle.

Binning CE, Young MD & Cripps E (1999) *National Research and Development Program on Rehabilitation, Management and Conservation of Remnant Vegetation*, Ausinfo, Canberra.

Commonwealth of Australia (1997) *Natural Heritage Trust: Guide to Community Group Applications 1997–98*, Environment Australia, Canberra.

Department of Local Government, NSW (1999) *Comparative Information on Local Councils*, DLG, Bankstown.

Duncan C (1995) 'Legal restrictions on the exercise of council powers', *Local Government Law Journal*, 35, pp 35–43.

Evatt Foundation (1996) *The State of Australia*, Evatt Foundation, Sydney.

Information Australia (1999) *Australian Local Government Guide*, Information Australia, Melbourne.

Lee R & Wills J (eds) (1997) *Geographies of Economies*, Edward Arnold, London.

Local Government Grants Commission, NSW (1999), *Annual Report*, LGGC, Canberra.

Morton A (1998) *Financing Options for Australian Local Government*, National Office of Local Government, Canberra.

National Office of Local Government (1999) *Local Government National Report, 1998–99*, NOLG, Canberra.

New South Wales Local Government Grants Commission (1999) *Annual Report*, New South Wales Local Government Grants Commission, Sydney.

Newton P & Bell M (1996) *Population Shift: Mobility and Change in Australia* AGPS, Canberra.

Osborn D (1997) *A Rationale and Approach for Applying Environmental Accounting Frameworks in Local Government*, Australian Centre for Regional and Local Government Studies, Canberra.

Pritchard W (1993) 'Land transport reforms and the economic geography of the Northern Territory' *Australian Geographical Studies*, 31(1), pp 39–48.

Productivity Commission (1999) *Impact of Competition Policy Reforms on Rural and Regional Australia*, AusInfo, Canberra.

Stuckey EB (1994) *Bluett Local Government Handbook*, Law Book Co, Sydney.

12
CONCLUDING THOUGHTS
PHIL McMANUS & BILL PRITCHARD

This book opened with the observation that complex roots underlie the intense social and economic challenges facing rural and regional Australia. It is easy to typecast the economic hardship and social dislocation experienced by many people in rural and regional Australia as emblematic of a national 'great divide'. Such a moniker does not contribute to an understanding of the degree of these processes, their origins or the appropriate policy responses. There is a need for national debate to move beyond these stereotypes, while at the same time acknowledging the seriousness of the plight of many individuals and communities outside the capital cities.

Australian governments still equivocate in their policy responses to rural and regional Australia. In Chapter Six, Pritchard notes that the Dairy Industry Package of September 1999 was noteworthy in that it linked (further) deregulation to compensation arrangements. This appeared to suggest a sea change in the government's attitudes to rural and regional Australia, at least in the field of agricultural policy. The broader policy canvas, however, is not painted so neatly. Two examples illustrate this.

In October 1999, the Deputy Prime Minister and Leader of the Federal National Party, John Anderson, hosted the Regional Summit in the Commonwealth parliament. This event was laden with the philosophies of community self-help and the social resilience of rural

Australia. In his opening address, Anderson made it clear that the Summit was not going to entertain claims for fiscal handouts to salve the pains of the bush. In stressing this view, Anderson was entirely consistent with the regional policy perspective espoused by the Howard government since its election in 1996 (see Chapter 10). In an immediate sense, this perspective also served to dampen expectations from the Summit's participants, signifying a political astuteness by Anderson. Yet after three days of deliberations couched in these terms, Prime Minister Howard addressed the Summit and announced funding for the Alice Springs–Darwin railway. The message taken away by many Summit participants was that largesse could still be bought.

Three months later, John Howard spent ten days in rural New South Wales, Victoria and South Australia on a self-described 'bush listening tour'. This event was planned, symbolically, to be the Prime Minister's first official duties of the new millennium. Howard wore an Akubra Hat throughout this tour as an apparent sign of his empathy with the people he met. Notwithstanding the symbolism, the outcomes of this tour were intriguing, to say the least. Upon the completion of his tour, Howard announced a moratorium on further reductions to Commonwealth government employment in rural and regional Australia. About a month later, however, the Prime Minister vociferously supported Telstra's plans to shed 10 000 jobs nationally. Many of these jobs were located outside the capital cities. Howard also perceived no legitimate grounds on which to intervene in the proposed merger of the Commonwealth Bank of Australia and the Colonial State Bank, which would encourage further reductions in bank branch numbers in rural communities. The Commonwealth government's approaches to rural and regional Australia, it seems, remain fragmented.

These episodes are retold not to expose perceived flaws in the Howard government's responses to current issues, but to emphasise the multiple domains of action that influence the livelihoods of individuals and communities in rural and regional Australia. Events in the boardrooms of institutions such as the Commonwealth Bank shape the futures of individuals, towns and regions as much as local meetings to galvanise community self-help strategies. The geographer Doreen Massey reminds us that regions are constructed as 'nets of social relations' that link human and institutional actors that exist within and outside these spaces (Massey, 1993). Specific places in rural and regional Australia are not islands, separate from the rest of humanity. Their futures rest with the networks of capital, people, ideas and images that serve to locate them globally. Some places in rural and regional Australia, such as Byron Bay on the New South Wales north coast, have experienced dramatic transformation over recent years because of the ways they have been repositioned by shifts in the global economy. Not too long ago, Byron Bay was an isolated whaling station. Now it is a strategic site within international tourism: a place characterised by the strong presence of backpackers and eco-tourism. The transformation of Byron Bay, like any place, rests on the interplay of internal and external economic and cultural processes.

The transformation of Cairns during the last two decades provides another example of the interplay of internal and external processes that shape regional futures. Cairns has developed as a major centre for international tourism, largely on account of its abilities to attract significant numbers of tourists from Japan and other Asian nations. But as Stimson et al., (1998) note, the place–formation of Cairns cannot be read simply as a process of the impersonal mechanics of global capitalism. Specific investors within specific historical junctures (Christopher Skase, the Daikyo Corporation) provided the agency to embed mobile financial capital into the built environment. In these tasks, they depended upon local actors: companies, local governments, politicians.

This leads us to the conclusion that understanding the futures of rural and regional Australia requires research grounded in local context. Grand theorising of the reasons for socio-spatial inequality, or the appropriate policy responses for its alleviation, are likely to lead to partial solutions. As noted repeatedly throughout this book, rural and regional Australia is extraordinarily diverse. Broad processes such as declining agricultural terms of trade have been enormously important in shaping many parts of rural and regional Australia over recent decades, but so have been the actions of individuals and communities. Failure to consider one without the other — for the purposes of academic theory or for the purposes of public policy — makes for inherently incomplete analysis.

Let us pursue these arguments via constructing a fictional small rural town in the Murray-Darling Basin of inland south-eastern Australia. While this town is fictitious, it contains an amalgam of the scenarios that occur to varying extents throughout rural and regional Australia discussed in the chapters of this book.

The first thing that strikes the visitor to this town is an enormous grain silo, situated adjacent to a railway siding. The silo is an artifact and reminder of an age of rural development and progress. The State government built it in the 1940s and upon its construction it became the nodal point for a vibrant regional community of wheat growers. These days the silo is owned by a private concern and is used less frequently. Much of the grain grown locally — which is no longer just wheat, but barley, canola and a variety of other grains — is now trucked to larger storage sites. The grain growers in the region sell their output to private agribusinesses rather than a commodity board, and hedge their contracted prices through trading on futures exchanges via the Internet.

But, as the empty bar stools in the pub opposite the silo attest, grain growing is no longer the main activity in the town. In the 1960s the council entered into a joint venture with a private meat marketing company to build an abattoir. This quickly became the major employer in the town, but in the late 1970s the company got into financial hardship and closed. At the time, the town was featured on national television as 'another small town facing oblivion'. A decade later, a transnational company bought the old abattoir site to construct a beef feedlot, specialising in the export of marbled beef to Japan and Korea. The council waived rates and local taxes, and the State Department of Regional Development entered into a scheme to supply the factory with subsidised power. The feedlot does not employ many locals, and there are legal issues pending with neighbouring properties over effluent run-off. Nevertheless, it is now the town's largest business.

The main pub in the town is little changed from decades past, except that it has a satellite dish on the roof. The town's only family of Chinese people, who are third-generation Chinese–Australians, runs its kitchen. Across the road from the pub is the town's only doctor's surgery. The town was without a local doctor for five years, until an immigrant from India was lured to the town, his Australian medical accreditation being granted after a wait of many years.

The town's main street has two cafes for the passing tourist trade. One of these was the former council chamber, made redundant by a council merger. Both the cafes advertise local 'farm stays' and 'bed and breakfast'. In 1988 the town received a bicentennial grant to establish a signposted heritage walk, but the paint on the signposts is now peeling. The video store on the main street has now closed because most households have pay-TV. The last bank branch in the town is still open for business, although one of its competitors has an agency relationship with the town's supermarket. The local farm supplies business closed last year after the long-serving owner died, and the storefront is now used to hang paintings done by children at the local primary school. On the opposite side of the street, another closed business has become the office for the local Aboriginal land council..

Evidently, the travails of this fictitious town are linked intimately to flows of capital, people, commodities and ideas that connect it with wider national and international spaces. Decisions affecting the town, and the daily lives of people living in or near the town, are often made in distant places such as Canberra, Sydney, Tokyo and Washington. But globalisation is not an all-powerful force that leaves little or no agency for people in rural and regional Australia to shape their own lives. The future of rural and regional Australia lies not with blaming the global for the local (a la Pauline Hanson), nor mythologising local resilience and enterprise. In thinking about and developing policies for specific places in rural and regional Australia, an accommodation and acknowledgement of different scales is required.

The situation of rural and regional Australia at the beginning of the 21st century is complex. The lack of an easy diagnosis of the problems is likely to lead to an absence of easy, effective solutions. This means that informed input is required to construct, promote and influence debates. It is our hope that this book proves to be a useful contribution to this debate and to effect policy development and implementation that results in ongoing improvement in the lives of the people in rural and regional Australia.

REFERENCES

Massey D (1993) 'Questions of locality', *Geography*, 78 (2), pp 142–49.

Stimson RJ, Jenkins O, Roberts B & Daly MT (1998) 'The impact of Daikyo as a foreign investor on the Cairns–Far North Queensland regional economy', *Environment and Planning A*, 30, pp 161–79.

INDEX

peri-urban 55, 57
Perth 56, 78, 80, 84, 106, 144, 152, 188
pests and pest control 107, 109
pluriactivity 41–42, 80
police 60, 126, 130
policy-making atrophy 123
population change *see* demographic
     change
Pork Council of Australia 99
Port Augusta, SA 212
Port Hedland, WA 152
Port Lincoln, SA 212
poultry 44, 99
Primary Industries, Department of, Qld
     111
Primary Industries and Energy,
     Department of, Commonwealth
     150
privatisation 62, 125
Productivity Commission 3, 35, 57, 63,
     91
protectionism 73–74, 90, 92–93, 95,
     99, 125
public choice theories 92, 101
public sector institutions 54
public transport 156, 175

quality of life 97
quarantine 99–100
Queensland 7, 14, 56–57, 59, 100,
     106–109, 111–12, 115, 156, 180,
     184, 186–87, 190, 196, 200,
     205–206, 210, 212, 214
*Queensland Fauna Conservation Act
     1974* 112
questionnaire surveys 77–78

railways 60, 63, 77, 126, 134, 142,
     144, 199, 219
RDOs *see* Regional Development
     Organisations
Regional Assistance Program 132, 179
Regional Australia Strategy 178
Regional Australia Summit, 1999 178,
     218–19
Regional Banking Services, House of
     Representatives Standing
     Committee on Economics, Finance
     and Public Administration Inquiry
     into, 1999 141, 161
regional development 67, 169–91, 209
Regional Development Organisations
     (RDOs) 177–78
Regional Development Program 174,
     176, 178, 183, 186

Regional Employment Development
     Scheme 174
Regional Forums Program 179
regional policies 87, 133, 169–91, 222
regional towns 81, 124, 142–43,
     145–46, 152, 155, 157, 188, 208,
     215
regulation
   growth of 126, 137
   theory 170–72, 185–86, 190
Reserve Bank of Australia 161
Ricardo, David 94
roads 145, 156–57, 187, 199, 214, 216
Rockhampton, Qld 135
Romania 118
Rotary 196
RRMA Classification 147–51
rural and regional Australia 5, 16, 53
   income disparities and poverty 2–3,
      124
   rural crisis 28, 123, 129, 138,
      140–41
rural community 19, 140, 187, 203
   decline of 64, 74, 81, 86–87, 125,
      130, 146, 157–58
   development and empowerment 26,
      127, 137, 204
   infrastructure 60, 147
   leadership 68, 140, 177, 209
   participation 26, 82–83
   sense of 82, 84
   sustainability 66, 87, 141, 175
rural idyll 73
Rural Industries Research and
     Development Corporation 74, 77,
     83, 85
Rural Partnership Program 173
rural population change *see* demographic
     change
rural producers *see* farms, farmers and
     farming
Rural Transactions Centres 132, 178
rurality 15, 17–18

salinisation 107, 111, 120
'sandstone curtain' 141
schools *see* education
science and scientists 24–26, 109
self-help policies 66, 69, 87, 119, 175,
     218
service industries 42–43, 54, 60–61
settlement patterns 143–44
sheep-wheat *see* wheat-sheep farms
Sidoti, Chris 20–21, 141, 147
single parents 3